FINDING
HOME

FINDING HOME

REAL STORIES OF MIGRANT BRITAIN

EMILY DUGAN

ICON

Published in the UK in 2015 by
Icon Books Ltd, Omnibus Business Centre,
39–41 North Road, London N7 9DP
email: info@iconbooks.com
www.iconbooks.com

Sold in the UK, Europe and Asia
by Faber & Faber Ltd, Bloomsbury House,
74–77 Great Russell Street,
London WC1B 3DA or their agents

Distributed in the UK, Europe and Asia
by TBS Ltd, TBS Distribution Centre, Colchester Road,
Frating Green, Colchester CO7 7DW

Distributed in Australia and New Zealand
by Allen & Unwin Pty Ltd, PO Box 8500,
83 Alexander Street, Crows Nest, NSW 2065

Distributed in South Africa by
Jonathan Ball, Office B4, The District,
41 Sir Lowry Road, Woodstock 7925

Distributed in India by Penguin Books India,
7th Floor, Infinity Tower – C, DLF Cyber City,
Gurgaon 122002, Haryana

ISBN: 978-184831-864-9

Typeset in Garamond 3 by Marie Doherty

Printed and bound in the UK
by Clays Ltd, St Ives plc

About the author

EMILY DUGAN is Social Affairs Editor at *The Independent*, *i* and *The Independent on Sunday*. Her investigations into human trafficking have twice been awarded Best Investigative Article at the Anti-Slavery Day Media Awards and her human rights journalism was shortlisted for the Gaby Rado Memorial Prize at the 2012 Amnesty Media Awards. This is her first book.

For Oly

Contents

Prologue

Prologue

It was an unusual way to start the New Year: a dawn flight to Romania followed by 52 hours on a bus back to London. I wanted to catch the first coach leaving Bucharest in 2014 and witness the journeys made by people coming to Britain amid hysterical headlines predicting floods of new migrants. The glimpse it offered into the experiences of those making a life in the UK is what prompted this book, which explores the unseen lives of ten migrants from around the world.

As the public debate about immigration gets noisier, it is too easy to forget that we are talking about a collection of individuals. In this hyped-up discourse, newcomers are often talked about in terms of numbers – or worse – using the metaphors of pestilence and invasion. Even those defending migration often do so with unhelpful generalisations or an over-reliance on cold statistics. Their arguments fail to calm a debate that has always been more about gut feeling and identity than economics.

Generalisations have sullied the debate on all sides. How can a huge variety of people arriving from across the planet all be faceless scroungers? Or, as some liberals might have it, a homogeneous mass of saints who are all better and harder-working than us?

Over the last year I have immersed myself in the experiences of ten people who have arrived on this island over the last decade and attempted to make it their home. I travelled across Europe with Syrians trying to sneak into Britain; went to a mosque in Newcastle with Pakistani men who would be killed for praying back home; attended a Polish-language Mass in Lincolnshire so popular that much of its congregation watch from the car park; trudged around Glasgow's homeless services with a man left stateless and homeless by a squabble between Zimbabwe and Britain; and witnessed a judge deciding in a court on an industrial estate whether one of the country's leading NHS therapists should be banished to Australia.

It was a privilege to spend time with them and be let into their homes, cars and secrets. But in the scheme of their lives I was there only for a relatively short time. For this reason, with the exception of the prologue and epilogue, I have edited myself out. My experiences as an onlooker do not merit making me a part of their history.

This is not supposed to be a definitive picture of every immigrant experience in Britain, but a snapshot of ten lives whose detail might otherwise be invisible to society. The drama of their stories is at times more far-fetched than anything a novelist could come up with. I hope that putting their personal struggles and triumphs on paper may help promote empathy with the migrant experience of coming to Britain.

Journalists rarely get the chance to return to the people they interview – let alone spend days on end in their company. The intensity of a project like this forces you to tread a fine line between reporting and friendship. Though I risk offending new friends, I have endeavoured to keep these portraits as faithful as any one-off interview.

Almost everyone in this book wanted their name to be published. A few were worried about the impact it might have on their immigration status and chose not to print their surnames. In two chapters, the names in the story have been changed to respect their privacy.

These ten people share many common experiences: the struggle to reach Britain and stay here; the tug of two homes; battling with the inefficiency of a Home Office recently declared unfit for purpose; the slog of work and the pain of separation from those they love. But once you hear any of these stories in depth it is the differences that stand out. These differences are what make them human. They have the power to transform each person in the eyes of a sceptical public from immigrant to individual.

London, March 2015

◆

CHAPTER 1

The bus

In Bucharest, a new life in western Europe begins at 4am in a draughty waiting room opposite McDonald's. It is one of thousands of locations around the world – drab, prosaic and exotic – where the long journey to Britain starts.

As the first four coaches of 2014 line up under floodlights, crowds of families gather to send off their relations on a long journey across the continent. The names of European cities are barked out and luggage-laden people shuffle forward, tickets in hand. The busiest bus is going to Hamburg, closely followed by others to Paris and Zurich.

The first coach to London in the New Year – a 52-hour journey – was expected to be the moment that a flood of migrants to Britain materialised. Excitable newspapers reported for weeks beforehand that Romanians' unfettered access to working visas would result in a mass invasion, with coach loads arriving daily.

But only one person getting on at the start of Eurolines route 441 is going all the way to London.

Most are off to Germany, Belgium and Holland – where work restrictions for Romanians and Bulgarians have also been loosened, seven years after the countries joined the EU.

Mihai drags his suitcase into the hold and climbs aboard. He is 29 and has been working in construction in London for the last year without papers. His shaved head makes him look tough in the half-light, but his easy smile dispels the image quickly.

For Mihai the biggest change in 2014 is not the first opportunity to work in Europe – but his first chance to get the minimum wage. 'Because I don't have papers the bosses take advantage,' he says. 'When I first came to the UK a Romanian man lied to me. When the boss paid us on Fridays, everybody else had their pay in an envelope but mine wasn't. I found out this guy had taken my envelope and was taking his cut from it so I only got £50. We had a fight and I never got my money back. He made me steal copper pipes from sites and take them to the Caledonian Road. I told the boss about his stealing and now he is gone and I get paid directly.'

He still works for the same building company and feels vulnerable to people taking advantage. He doesn't trust the men he works with. This year, he says, will be different. 'I want a National Insurance number so much. I want it to work, not to take benefits. We work more than ten hours a day and my boss pays £60.'

He understands the bad press some migrants have received and sometimes shares British prejudices against his compatriots. 'Nobody wants them but I understand because there are a lot of Romanians and Bulgarians who do bad things. They are stealing and killing for drugs. Because of them, we who work get a bad reputation. There are a lot of poor people in Romania and it makes them bad because they are desperate. When people ask: "Where are you from?" and I say Romania, they run away. They think you're a gypsy.'

Mihai works in King's Cross and lives in Hendon, north London, in a flat with twelve other builders, most of whom are from Romania. He was home in Bucharest for Christmas to see his partner Roxana and their four-year-old son, Mario. 'I want to bring my girlfriend and child to England. I miss them very much and it makes me cry because I love them so much, but the rent is a problem.'

To rent even the tiniest flat for him and his family would leave almost no money under his current wage and make saving for a better life impossible. It could also be even harder for his family to get food and other essentials than it would be back in Bucharest, where the cost of living is relatively cheap.

In Romania he worked as a driver and was in the army as a fireman but he says that did not make enough money to keep a family. The minimum salary in Romania is 850 lei a month, about £160. 'People leave Romania for one reason only: money,' he says. 'It's the hope for a better life.'

Mihai taught himself English watching the Cartoon Network and 90s films (his favourite is *Titanic*). He has also worked in France and Italy but likes London best and hopes one day to make it a proper home. That does not make him unfamiliar with how rapidly things can go wrong in Britain. 'I have a friend who lived under the bridges in London. He tried to find work and was washing dishes but he had nowhere to live. He started working for some Albanian guys selling drugs. When you're that desperate for money it pushes you to do bad things. Now he's back in Romania and says it's too hard to make a living in the UK.'

The 1,600-mile bus trip is favoured by many since it costs under £100 and you can take more luggage than on a plane. The first five hours are spent navigating hairpin bends on single-lane roads covered in black ice. It is still dark but the mountains are lit by a dusting of ice reflecting back the moonlight. Gazing out, Mihai says, 'I'm going to miss this. It's so beautiful.'

His eyes prick with tears after calling his partner and son. 'My girlfriend is crying,' he says. 'I didn't let her see me off because it's too hard. I'll try everything to bring her next time. In a situation like this you realise how much you love somebody.'

Sitting at the back of the bus are Vali Draghici, 40, and Julian Oprea, 29, from Buzău. They are going to Frankfurt to work in steel welding and construction. Vali tried to work there two years ago, but without papers he was exploited, he says. A Romanian agent promised him 1,500 euros a month but paid only 700 the first month and then nothing in the next. Vali says: 'We only stayed for two months last time because the pay was bad. But this time it's eight euros an hour.'

Despite being victims of it themselves in Britain, casual racism is common among the passengers. Over a lunch of gruel at a rest stop, Vali asks: 'Why don't the English want us? There are other immigrants in the UK like Indians and niggers so why don't you want Romanians and Bulgarians? We are better.'

Marin Ninca, 58, is one of three drivers working on rotation on the coach. He has been a driver for almost 45 years and has noticed little change in the numbers going to and from Europe over the last decade – despite the recent hype. 'There's no difference. All the routes I make I go with a full bus and I come back with a full bus. I take people to work and I bring them back when they've collected their money. Germany, Holland, Belgium, they are all more popular than Britain. They are the most well-known places to go.'

At 2pm the bus reaches Deva, the shabbiest city so far: crumbling brutalist apartment blocks fed by huge rusty pipes, dirty roads, dilapidated houses. Later, as darkness falls, the coach arrives at the north-western Romanian city of Arad, the last place to collect passengers before the journey across Europe begins. Families seeing off relatives are caught in the headlights, their smiles cracking and turning to grimaces as the bus pulls away.

Most of the 50 passengers are returning to existing homes in western Europe, where some have been living for decades. The loudest is a 32-year-old brunette who calls herself Pamela. Her real name is Alexandra Benitez-Pozo. She lived in Barcelona for twelve years and, since last summer, Cologne, making money as a pole dancer and sex worker.

She is on her way back from a Christmas break with her family in Bucharest. Her boss gave her ten days off, and to save money she has spent five of them on a bus. She leaves her four-year-old daughter, Esthella, with her sister in Romania.

'I've been a go-go dancer for twelve years and I can't lie, I do a bit of prostitution to make money. I can make 200 or 2,000 euros a night. I send home about 800 euros a month – that supports my mother, father, sister and two nephews.'

She has family in Britain, but prefers to work in Germany where prostitution is legal. 'I have two brothers, one in Manchester and one in London,' she says. 'The one in Manchester has babies and works as a cleaner. The one in London steals and takes drugs. He was there a year and nobody helped him, so he steals.'

She interrupts the journey periodically to shout criticism at the driver, or exchange ribald jokes with a group of builders who have gathered at the back of the bus to keep her company. 'You can't afford me,' she keeps reminding them.

At a rest stop just before the Hungarian border, several people get off and change their last fistfuls of leis into just a couple of €5 and £5 notes. Once all the passengers are back on board, Pamela passes around a large brown envelope, demanding three euros each to bribe the border officials. 'Otherwise we'll wait hours while they search our bags.' Everyone pays up.

As it turns out, it isn't the luggage that delays things. When border police get on the bus they stop at the seats of an unlikely couple. Aziz, a man from Afghanistan in his thirties, travelled from Bucharest with a very young woman, Georgiana, and they argued for much of the journey. The ID Georgiana hands to officials is cracked in half along the photograph and stuck together with Sellotape. When they take her off the coach, Aziz stays inside, staring ahead impassively. It turns out she's seventeen and travelling on her older sister's card. Strict laws to prevent trafficking mean it is illegal for her to travel without a parent or papers proving parental consent. The consensus on the bus is that she was being taken to Belgium to work as a prostitute, but Aziz says later that he met Georgiana in his cafe in Antwerp and that they were just on holiday visiting her family in Bucharest.

After three hours of deliberation, Georgiana's luggage is taken off the bus and Aziz leaves her with a few euros. As it pulls away, Aziz stares resolutely ahead. She's left standing alone in the cold, sobbing.

Twenty minutes into Hungary, the sound of retching brings the bus to an abrupt halt. A Dutch tourist has guzzled half a litre of Pálenka, Romania's moonshine, and coated the back of the coach in vomit. The driver is apoplectic. 'Baggage! Passport!' he barks, before dragging the drunkard from his seat. The man, who can barely stand, shouts 'fuck you', but stops fighting when he sees how angry the driver is. He is jettisoned at a dark petrol station in the middle of the freezing night.

Every passenger has a story of separation, a sacrifice made for a shot at prosperity. Roxana, 28, who joined the bus in the mountain city of Sibiu, Transylvania, is leaving Romania for the first time. Roxy, as she likes to be called, has left her husband Laurentiu behind while she takes a job in London as a live-in au pair. 'We've been together five years and we've never been apart,' she cries, tissues clasped in her lap. They married in 2012 and her phone is full of smiling pictures of them. 'Look!' she says proudly, comparing recent photos to one on their wedding day. 'My cooking made him bigger.'

At the top of her handbag is a velour heart-shaped pillow with a silhouetted couple dancing on it and the words 'love you for ever' written in Romanian. Periodically she picks it up and holds it close. In another's hands it might seem tacky, but it was a parting present from Laurentiu and when she hugs it she can almost feel him there with her.

Roxy is leaving behind a good job in a restaurant which paid 1,000 lei (£185) a month, not enough to start a family. 'In Romania you have to work so hard for little money,' she says. 'I've prayed every day. I thank God I've been given a chance to change my future. I wish to make children but I don't have money to buy a house. Once I have money I can come back, buy a house, make children and be happy.'

She got her new job as an au pair to five-year-old twins after she was recommended by a friend who had previously worked for the family. She's already spoken to them on Skype and is optimistic. 'The twins are very sweet. On Skype the kids say "Roxy, Roxy!" and kiss the computer. I can't wait to meet them. I think they are a nice family and I am very lucky.'

All she knows is that their father will meet her at Victoria coach station. Her own family history is less rosy. Her mother died when she was thirteen and her father turned to drink. He flew into drunken rages, she says, and would disappear for weeks, leaving her to bring up her four-year-old younger sister. Roxy was forced to bake cookies in the evenings after school to sell and support the family. At fifteen her father once beat her so hard that she was in a coma for a week, she says. 'But he's ill now and dying so I have forgiven him.'

Roxy's travelling companion from Deva is Mihaela Sirbulescu, 24, who is on her way to Rotterdam, where she has lived since she was nineteen, making flower bouquets. She first went there with a Romanian boyfriend but around six months ago he broke up with her and now leaving home after a Christmas break is harder than ever. Though she and Roxy have never met before, the two talk softly together, ahead of a journey that is making them both apprehensive. 'Nowhere is better than home,' Mihaela says later. 'In the beginning it was good but since my boyfriend ended things it just doesn't feel like home. Yesterday I cried all day, from eleven in the morning until eleven at night. It just hurts too much to go.'

Through Hungary and Austria, Romania's single-lane roads are replaced with fast motorways. The coach speeds through the night. Once the sun is up we are in Germany. In Frankfurt, a dozen people get off. As the bus nears Cologne, Pamela gets changed and puts on make-up, ready for a night with clients. 'Today I go back to work. Tonight I will finish at around 7am. Then it's Friday and Saturday and it's open all the time. What can I do? If I don't work I don't get paid.'

In Cologne, five people change coach for the last leg to London. Four of them are Romanians: Roxy, Mihai, and two brothers in-law from Turnu-Severin, Romeo Dinescu, 33 and Gelu Ipsas, 39, who have been working as builders in London since 2009. The fifth person is Mark de Groote, 24, a Dutch jewellery maker living in London, who is returning from holiday in Romania. Roxy has to wait longest for all her bags to come off the coach. 'I didn't know what to buy or what to take,' she says, looking abashed. The indecision seems to have resulted in an unfeasible amount of baggage – three suitcases and a carpet bag. One of the bags, she says, is just shoes.

On the new coach Roxy is told that her four suitcases are too many, and that she will have to pay a ten euro charge. Her face blanches. With only a few cents to her name she starts to panic. But other passengers step in and soon the cases have been spread among the group.

The bus is already almost full of people looking settled into the journey. When many refuse to give up the spare seats next to them, Roxy looks more nervous than ever. Such unfriendliness wouldn't happen in Romania, she says.

After dropping off people in Brussels, the bus arrives at Calais at 2am. Wind and rain lash the windows. A neon sign flashes 'The port of Calais wishes you a Happy New Year 2014!' The ferries are delayed because of the storms and in the normally calm port, the waters rage. Roxy is afraid of the sea and has never been on a ferry before. As the coach pulls onto the ramp she looks wide-eyed at the tempestuous water below.

Inside the boat people stagger around, holding onto rails as it is buffeted across the Channel. As the waves get bigger Roxy excuses herself to the bathroom and comes back white-faced.

In the hope of perking people up, Roxy offers to buy coffees, which at service stations in Romania cost one lei (18p). On her way back from the Costa bar with a latte and an espresso she looks shocked: 'This is a day's work in Romania,' she says, aghast.

At 4am the bus comes off the boat – and is hauled straight to an enormous warehouse for a full baggage search. Only then can the bus finally leave for London.

But minutes after passing the White Cliffs it turns around and comes back again. The steering is broken and everyone must wait for a replacement coach that has space for just 30 of the 40 passengers. When the new bus arrives a stampede of people rush through the heavy rain clutching their belongings. Inside, Roxy looks out at the streaming windows and laughs: 'Welcome to England.'

The bus is freezing while the engine is off but there is a CCTV camera above almost every seat. 'They have cameras but no warmth?' she asks, incredulously.

As London starts to go by, she smiles with recognition at the red buses and looks excited. Peering up at the dark buildings, Mihai recalls the first time he stepped out in this new city. 'I was so lost; all the buildings are made with red bricks and it was hard to remember where I was because everything looked the same.'

As the coach turns into Victoria, though, Roxy holds her red pillow closer and looks frightened. 'My heart is going like this,' she says, tapping her chest fast. Mihai stays to make sure she meets her new family safely. A man in a hoodie walks past twice before deciding that Roxy is the woman he is looking for. This smiley man is her new boss, Jas, a 45-year-old jewellery importer from Ealing, west London. He proudly shows phone videos of his five-year-old twins, Rohan and Karena. Back out in the rain, Mihai and Roxy follow him around the corner to a silver Lexus where her cases are piled into the boot.

On seeing Roxy go, Mihai looks unsure of himself. Standing on a rainy intersection, he turns on his heel and begins to head back to the bus stop and a night in a house with twelve workmates he still struggles to call friends.

The *Daily Express* predicted an influx of migrants by coach under the headline 'Benefits Britain Here We Come' – but on this bus, Roxy is the only Romanian arriving in London for the first time. Once in the car, she waves goodbye and looks ahead, ready to start her new life. Working Britain, here she comes.

◆

Working without a National Insurance number weighs heavily on Mihai. Being an illegal employee makes him feel unwanted in Britain and he is desperate to join in and pay taxes. For more than a year he has felt uneasy about his illicit income, knowing that without being registered he risks prosecution. A few days after arriving back in London in the New Year, he goes to ask his boss for help applying. Working regulations have been lifted for Romanians, so there is no longer any reason to be in the shadows. His boss just says he is too busy to help and changes the subject. After this happens a couple of times, Mihai decides to do it himself. Not confident of his English, he gets a friend to call the helpline and book an appointment in Camden Job Centre Plus.

A fortnight later Mihai is standing under the green Job Centre Plus sign near Mornington Crescent station. He is half an hour early and his hands are already quivering with nerves. He worries what will happen if they realise he has already been working without permission. A G4S security guard on the door takes his papers and ushers him in. No guests are allowed inside, so Mihai sits alone waiting to be called.

He is ushered inside and when asked why he has come, Mihai's explanation comes tumbling out. He recalls later: 'I told him the truth – that I'd always worked; that I washed dishes and I'd done driving and building. He said it's OK and it's better to show that I've worked and not been stealing things. I said, "I want to pay taxes. I want the people in the UK to know that I'm working hard and I want to pay to live here."'

When the interviewer asks if he wants to go on benefits. Mihai is quick to reply: 'Why would I want to do that? On benefits I'd get maybe £800 but if I work I could get £2,000.' To illustrate his point, he says, 'I like working – look at my hands!' and upturns his calloused palms to the interviewer, smiling. But Mihai is not offended by the question and often remarks that the prejudice is a fair one. 'Some Romanians in Britain are just here for the benefits. In the communist time if you had more than seven children, especially boys, you were a hero mother and got more benefits. That has been in our culture.'

As the interview goes on and Mihai's fingers continue to tremble, the man tries to reassure him. 'Don't be scared', he says, 'I'm not going to kill you.' Mihai is asked for all the addresses of the places he has lived – on the Holloway Road, in Finchley and now in Hendon – before being told that he will hear back in three weeks' time.

When he walks outside he is still shaking, but smiling too. 'It was OK – he was nice,' he says, relieved. His reasons reveal the prejudices still common among his fellow Romanian exiles – he struggles to adjust to the idea of Britain being multi-racial. 'I was nervous I might get an Indian guy because my friends told me they'd be racist to me. I heard people got rejected by them. But it was a black guy and he was nice, funny.'

Mihai does not want to bring his girlfriend Roxana and their son Mario to join him until he has found better work and can afford a place of their own to live in. 'My first four months in Britain I didn't have any accommodation, I was just walking round like a dog in the rain. I slept in hallways and I was depressed. I don't want Roxana to be depressed.' The current home would never be suitable for them, he says. His terraced house in Hendon, north London, is now shared with twelve other builders, all men, who are squashed into a handful of bedrooms. The conditions are cramped but he is still charged more than £250 in rent. When the heating turns off it is Mihai's job to gather £5 each for the meter from his reluctant housemates. He is stuck – unable to afford to leave but desperate for his own home so he can be reunited with his family. He hopes a National Insurance number may help him towards a better-paid job as a driver, which he prefers to construction labouring.

A fortnight later Mihai calls, elated. 'I got the letter, I got it!' A card with his National Insurance number has arrived in the post and now he is part of the legal workforce. His British driving licence has also come through and his dream of a career as a driver now feels within reach. The two small cards are the only prompt he needs to begin planning a future in Britain with Roxana and Mario. 'I miss them so much. I worry about her; she went back and took her high school exams recently but she failed some. She works at McDonald's in Bucharest until late every day and had no time to study. I hate McDonald's now. Whenever I pass it I feel angry; they make her work from six in the morning until eight in the evening. That's fourteen hours. I won't even eat there in London now.'

Mihai wants to get married in September. He and Roxana had not planned to have a child and until now have had little time to think about a wedding, which in Romania means saving huge sums so you can entertain several hundred people.

When he suggests an autumn ceremony, Roxana is coy. 'She says I have to ask her properly, not on the phone,' Mihai explains. 'I love her and I want to marry her. If we do it in September then she and Mario come to Britain afterwards, and it will be easier to find a home.'

With Roxana's words at the top of his mind, Mihai decides he will drive to Romania at Easter and surprise her with a proposal. He often does the drive to Bucharest, delivering cars that friends want brought over from Britain. They pay his expenses if he drives the car and it means he can avoid the slower bus route. He loves driving, despite a near fatal accident in his early 20s, when he was driving fast on the motorway with no seatbelt and careered into another car. He had to have both his legs reconstructed after his knees were crushed under the steering wheel.

He is excited to be going back, and looking forward to seeing the Romanian countryside on the journey. He often reminisces about the mountains near Bucharest. His aunt lives there by a lake where they would all go fishing for catfish and carp. 'The carp are so big there that even the army divers are scared of them,' he laughs. 'One said he saw one with a giant head and wasn't going in.'

The night before leaving he buys some ear plugs to make sure he gets a good night's sleep, undisturbed by his house-mates' Friday night drinking. 'They like to drink moonshine all night and say nasty things about the people at work. I prefer to stay in my room. I have to sleep because I'm not going to stop on the journey, I will drive all night because I just want to get there and see Roxana.'

◆

When Mihai arrived in Romania he could hardly wait to get to Roxana. He had not told her he was coming, keen for his arrival – and proposal – to be a surprise. But when he opened the door to her flat, Roxana and Mario were not alone. Sitting with the two of them on the sofa was another man. The three were easy together, like a family, and Mihai's stomach flipped with jealousy.

Friends of Mihai's had hinted there might be someone else – 'We've seen her in bars with other men,' they told him, trying to warn him of what might be happening. But Mihai did not want to believe it. He thought they were stirring up trouble. He loved Roxana, quietly enjoying the responsibility of looking after her and Mario, regularly sending home almost everything he earned once he paid the bills.

With little explanation for the intimate scene, Roxana opted for the truth. 'I'm in love with him,' she said, 'and my feelings for you won't come back.' Mihai left the flat in a rage. He went to his sister who tried to calm him down. 'Don't be angry,' she soothed, 'you'll only regret it later.'

He would pick over Roxana's words for months afterwards. 'I don't know how long they were together and if she told me I wouldn't believe her', he said in the weeks afterwards. 'Everybody lies to me. I know that guy, he doesn't make money – he just likes to party. He doesn't like to work and she works so hard. I don't know, maybe he knows how to talk to a woman but I always tried to protect her and give her a good life. I don't hate her. I just fear what may happen to her.'

In retrospect he notices the signs that things were wrong. 'I would call her maybe fifteen times a day and she barely ever answered. She would just say, "I don't have time to speak, I have things to do." You can feel it when a person changes; you feel it in your soul.'

He returns from the trip more motivated than ever to make his life work in Britain. 'It broke my heart. All my feelings for her, she didn't feel them on her side. I'll be in London for a long time now because I don't want to go back to Romania. After that trip I hate Romania.'

The cousin of the boss, Enache, has moved into the house in Hendon, where he was given the whole top floor to himself. After becoming a good friend to Mihai, who is quieter than the others and less fond of moonshine, Enache asked Mihai to take the other room on the top floor with him. The friendship is a great support to Mihai, who confides in him some of what happened when he went to Bucharest. 'You are Spartan,' Enache told Mihai when he heard the story. 'You have to stand up straight; she's not worth anything.' The separate quarters mean he can stay away from the chaos and noise of the other twelve builders and he becomes less bothered by the idea of moving out or changing employers.

With a British driving licence sorted, Mihai persuades the boss to take him on as a van driver, buying and delivering materials to the company's sites across London, Kent and Brighton. Not wanting to think about his imploded personal life, he drives all the hours he is offered. The work numbs the sadness and soon he is making up to £2,500 every month, working fourteen hours a day. Within four weeks he has driven 4,000 miles, stopping only to sleep and barely remembering to eat.

He likes delivering things for the company and feeling useful, taking pains to find the best deals on his smartphone before picking up materials from suppliers. He misses having a job with a civic purpose. When he was nineteen he worked as a firefighter as his army national service. He loved it in spite of the risks and built a reputation for courage. One day he saved two children from a burning building, giving them his own oxygen mask and his spare as he carried them out. The smoke inhalation left him in a coma for several days afterwards.

Saturdays are the only day off, as some of the management are Jewish and want to observe the Sabbath. Most of the workers spend the Friday night drinking followed by the Saturday in a hungover stupor, but Mihai uses the time to help out friends. Since he is allowed to use the van as his personal car, he drives them to the supermarket to carry their food home and to run errands. With good English he often goes to translate for people needing to pay bills or organise a mobile phone contract.

In the months after discovering Roxana's infidelity, one thing keeps gnawing away at Mihai. His son Mario never looked much like him – or anyone in his family – and he is beginning to wonder if the boy may have been a trick to exploit him for money. He had been in a relationship with Roxana when she fell pregnant six years earlier, but not for very long. She had been only sixteen and didn't take life very seriously. 'Just get a DNA test,' one friend advised. Mihai wanted to go back to Romania and visit his grandma anyway, because she had fallen ill with worsening diabetes and heart problems, so he called Roxana and said what he wanted to do.

Roxana was not enamoured with the DNA test idea but when she continued to refuse, Mihai threatened to take her to court for it. He was still sending around £400 a month for the upkeep of his son, more than the legal requirement for a father, and he did not like the nagging feeling that he had been duped. 'OK, OK', she acquiesced, making him hope that his worries had just been paranoia.

In July, Mihai arrived back in Romania. He did not tell anyone he was coming, except his grandmother, though even she was unaware of his real business there. At a hospital in Bucharest, he paid almost 1,000 euros to have himself and Mario tested. A nurse took a blood sample, as well as a piece of fingernail and hair. The results came back: Mario was someone else's son.

The news crushed Mihai. He replayed the early years of his relationship with Roxana, remembering, 'I never wanted to believe the people who said "Mihai, I saw her out in pubs late at night" when I was in London, or before that, in Italy. I didn't want to trust them because when you love somebody you need to trust them, but they were right.'

As soon as he found out he went back to his grandmother's house and fell apart. He was in the country only for a couple of days and he spent the rest of his time lying on the bed in her small flat with his head in her lap like a young boy, while she stroked his hair and told him stories about her life. He could not bring himself to tell her the details about what happened, just saying 'I broke up and it wasn't OK'. His explanation was enough for her. She had always provided the love his parents failed to. His mother and father were indifferent to him when he was growing up, caught up in alcohol problems and their own failing relationship. 'To live with your parents and feel alone is a hard feeling,' he would say later, 'but my grandma loves me unconditionally.'

In August Mihai worked more than ever, blocking out the pain of the last few months. Much of the work had moved to Brighton and involved long drives to and from London lugging around supplies. One night he came back so tired that when he sat down at the table to eat his soup he fell asleep, the spoon still in his hand. When he woke the next morning in the same position, the bowl of cold soup next to his head, he simply began eating it. Once he'd finished, he went out to work again.

◆

It is autumn 2014 and the boss at Mihai's construction company has finally registered all his staff with National Insurance numbers. Restrictions on Romanian and Bulgarian labour were lifted many months earlier, but he tells Mihai he had not had time to do it before. 'I'm close to the bosses now', Mihai says. 'They don't make dirty things, they are good men and they always pay. I've worked for them for more than two years now and there's no day they didn't pay.'

Driving around in his own van makes him feel very fortunate. 'I was very lucky with this boss. When I go to the builders' depot or to Wickes I see a lot of people and they are mostly Romanians who are searching for work. They ask everyone who goes outside if they have work for them. When I drive in they're looking at me and asking me for work. I feel sorry for them. Usually there are 30, 40, or even 50 people waiting on Staples Corner. They wait hoping for any work. Sometimes they find work, sometimes they work and don't get paid. Most don't have a National Insurance number. I have a lot of friends in Romania who want me to bring them to London to work. A lot don't know what it's like here, though. They think: "Oh, it's London, I'll find honey on the street." They don't realise how hard it is to find a job.'

The twelve other builders who Mihai lives with in north London are keen to set him up with a new girl after Roxana's betrayal. He was uninterested at first; he was badly hurt and just wanted not to think about women for a while. Then one of his housemates with a girlfriend in Romania started to tell him about this girlfriend's widowed sister, Irina. The more Mihai heard about this gentle woman and her young daughter Maria, the more he liked the sound of her. They made friends on Facebook and soon they were messaging each other all through the day, Mihai sneaking a look at his mobile whenever he stopped the van. Irina is six months older than him and had just turned 30. Her husband died in a car accident two years earlier, leaving her behind with their daughter Maria, now seven. Where they live, a village about ten miles outside Bucharest, there is no pavement and the car had mowed him down on the road's edge. Now she survives on the proceeds of a small garden-farm, raising pigs and selling corn. She cannot work full-time because of her daughter and she never has more than around £70 a month.

'I like her because she's fighting with life and she doesn't expect anything from anybody,' Mihai says. 'She doesn't complain about life. I haven't met her yet but when I come back to Romania I want to come and see her. I think she's a little bit afraid in case I'm that kind of man who only wants to sleep with her but I don't want anything from her.'

The friendship gives Mihai a renewed sense of purpose. When he hears that Irina has an old Nokia phone with no Facebook messenger on it, he sends her a Samsung smartphone for her birthday so they can chat whenever they want. He asks if her daughter Maria would like anything and Irina is suspicious. 'You're a stranger, why do you want to buy something for my little girl?' Mihai could not really explain. 'I just feel I'd like to do this.' It made him feel good to help out when they had so little. Eventually Irina put

Maria on the phone to Mihai one day and she asked for a doll. 'She didn't want gadgets or phones or tablets, she just wanted a doll. It was wonderful. I felt wow, I want to meet both of them.'

With no money now being sent to Roxana, he enjoys the chance to spoil others. On his sister's birthday he sends her an enormous flat-screen television.

Over the late summer and autumn Mihai grows to like Irina more and more. 'I like her because she doesn't want anything for free; she works for what she has. When I call her she has her headset on and she is always working, cleaning, cooking or out on the farm. She doesn't know but she gave me life lessons. I spend £700 here in London on nonsense, on Playstation games and junk food and things like this. She only has £70 a month and she is raising a child.'

She never asks him for anything, despite her situation, and the contrast with Roxana is striking. 'She never complains. When I called Roxana she always complained and said "It's hard, I have nothing." When I call Irina I don't hear any of that; she's only telling me what she's doing, like "Now I'm taking care of my flowers, or now I'm washing, or playing with Maria."'

There are not many pictures of her on Facebook, but the few there are show a beautiful young mother with dark glossy hair. Mihai resolves to go to Romania in October to meet her. He has only five days off but he can do it cheaply; his boss is letting him take the van. The week before he leaves he feels like an excited teenager. Irina is planning to cook for him and he is desperate for it to go well. 'I'm nervous about it but I will ask her if she will go out with me. I told her I want to know you better because you're a nice person. I saw good things in her and I know I need to fight for her if I want her, to gain her trust.'

♦

The previous two times Mihai returned from a trip to Romania it had been under the shroud of a fresh betrayal. First the discovery of Roxana's infidelity – and then the realisation that Mario was not his real son. But his last trip of 2014 ends differently. Irina has agreed to a relationship and as he goes about his deliveries in London it is with a smile fixed permanently to his face.

The October visit to Irina and her daughter Maria was a success. They talked and talked at her farmhouse and he sat with Maria while she played with the doll and toy pram he had given her. He got to see his grandma, who cooked his favourite dinner of pork meatballs and cabbage pickle, and he visited his sister. Though he rarely sees his mum and dad, he is close to his sister and her son, who was named Mihai after him and is also his godson. Mihai junior is nine and spending time with him eases the pain of losing Mario. They play football in the garden and Mihai tells his namesake that one day he can be like Lionel Messi if he works hard at the football academy he is training at.

Reminders of the hurt he felt at losing Roxana and Mario still return sometimes, but seeing seven-year-old Maria and his nephew Mihai help him recover. 'It's not Mario's fault, I don't hate him. But I won't see them any more because it harms my soul. I don't want contact with them. There's something here for Mario,' he says, patting his chest, 'but the deception was too big. To raise a child for six years and then discover it's not yours … They are feelings you can't find words for.'

When he returns to Britain he feels torn between the two countries for the first time all year. But he still sees the flaws back home. 'I miss my grandma and my sister and my nephew but that's it. People say: "You don't miss Romania, you traitor." I love my country but life is very hard there.'

He has found a Romanian shop in Burnt Oak that sells his favourite Fruity Fresh pear juice from back home. Every few weeks he drops by to replenish his supplies. He is easy-going again, enjoying the company of his housemates and even going out drinking with them occasionally. But mostly, he drives. In the first nine months of being in charge of the van he has driven more than 35,000 miles. Next Easter he will make another long drive, back to Romania to see Irina. He would like to bring her to Britain but he knows she loves the farm and, with little English, would struggle to make a living in London.

As the days wear on his plans for the future change. When he first heard of Roxana's betrayal he was convinced that his long-term future was in Britain. Now he thinks he may save up for five years and build a better house for him and Irina in her village outside Bucharest. To have enough for a house – and to supplement what would be a lower income in Romania – he will need to save more than ever before. The prospect is not daunting to him. 'I am powerful,' he says, curling his bicep with a cheeky grin. 'I can work as long as there are days.'

◆

CHAPTER 2

Ummad

It took a YouTube video to persuade Ummad Farooq that Sunderland was the university for him. While the promise of decent wages drew Mihai to Britain, for Ummad it was the lure of a peaceful education in the country of dreaming spires. From his bedroom in Karachi, he scrolled through university websites on his laptop. He had whittled the decision down to a handful of MBAs with affordable fees that might offer scholarships as a reward for his First Class degree. Then he saw the Sunderland video. The slogan was 'Life-Changing' and its slick visuals cut between students in the pool, the bar, and finally in their graduate jobs. The campus looked calm and idyllic, far from the bustle of Karachi's 23 million people – and even further from the threat of violence that had begun to hang over his family.

Ummad had wanted to live in England for so long that when he made it to Sunderland aged 21 he embraced a new Mackem identity. He was enthused with a desire to learn the local culture and history, bounding around campus in a hoody, jeans and a bright white smile. As a practising Muslim he did not drink, though he did not mind when his friends did, within reason. He would go to a local Wetherspoon pub, the Lampton, eat fish and chips and watch the football with them.

He believes Muslims must assimilate and adapt to their surroundings. 'If you wear a shalwar kameez and bathroom slippers in Britain I think it's weird and disrespectful,' he says. 'Why not use camels instead of cars then? It's not like you have to look like that to be a Muslim in Britain. It was a necessity of the time having a beard because of the dust in the desert. I'm not an Arab, I'm a Muslim. For me if you're living somewhere you need to respect the values of local people. We are very clear on the need to cover our bodies but Islam doesn't restrict you so that you have to wear a burqa and sunglasses and gloves. Why would God make religion that hard?'

Ummad had reason to savour his new life and religious freedom in Britain. His family had the superficial trappings of comfort in Karachi: an enormous villa, several maids and a successful business, but danger beyond their gates meant they were living in a gilded prison. Ummad's father Farooq was a prominent businessman with a company importing generators. He was also a leading Ahmadiyya Muslim, which increasingly put his family in the cross-hairs of extremists.

Ahmadiyya is a sect of Islam whose followers believe that another prophet came after Mohammad in the nineteenth century, called Mirza Ghulam Ahmad. This idea has seen them condemned as heretics by other Muslims and their right to worship is now forbidden under a series of draconian laws in Pakistan. It has been illegal for an Ahmadi to call themselves Muslim since 1974, when the otherwise liberal leader Zulfikar Ali Bhutto introduced the law to appease conservative critics. Ahmadis' freedom to practise their religion was outlawed entirely a decade later, when the country was under military dictatorship.

Now, just touching a Quran, wearing Islamic clothing such as a skull cap or shalwar kameez, or calling their place of worship a mosque, can result in thousands of pounds in fines and up to twelve years' imprisonment. Even having a building that looks like a mosque is illegal and police have torn down Ahmadi minarets, so that most of their mosques in Pakistan look like houses. Ahmadi graveyards have been desecrated because the tombstones contained Quranic passages.

Ummad thinks this persecution is less about their perceived blasphemous beliefs and more because of the strong stance the community takes on promoting peace and tolerance. Their motto is 'Love For All, Hatred For None' and they are outspoken in saying that no killing can ever be justified, particularly not in the name of Islam. 'Politics has nothing to do with religion but in Pakistan they're all connected and that's where things go wrong,' Ummad says.

Prejudice against Ahmadis is so enshrined in law that police are even accused of turning a blind eye to violent attacks. In 2010 when the Punjabi Taliban besieged two Ahmadi mosques in Lahore and killed more than 90 people, police arrived late and were accused of doing little to prevent the massacre. Three days later a Lahore hospital's intensive care unit, where many victims were being treated, was attacked and another twelve people killed.

Where once Ummad's family got by living quietly and keeping a low profile, now they feared leaving the house without an armed escort. On the few occasions they did they carefully timed their movements to avoid a predictable routine that could be exploited by would-be attackers. Despite the danger at home, when it came to the youngest of their three children leaving Pakistan for England, Ummad's parents worried. Before going, his mum piled up his suitcase with pots and pans until it weighed more than a fully stocked kitchen cabinet. 'Mum,' he groaned, 'you know they have pans in England, right?'

Ummad had always lived in Karachi and loved his home but that wasn't enough to stop the rush of relief when he left. He'd spent so many hours poring over websites and imagining his life in Britain that when he finally arrived it could have been a disappointment; instead the anticipation only added to the excitement.

It was nighttime when he landed at Heathrow in September 2011 but it still took him a while to get through customs. 'Can we check your bag, there's something suspicious,' a man in uniform demanded. Ummad undid the zip and looked down sheepishly at its heavy metal contents. 'What's all this?' the officer asked, sifting through piles of heavy pots and pans. Once Ummad's embarrassment was complete, he was ushered on.

At Arrivals he was met by Ahmed, an old friend of his father's who had recently moved to Britain. They set off for his home in Wandsworth near Britain's first Ahmadiyya mosque. Even the most prosaic things astonished Ummad. 'The whole of London seemed amazing,' Ummad recalls of that night. He saw a fox walking around the street – something he had never seen in Pakistan – and at the supermarket he was transfixed by the sight of people scanning their own groceries at automated check-outs. The next day at Kings Cross station, a place he had only ever seen in Harry Potter films, the excitement had still not dissipated.

When he got out of the train at Sunderland he hailed a taxi and asked to be taken to his halls of residence. The driver's reply made no sense at all. It did not even sound like English and Ummad began to doubt himself. 'I thought "I'm not that bad at English, I'm quite fluent even,"' he remembers. That was his first experience of a north-east accent, one which after five years of living in the region, he has adopted himself. Now his sentences are peppered with the word 'like', which in his Geordie twang sounds more like 'lake'.

After Karachi, Sunderland was a kind of paradise. Acutely aware of his good fortune, he put everything into university life. Within days of beginning the MBA he was elected to represent all 70 students on the course and had joined a host of societies and clubs. He was surrounded by people from around the world: China, Malaysia, America and Singapore and his whole life seemed to be opening up. Having already studied chartered accountancy he found the work pretty easy and got on well with his teachers.

His first December brought a sighting of snow. He was in his halls of residence with two friends, fellow students from South India who had also never been in a cold country before. They ran outside like excited children and stopped, staring, delighted, unsure what to do next. When the flakes piled up in drifts after a few days, they went out to build snowmen.

To Ummad, the riverside campus was just as beautiful as it had seemed in the video and he split his time between lecture theatre, library and gym. With an easy smile and the kind of bright eyes that come from optimism, regular exercise and no booze, he looked like a cast member of an American High School film. Looking back now he says that time was the happiest of his life. He liked being a person that other students turned to when they had problems. Sunderland isn't a big place and at first he was struck by how old everyone was. Aside from the students there were few young people and he could see more funeral homes than places to play. But he grew to love the small city and liked being stopped in the street and recognised by other students. In Pakistan he was quite shy but here his confidence grew.

'Thanks so much for sending me', he told his father in an emotional video call to Karachi. He lifted up his laptop and moved it along the horizon, showing him the library and campus. It's great. Coming to England was the best decision.'

◆

Ummad's mother missed her youngest son terribly. He had been away for almost a year when she began to beg him to come back for a visit. It was August 2012 and she wanted him home to celebrate Eid. His older brother and sister would both be there and if Ummad came the whole family would be reunited. Ummad decided to surprise her. His older sister Saba was travelling back from America, where she worked as a doctor, so they both booked flights to Turkey and flew to Pakistan together from Istanbul.

Ummad spun his mother along, saying he had too much work. Even when he was at Heathrow and about to catch the plane he called her to say he was in the library. When he walked out behind his sister into the Arrivals hall at Jinnah International airport his mother squealed with excitement.

The joy of the reunion was exquisite, but short-lived. Even in the brief time Ummad was away, life had become more frightening for his family. Or perhaps the distance just meant he noticed it more. As leader of the Ahmadi community in Baldia Town, western Karachi, Ummad's father was a target for local hatred. He was responsible for organising some 80 families in their secret worship. That role, combined with his business success, angered local extremists. They began to send him death threats.

As children, Ummad, his older brother Saad, and sister Saba had few opportunities to play with non-Ahmadi kids. Ahmadis often get teased and called Qadianis, a reference to the city of Qadiani in India where the sect originated and to which Ummad has since made four pilgrimages. When Ummad tried to play with other kids in the street they would shout 'Qadiani,' laugh and run away. They said they couldn't eat with him or have an Ahmadi in their homes. So Ummad was relieved when he went to study at a private Catholic school in Karachi, St Patrick High School, which has two former presidents among its alumni and doesn't tolerate religious bullying. Mostly he and his siblings learnt to stay in their home or play only with other Ahmadi kids. To do otherwise was inviting trouble.

Staying at home was not as bad as it could have been. Their house was a spacious five-storey villa with three maids, including one who just washed and ironed their clothes. Ummad's mum worked as a nursing sister and when she came home from work she would help the maids make everything ready for dinner. A lot of the time they were happy, though their gates were high and always closed. They learnt to ignore the pocking sound of stones being thrown at the ironwork.

Even while Ummad was at school there were risks involved in going out of the house. 'If you want to go out just make sure it's for a good reason,' his father insisted. As Ahmadi children, Ummad and his cousin Zain were at risk of kidnap even on their journey to school, so they would get into a chauffeur driven car and lock its doors before even opening the gate.

Ummad's father Farooq set up the family business FG Prime Power in 1992 and it was getting stronger and stronger, supplying power generators to some of the biggest industrial players in the country. They would import them from Singapore to save money and they had built a reputation across Pakistan. They were a wealthy upper-middle-class family but because they were Ahmadi, their enemies accused them of getting rich on Israeli money, which Ummad says is pure invention.

Growing up behind high walls meant Ummad was accustomed to feeling uneasy in Karachi, but on returning from Sunderland he suddenly saw how frightened his father had become. He had started receiving ominous messages ordering him to leave the religion, leave the area or expect to die. A peaceful, quiet man, he had grown up in a poor family in rural Punjab and built his business up from nothing. He had been so desperate to better his family's circumstances as a child that he once looked at a gleaming tractor and asked if he could tie it to a tree; that way, like caught livestock, it would not leave their land. The idea of abandoning a successful business two decades in the making was anathema to him. He also felt for the rest of the Ahmadi community. If he ran away, what would happen to the 80 families in the neighbourhood who relied on him?

Ummad could see the seriousness of the threats but hoped life might be able to continue as before. Then he saw the gun on the dining room table. Nobody in his family had ever owned a firearm; they were peace-loving and his father Farooq had always taught him to reject violence of any kind. But there it was, next to his keys and wallet as if it was the most normal possession in the world. The sight unsettled Ummad who looked up to his father and knew it would have taken a serious threat to push him to such an extreme.

Ummad's father and uncle were business partners and they worked in the same office. But they were so afraid of an attack killing both of them, leaving their families with no support, that they always travelled separately and regularly changed their working hours. Because of the state's complicity in the persecution of Ahmadis, police protection was not an option so they had to use their initiative. At Friday prayers, which had to be at a set time, the young men of the community came together. They formed their own armed motorbike protection detail, escorting the cars of worshippers under threat.

They stopped eating out or shopping locally, instead driving to the other side of the city where they wouldn't be recognised. Ummad's dad began to notice people following him, motorbikes trailing him for long distances. One morning they woke to find graffiti on the wall of their house. It had been carefully painted in black on white and it read: 'Ahmadis should be killed'. It was signed 'JTI,' the student wing of a legitimate political party, the fifth largest in Pakistan, that has fifteen seats in the National Assembly.

The short trip home frightened Ummad. Before he went back to Sunderland he spoke to his father about wanting to stay in Britain. 'Maybe I could claim asylum,' Ummad said, picturing a life without threats. But his dad stayed firm. 'No. It is wrong to take political asylum unless you know for sure the alternative is death. Nothing has happened to you so it would be false. To ask for it would be a lie.' Ummad respected his father but still hoped to persuade him. 'We're not safe here, papa,' he reasoned, 'So how is it a lie?' His father wouldn't budge. 'Do your studies and then get a visa to work in Dubai.'

◆

A less buoyant Ummad returned to Sunderland for the new term. He was scared for his family and though he loved what he was doing, he was distracted by the thought of his father being followed by unknown assailants. Soon he was back in his routine of studying, going to the gym and seeing friends. He even joined the university's rowing club, not to compete, but just to enjoy the exercise and being out on the Wear with friends.

Not long after graduation, Ummad's life lost all of that simple joy. It divides into two halves: before the tragic events of Saad's wedding – and after. Ummad went to London when he finished his MBA in August 2012, where he was quickly offered a job at an accountancy firm in Tower Bridge. A financial job in Britain was something he had dreamed of, but there was one small problem. His brother Saad's wedding was in October and to get his new visa processed by the company he would have to hand over his passport and miss the wedding. His family were clear: he could not miss the party. So reluctantly Ummad walked away from the job.

Ummad flew back for the wedding and was glad he had been able to go. The family were so excited after more than two years of anticipation and Ummad wanted to share it with them. Saad knew his fiancée Shaiza from childhood and they had married on paper two years earlier. But his parents wanted him to finish his studies before he had the proper ceremony. Saad's electrical engineering degree was going well in Pakistan and he was learning his father's business while Shaiza was living in New York with her family, working in health administration. Ummad's mum had relished the preparations, going all across Karachi to find dresses for her new daughter-in-law. Each one was designer made and spent a month to complete and she went back and forth to check alterations. 'It's not safe, why are you going so far, can't you shop somewhere nearer?' Ummad's father would ask in exasperation. But she was happy to take the risks – this was her first child to get married and she wanted it to go well. Saba was the oldest of the three siblings but she had been let off the hook by parents proud of her dedication to medicine.

Saad loved Shaiza. Although the marriage was arranged by their families they were already close and had been like courting teenagers in the two years they lived apart, talking on Skype for hours at a time, plotting out their dreams for a life together. Saad was fun and mischievous and used his electrical engineering skills to play around with robotics. He liked to make robots strong enough to fight in RoboWars and he went to every robot competition in Pakistan, once making one so big he could sit on it. When he was younger he used to open up Ummad's toys to learn what was going on inside. Invariably he worked it out.

Even in what should have been the happy run-up to the wedding, though, the security risks hung over them. Some guests were too afraid to come and the venue had to be chosen carefully. As president of the local Ahmadi community, Ummad's father was obliged to invite all the local Ahmadi families as well as all the other Ahmadi leaders in Karachi. The guest list was around 700 people and he felt a huge burden of responsibility to keep them safe.

They decided to hold the wedding in the military quarter of the city. It had the best security and there was an army wedding hall which could be hired for private parties. They knew the secure area was not a guarantee of safety though – the Taliban had successfully attacked it before. When the day of the wedding came, Monday 15 October 2012, the family was so nervous that Ummad's father kept a gun on him the whole day. He organised extra safety precautions for guests so that coaches would pick them up at a pre-arranged location and then drop them back at their homes so they did not return to the same place. Their efforts paid off. The day went without a glitch: the bride and groom looked beautiful, everyone had a good time and all the guests got home safely.

Nobody guessed that the real danger was yet to come.

Over the next few days Ummad remembers thinking he had never seen his brother look happier. Saad was goofy with his new wife, letting her fuss over his clothes and rarely being more than a few metres away from her. It was the Friday after the wedding and the couple had been married for four days. The men were all getting ready for Friday prayers and Saad was still in the shower, running late. Shaiza was sorting Saad's outfit and Ummad was struck by how vividly happy they both were.

Their father Farooq's routine was to go to Friday prayers with young Ahmadi volunteers escorting his car by motorbike. Travelling by motorbike made it easier to pull out a gun and defend the convoy if someone started firing at them. As head of the student volunteers in the community, Saad was often one of the guards, taking his position behind the car to make sure his dad arrived safely. But this morning his father was getting impatient at Saad's slowness and said he would drive the other men to the service alone; Saad could come later on his motorbike and catch them at the mosque. Saad wasn't having it. 'No, it's not safe Dad,' he said, and rushed to get himself ready. He drove behind the car carrying his father, his new father-in-law Nusrat, two uncles and Ummad. At the mosque the men went in for prayers but Saad stayed behind guarding the entrance with two other youth volunteers. Since the attacks in Lahore, nobody trusted the police to provide security in an Ahmadi mosque, so they did it themselves. CCTV was installed at the entrance and whenever people were inside praying at least three young, armed Ahmadis would stand guard.

When the prayers were over, Saad asked Ummad to wait. Guarding the mosque meant he had not had a chance to say his own prayers and he wanted to go inside and pray. Saad's favourite food was biryani – whenever their mum asked what they would like for dinner, he always said, 'That's a silly question, always biryani'. When he came back from his prayers he was hungry, and asked 'Ummad, biryani?' Ummad declined. It was hot and he wanted to get into the air-conditioned car. Those were the last words his brother said to him.

The men had piled into the car again: their father drove with Saad's new father-in-law sitting beside him and Ummad in the back beside two uncles. Saad got on his motorbike.

They had only just begun their journey when they heard the gunshot. They could see nothing until a gunman on the back of a motorbike suddenly pulled up alongside them. Before they could react, a volley of bullets tore through the car. A bullet hit Ummad's dad in the neck and as Saad's father-in-law Nusrat turned to see what was happening, he too was shot in the neck. Then the bike accelerated and turned sharply in front of the car, blocking it, and the attacker fired another burst, hitting Ummad's father Farooq again, in his lungs, chest, and arm. But Ummad didn't see this part – one of the bullets had hit him between the eyes and blood was pouring from his head. Everyone in the car was wearing a white shalwar kameez for their prayers and in an instant all the white inside the car

turned red. Ummad screamed 'I've lost my eye'. He couldn't
see anything and the searing pain in his eye socket convinced
him it had gone. The shooters ran away and one of Ummad's
uncles got out to find Saad. 'Saad's down' he shouted back to
the car, 'he's down.' People coming back from prayers helped
carry the motionless Saad into the car and laid him across
Ummad's lap. He had been hit by the first bullet, a single
shot to the neck. Ummad noticed how heavy he was, lying
there across his knees. He had always admired his big brother's
strength but suddenly he was powerless. 'Saad's name means
lion and he was brave like a lion,' Ummad remembers. 'I'm
sure if he had been shot anywhere else he wouldn't have let
those people go, he would have chased them. He was so brave
and so strong.'

Even with five bullet wounds, their father was determined
to drive his family to safety. He hurtled the car across Karachi
for twenty minutes, his lungs rattling for air where the bullet
had punctured them. Ambulances are notoriously unreliable
in Pakistan and some hospitals won't accept gunshot patients
until the police arrive because of the risk of attracting further
terrorism. Their father knew that if his family was going to
survive he needed to get them to a private hospital. Saad's
father-in-law Nusrat was drifting in and out of consciousness
and Ummad kept asking him 'Are you OK? Are you OK?' His
only whispered reply was 'How far is it?'

Once they reached the hospital Ummad tried to pull Saad
out of the car but he couldn't do it. There were no police and
nobody to help. In the end it was other Ahmadi volunteers
who had rushed to the hospital after them, who helped get
him out. As they went inside, Ummad took the gun from his
father in case they needed defending again. His father could

barely understand what was going on. Having completed the drive on adrenaline, his body finally gave up. The hospital staff were so accustomed to seeing the trauma wounds that they hardly spoke to Ummad and his family. Without painkillers they stabbed his father in the chest with tubes to drain the blood from his lungs.

Ummad pleaded with the staff to pump Saad's heart and give him life-saving injections. They told him to 'calm down' and that there was no point in trying. 'We see this every day,' they chastised, before making what seemed to Ummad to be a cursory resuscitation attempt. Shortly afterwards, his sister Saba arrived, desperate to save Saad. She had a friend working there who was also a doctor and they both set to work on him. As she worked, Saba was crying with an intensity that Ummad had never heard before and it frightened him. A peaceful family that had not seen blood was now covered in it.

Ummad couldn't look at his brother. A part of him knew he was dead. 'Papa, he's alive, not dead,' he said over and over to his father. But Saad had been killed instantly by the bullet, a martyr at 26.

His new bride, Shaiza, meanwhile, was still at home, oblivious to the scale of the tragedy. She had not been told on the phone that Saad was dead, just that he had been in a shooting. Even as hospital staff tried to treat Ummad, his father and Nusrat, the family knew they had to prepare to move. The hospital wasn't safe; when Ahmadis were taken there after previous attacks it had come under siege. The community volunteers came armed and packed the three of them into an ambulance and on to a secure hospital.

Ummad's dad was taken into intensive care and Saad's father-in-law was taken into the operating theatre. Nusrat had been partially paralysed by the bullet to the neck and had lost a lot of blood. On the journey to the second hospital Ummad lost consciousness. His now red Shalwar Kameez was cut off his body and they checked him everywhere for other wounds. An x-ray was taken of Ummad's head – the bullet was still there. It had pierced the skull and was sitting between his eyes on his brain. He still couldn't see out of one eye but the surgeon said operating was out of the question. They knew one false move with a scalpel could kill him – but he couldn't carry a bullet around in his head indefinitely either. When night fell the rest of the family were taken to a safe house by an armed escort of eighteen Ahmadi students on motorbikes.

Back at the family home that evening, one of Ummad's uncles was dropping by to give the happy couple his best wishes. He rang the bell at the gate, oblivious to the afternoon's tragedy, when several menacing characters approached. They had been staking out the house. He got back on his motorbike, the thugs trailing him for miles, until he lost the tail.

Ummad stayed in hospital for three days with an armed guard keeping vigil outside his door. As he rested, Ummad kept looking over at the other two beds where his father and Nusrat lay, and asking, 'will they be OK?' Nobody could think of an honest answer to calm him.

Ummad was discharged with the bullet still sitting on his brain because the surgeons were too afraid to operate. He was taken to join the rest of his family in the safe house, run in secret by the Ahmadi community as a haven for those who come under attack. He had been afraid in the attack's aftermath. Now he felt fortified by new courage knowing he would have to be the man of the family. Nobody was allowed to use a mobile phone in case the call could be traced, so Ummad used Skype to contact friends. Since the family suspected the government was backing their persecution, no precautions seemed too paranoid.

Ummad's father got out of hospital after a week. He was determined to show strength and when he got out of the car at the safe house he walked inside unaided. Shortly afterwards, Nusrat's struggle to stay alive ended. His death left Shaiza with no husband and no father. Three months later her mother died of cancer. She had been ill before the wedding but it seemed the sudden grief had finished her.

◆

Ummad's family wanted to get him out of the country, somewhere he had a chance of treatment and a peaceful life. They hoped if he went back to England he would get the surgery he needed and that, with several months still left on his visa, he could apply for asylum in his own time. His father could no longer say the risks were too abstract to seek sanctuary.

The swelling on Ummad's face had started to go down and he had some sight back in the damaged eye. He put a dressing on the bullet wound and left for the airport on 27 October, eight days after the attack. An Ahmadi friend in airport security helped him get through without too much hassle. Pakistani Ahmadis are legally required to declare their religion on their passport – and once the fact is known by an immigration officer it often leads to a sudden bureaucratic delay. That evening was no exception but it was comforting to have a friend by his side, who was able to stay almost until he got on the plane. Remembering the heartbreak of that night, Ummad says: 'It was so sad. You're waiting for the time you can leave the country you love and the place you were born.

You don't hate the land, it's just the people who don't know what they're doing.'

He got on a flight to Turkey and fell into a deep sleep. In Turkey the security officers asked him a lot of questions. Any flight from Pakistan going to the UK or America prompts scrutiny and Ummad knew if he revealed the real reason for his head dressings they might not let him fly because they would know he was trying to claim asylum. So he made his explanation vague, saying he was returning to his studies and that the injury was caused by an accident. 'Oh, you must've been riding a bike,' the security guard said kindly. Ummad just nodded and managed a weak smile. It was enough to get him through.

When his flight landed in Heathrow he was met by the same old family friend who collected him the first time he arrived in England, Ahmed. But this was a much more sombre arrival. The head of the Ahmadi community worldwide, Caliph Mirza Masroor Ahmad, had heard about the attack on Ummad and his family and told his private secretary that he wanted to meet him. The caliph is the spiritual leader of millions of Ahmadis and has been based in London since the forced exile from Pakistan of his predecessor in 1984, when persecution reached its peak. The headquarters of the Ahmadiyya faith is now split between two mosques in Wandsworth and Morden.

Ummad was taken to Ahmed's house, next to Fazl mosque in Wandsworth. His head dressing meant he couldn't take a shower before meeting the man who, for him, was bigger than the Pope. He just had to change his clothes and head back out.

The meeting with the caliph didn't disappoint. It was meant to be three minutes but it overran, the time stretching as he comforted Ummad, even giving him a hug, which he still remembers for its restorative effect. 'It gave me a sense of calm. When you're that close to religion you get a sense that people love you.'

It was Eid that day, a time Ummad would normally be celebrating with family. Instead the caliph's secretary sent him to the house of the man who leads the Ahmadi community on non-spiritual matters; a chartered accountant living near the mosque. His host gave him tea and sweets and even though it was already ten in the evening, made a phone call to one of the best trauma surgeons in the country who also happens to be an Ahmadi Muslim. Shahzada Ahmed is a specialist in ear, nose, throat and skull surgery, based at Queen Elizabeth hospital in Birmingham. He took the call and when he heard about Ummad's situation he asked him to come to the hospital the next morning. The Ahmadi community clubbed together to fund his treatment and Ummad was admitted as a private patient the next day.

At the same time as Ummad was receiving care at the Queen Elizabeth, Malala Yousafzai, another exile from violence in Pakistan who later took the Nobel Peace Prize for her brave pursuit of girls' education rights, was upstairs, undergoing surgery on the skull shattered by a Taliban bullet. Malala was being looked after in a secure room at the top of the building where dignitaries including Pakistan's President and a host of British politicians visited her. The hospital is famous for rebuilding soldiers mangled by war and its expertise proved invaluable for two young victims of another kind of violence.

Mr Ahmed, who was also involved in Malala's treatment, examined scans of Ummad's head. He now understood why Ummad had lost most sight in one eye: parts of the bullet had forced the muscles around his eye to stick to the shattered bone of its socket. To save his sight, the muscles had to be removed and then put back in place. But the hardest part was removing the bullet. Walking around with a piece of jagged metal sitting on his brain was not safe and the surgeon was keen to remove it as soon as possible.

A week later Ummad had the operation. Knowing the risks of removing an object so close to the brain, Mr Ahmed tried a new technique to extract the bullet. He went up through Ummad's nose using a revolutionary piece of technology – and it worked. Most of the bullet was removed, without extra scarring. Now you have to look closely to even see the scar where the bullet went in.

When Ummad came round from the anaesthetic and saw a friendly nurse, he was amazed at how well he felt. He was not in any pain and he knew exactly where he was. The nurse wanted to throw away the bullet but Ummad insisted on keeping it: 'I wanted it as evidence for the Home Office.'

Ummad's eye had been saved and his vision returned. 'You're lucky, extremely lucky,' said an eye surgeon who saw him after the operation. 'I've never seen such a lucky person.' Ummad later recalled: 'That windscreen saved my life. I've never heard of anyone who was shot in the head and survived. I've got a strong head I guess. A strong skull.'

Ummad recovered at a nearby private hospital and would later be horrified to read comments on a local news report about his operation. 'They were saying 'Why do these people come over and use the NHS?' but I hadn't, the Ahmadi community paid for it all.' The Ahmadi community commonly stumps up such costs. Charity, volunteering and fundraising is a huge part of their ethos and they raise huge sums in Britain for causes as varied as Macmillan Cancer Support and Help for Heroes.

When he was released from hospital Ummad had an appointment with what is now the Home Office to discuss a claim for asylum and he wanted to rest and prepare. He went back to London and stayed in a special guest house for Ahmadi visitors opposite Wandsworth's Fazl mosque. When the day came he went with the bullet fragment in his pocket. 'Why do you think your life was at stake?' the interviewer asked. Ummad replied: 'Look, I was shot and here's the bullet,' pulling it out of his pocket to show him. The interviewer looked shocked. It had the desired effect: within a few weeks he had asylum and knew he could start to build a life in Britain.

◆

Before his brother's wedding Ummad had been desperate to start a career in London but now he couldn't face it. He had become a minor celebrity in the Ahmadi community, with people clamouring to meet him and journalists wanting to interview him. He knew he needed rest, so he decided to head back to Sunderland, the last place he had felt safe and happy. He found a room in a shared flat with old student friends and gradually started putting his life back together. He struggled initially to relax. His sister had gone back to work in America but was finding the long shifts hard – and the days off inside her head even harder.

Their parents were still in Pakistan trying to sell their business and Ummad was desperate for them to escape to safety. They had left Karachi for Punjab and were doing their best to flog what they could. Selling property as a prominent Ahmadi is challenging – if a buyer gets wind of its provenance the purchase usually falls through. Eventually they managed to sell the house to someone from another town but the business

was harder to cash in. As Ummad's father became more desperate to get him and his wife out of the country, he decided to
get rid of the remaining stock of generators at half price and
not even attempt to make money from the land. They applied
for American visas to go and live with their daughter Saba and
began the long wait.

In Sunderland, grief caught up with Ummad. 'It was only
there that I finally realised what had happened to me. When
you're going through it you don't really feel the pain. But
when I was back in my same life I suddenly realised how much
I'd been through and I didn't know when I'd see my parents
again.'

Their family was splintered with no way of grieving
together. As a Pakistani refugee in Britain, it would be almost
impossible for Ummad to get a US visa to visit his sister, and
she would have to wait a long time to get a visa to visit him
in Britain. His parents couldn't come to Britain either – with
no visa they wouldn't even be allowed on the plane. In June,
eight months after losing her eldest son, the pressure became
too much for Ummad's mother: she had to see her children.
She arranged a meeting in Dubai, somewhere they were all
hopeful of getting a visa for, and rented an apartment for two
weeks. The fortnight was restorative for the family and when
Saba went back to America, she did not have to wait long for
her parents to join her – they claimed asylum and moved in
with her that October.

Returning to Newcastle airport, Ummad was stopped at
immigration by two men who introduced themselves as police.
They took him to a back room and asked what his status was
and where he lived. 'You understand I'm not a police officer,
right?' one of them said. Ummad remembers him being vague,

and saying 'We're working with communities and we're fighting extremism.' They asked if he wanted to report to them
anything that happened in his mosque and Ummad said that
would be fine and they were welcome to come and visit it – but
there would not be much to report. When they asked where it
was, they were even more confused. The mosque was meeting
in a church hall.

'I was in there for hours. They didn't know about the
Ahmadiyya community and they went out to research it and
came back. Once they knew what an Ahmadi is they said
'Yeah, it's alright' and they let me go. It's not like we've got a
mosque that no-one has access to. I told my dad about it and
was laughing – what would I tell them, it's all about peace
and love!'

Ummad still felt unable to settle at anything. He had good
friends in Sunderland but no proper job and had lost the motivation that once made him capable of working day after night
in the library. He took an internship with the NHS's internal
auditing service, travelling around the North-East checking
the finances of its ambulance services. He enjoyed being on the
road and getting immersed in the figures, but then someone
in the office googled his name, saw a local news story about
the shooting and people began to gossip. 'There was a behav-
ioural change,' he remembers. 'That was one of the reasons I
left, because they changed. If people hear about these things
they don't want to work out whether you were at the receiving end of the trigger or whether you were behind it. If they
don't follow news and know who is the victim then they have
a bad idea of you.'

For a while he couldn't work out why people seemed to be
treating him differently. Then one day a lady he was working

with told him about her insomnia and depression and he got frustrated. He said 'there are people in the world with bigger problems' and began to explain what had happened to his family. Before he had a chance to finish the story she said, 'actually, the whole office knows.' Ummad recalls: 'It wasn't a nice feeling knowing that everyone knew and were not talking to me about it. It was weird.'

For nine months he went back to London, living in Hounslow and working in Ealing in the accounts department of an online retail company. Then his uncle moved to Britain with his wife and their son Zain, Ummad's teenage cousin. They moved to Newcastle and Ummad was desperate to be near them. He also missed the North-East and wanted to help them settle, so he moved in with them, deciding he would study for his accountancy exams and look into starting his own business.

Newcastle suited Ummad and he slipped into a routine. He would jog in Jesmond Dene Park in the east of the city, run up to the waterfall and just stand there, watching, thinking. These days he knows the city better than many people who have lived there all their lives. He can point out the Roman fort and the homes of the first steam engine and matchboxes. 'I like to know the history. Newcastle used to have so much coal that people said it's like sending coal to Newcastle,' he enthuses, rattling off a list of local discoveries in the Industrial Revolution.

In the year after he got asylum he rewarded himself by taking trips around Europe, relishing the freedom and anonymity of being in a strange place. Amsterdam, Italy, Spain: everywhere in Europe seemed so cheap and quick to reach. Travelling made him feel free.

Being in Europe allowed him to look at other religions too. 'Some Muslims say never talk to other people about faith but I like to,' he says later. 'I went to the Vatican and I found it really nice. I spent hours standing at the top of the dome, it was amazing there. People came to find God and I attended a prayer session. I think observing other religions you can learn from them. Every Muslim should be strong enough to do that.'

Ummad found work as a delivery man for Domino's Pizza, 'the easiest job I have ever done'. He studied in the city library until 4pm and then took his Nissan Micra down to Domino's. Often he worked until midnight and clocked in twelve-hour shifts at the weekend. His record was 42 deliveries in one night. He saved money and studied hard.

The work showed him 'both sides' of immigration, he says. 'The guy managing the shifts in Domino's practised law in Bangladesh and he is doing a PhD. He is just here to make his life better. Someone earning and doing a PhD is not a burden on British people, Britain can get so much from him if he shares his knowledge. But then there are two Romanians on the shifts who don't want more than sixteen hours a week because then they won't get benefits.'

He began to enjoy the work, taking pleasure from peoples' reaction to the arrival of their pizza (one girl was so excited to see her delivery she jumped up and down and clapped her hands). Ummad's new routine was made happier still by living once again with his cousin Zain, who had always been like a brother to him – and especially so after they lost Saad. At eighteen, Zain is a few years younger, but serious about his studies in a way Ummad can relate to. He is also quick-witted and fun when he can be drawn away from his books. Zain attended a good school in Karachi and was studying for his

A-levels when the attack happened – he had to skip a year. He couldn't go to school in the safe house and after the disruption he thought it better to start again.

Zain wants to study medicine and looks like a surgeon already, in immaculate tucked-in Tommy Hilfiger polo shirts, rimless glasses and neatly combed hair. He's frustrated by the perception that migrants are here to take benefits or have come from poverty and makes it clear he has not. Sitting at the family home in a quiet suburb in east Newcastle, Zain speaks formally, his back straight and his English impeccable, while he tells the history of Ahmadi persecution in Pakistan. He describes what happened when the Ahmadi physicist Dr Abdus Salam became the first Pakistani to win the Nobel Peace Prize in 1979. Pakistan's leaders didn't know how to react. Salam had moved to London in protest five years earlier following a parliamentary bill calling his religion un-Islamic. In his acceptance speech he quoted a passage of the Quran – something he was forbidden from doing in public in his country of birth. Even after he died in 1996 his early work characterising the Higgs boson went almost unacknowledged in Pakistan. His gravestone has been altered so he is no longer described as a Muslim.

◆

Shaiza had only been Saad's wife for four days but a few weeks after his murder she realised she would have more than grief to show for their marriage. She was pregnant.

In July 2013, Rameen was born, a beautiful baby girl with enormous brown eyes like her father. But Shaiza, who had lost her husband, father, and, soon after, her mother, longed for family. She had returned to New York to give birth, staying with an uncle, before going to see her brother in Toronto. But she still could not settle.

Shaiza's in-laws doted on Rameen; the little girl was all they had left of their son and brother, and in the nine months since Saad's death, Saba and Shaiza had become as close as sisters. Shaiza decided she wanted to be nearer the family of her lost husband and moved to live with Saba and her parents in Memphis, where Saba was completing a medical residency at the University of Tennessee.

With Shaiza living with them, Ummad's parents had an idea. If a man is killed and leaves behind children, there is an old-fashioned tradition in Pakistan that his younger brother will step in and marry his widow. The custom developed to protect the child from becoming unwanted by a new family or falling into poverty as the mother struggled to remarry. Ummad's family was modern – after all they had let their daughter travel to the other side of the world to work as a doctor and even though she was now in her thirties they were relaxed about her being unmarried. But as they watched Rameen grow and became more involved in the little girl's life they became desperate to keep her and Shaiza in the family.

When they first called Ummad in Newcastle and suggested he marry Shaiza he was shocked. He loved her as a sister-in-law but had never thought of her in that way. He was also terrified by the responsibility. He was 24 and the union would mean taking on the responsibilities of a husband and a father. He also worried about how much they would have in common. 'She was perfect for my brother,' he said, 'but how do I know if she is right for me?'

The main problem was that Ummad didn't feel ready for marriage. He wanted to complete his studies and start a career.

But he also loved Shaiza and Rameen as part of his family and was desperate to do the right thing. 'She's been through so much,' he would say guiltily, whenever he contemplated his doubts.

Ummad felt like his youth was coming to an abrupt end before he was ready.

In the months while his family tried to persuade him, he couldn't concentrate on his revision in the library. It was autumn and he had his accountancy exams to think of in December, the qualifications he hoped might one day see him working on Wall Street.

With all this swirling around his head, he decides one day to drive back to Sunderland and revisit the university campus. He gets into his Nissan Micra, a Minion toy from the cartoon *Despicable Me* swinging from his mirror, and begins the drive. The trip is tinged with a sense of finality; the Ummad who studied here didn't carry the weight of impending marriage and fatherhood. He goes to Clanny House, the accommodation block he had run out of that day he first saw snow. Walking up to block ten, where he stayed, he hesitates near the door, knowing that he has no reason to go inside now. It looks like any other student housing, nondescript blocky architecture around a patch of grass.

At the university's Murray Library, he walks around it with the kind of nostalgia that many former students feel for the union bar. Beyond the modern, glass-fronted building are the Wear and heavy cranes pulling cargo off the docks. Seagulls caw around two young teenagers in tracksuits who are fishing for crabs over the wall under a grey sky. It is September but the wind off the water is already bitterly cold. 'I hadn't seen such a beautiful place in my whole life before I came here,' he says, watching from a bench with a cup of steaming coffee. 'I think this year that I spent here was the happiest of my life'.

Driving out of the city, he points to a green bridge and says proudly, 'That was the longest on the planet when it was built, can you imagine?' He talks of the area with proprietorial pride. 'Sunderland was the biggest shipping place in the world; it used to be an economic hub for the UK and was so strong that when Hitler attacked, this was one of the first places he wanted to hit. Sunderland was a prime target.' Pointing out St Peter's church near the campus, he says 'that has been there for more than 1,300 years. It's awesome.'

Though he idealises his time in Sunderland, not all of Ummad's memories there are pleasant. One of his friends got his arm broken in a fight, picked on for being Asian, and Ummad once had eggs thrown at him and his friends while they walked down the street. 'Sunderland doesn't really welcome a lot of foreigners,' he recalls, 'They were shouting at us, these teenagers, and they didn't even run away.' There are signs the situation has not improved much since. A mosque is planned next to Aldi, a development which has caused demonstrations in the city among far-right campaigners.

The nostalgic trip doesn't postpone the inevitable. Ummad's parents are insistent he gives the idea of marriage a try and they book Shaiza and Rameen on a flight to the UK the following month.

◆

Shaiza and Ummad sit on armchairs at opposite ends of the sitting room in the family home in Newcastle, looking unsure of each other. Between them, eighteen-month-old Rameen totters around, wide-eyed in patterned tights and a denim dress.

Shaiza is beautiful, with glossy dark hair, sad eyes and a perfect smile. In the background, an episode of *EastEnders* plays out on TV, with its usual soundtrack of mild swearing and misery.

It's a cold Thursday evening in November 2014 and Shaiza arrived in the country less than a month ago. Ummad talks about his new job; he has finally left Domino's and got work in an office for Home Group, a company he proudly describes as 'One of the UK's largest accommodation groups', before reeling off its annual turnover (£300 million). Ummad has a temporary role in customer service finance, reconstructing lost data. He finds the work tedious but is hopeful about other jobs advertised within the company that he's applied for. He had delayed his accountancy exams to the following year.

After several minutes of conversation about the new job, Ummad says out of nowhere: 'So, we got married.' Still looking serious, he adds: 'We had the ceremony on Monday.' Neither of them smiles as he announces the news. He managed to get a day off work from the new job, though he was too shy to explain to his employers why he needed it. In the morning they went to the registry office at Newcastle's Civic Centre, then on to a ceremony at lunchtime in Hartlepool Mosque attended by a handful of people. His parents couldn't get a visa to attend but his uncle and aunt were there and Shaiza's brother came from Canada for two days.

Ummad missed meeting his bride-to-be at Heathrow because it was also his first day in his new job. Instead his aunt and uncle went with Zain to pick her up. Recalling what she was feeling on the journey to England, Shaiza says: 'I was nervous. All of a sudden that happened two years back and I have to ...,' she pauses, 'I was worried about what's my fate going to be with Ummad. I was with his brother first and we were happy and now …' She trails off again, not wanting to articulate the difference between the two weddings.

Shaiza looks sad as she talks about her new life. 'I'm just staying home. It's a big difference after America. It's crowded here and the traffic is too much. It's so congested; the houses are small and the roads are small.' It's unclear whether they will stay in Britain or try to get Ummad a visa for a move back to America. The subject is causing tension, particularly given Ummad's excitement at the new job. 'We're just deciding,' Shaiza says, and they both exchange a nervous look. 'Maybe we can go back to the US in a few months,' she adds, more in hope than certainty.

Shaiza moved to America with her parents when she was eighteen, after the family's visa was sponsored by an uncle. She had thought she would study when she got there, but life was tougher than they expected. Her father was a manager at a huge sugar mill in Pakistan but in America, with little English, the only work he could find was in a Seven Eleven store. 'He didn't mind, he was strong and happy,' Shaiza recalls. The small income from her father's job meant she needed to work too to support the family, so she took a job as a medical biller. Now 26, and with five years' experience at it, she hopes to set up her own company specialising in medical billing but thinks that will be difficult in Britain where the NHS makes private healthcare plans less common.

Which country is better? It's a recurring discussion between them. Shaiza express scepticism about the British health system. Ummad steps in to give an impassioned defence of the NHS. 'It's not about capitalist or communist, it's about caring for people,' he says. 'It should be in every country in the world, or the developed ones at least. It's like *Breaking Bad*, have you seen that? He wants to get out of the ambulance because of the cost. That's so sad that you have to run away from help because you can't afford it.'

Shaiza recalls how she managed her parents' health needs in America. 'I had health insurance in my job so I was covered, but my parents weren't. Every time my mother got sick I would go and say I had a stomach ache so I could get her treatment.'

Cousin Zain comes downstairs on a break from his A-level revision and joins in the debate. He says of Britain: 'It's got everything. There's no racism, there's no extremism. A friend won't consider my religion before talking to me.' Then the conversation changes to London versus the North-East. Having lived in New York, Shaiza misses the bustle of a big city and says quietly 'My big dream was to visit London.' Ummad defends his home: 'I love living in the North-East. I'm the only Asian guy in this company, but people have been so friendly."

Shaiza has made pasta and chicken for dinner. 'It's the first time you've cooked for me,' Ummad notices, without malice. Over dinner, the debate about where they will live intensifies. 'What about Florida?' Shaiza suggests, 'Then we can go to Disneyland whenever we want.' Ummad is unimpressed, 'but we couldn't go to Disneyland all the time'.

He looks slimmer than a month ago, his features chiselled by lost appetite and increased exercise. For the last few weeks he has been cycling everywhere. Days before the wedding, Ummad hit a pedestrian in his car. He was nearing the end of a shift at Domino's, delivering a last pizza in his Nissan Micra, when a man stepped out into the road. Ummad was driving under the 30 mile-an-hour limit, but he couldn't brake in time and hit him hard. It had been a long day; the shift started at 10am and it was 11pm. The man lay in the road motionless, unconscious, and Ummad couldn't hear him breathing. Desperate to help, he called an ambulance immediately. Ummad felt guilty but he had not been on his phone or playing music. When police arrived at the scene they asked if he had been drinking, he said no and a breathalyser test confirmed he was telling the truth.

The next day he saw on the news that a man was in critical condition after an accident but they gave no details of who he was. Ummad wanted to visit him in hospital to apologise and see if there was anything he could do but the police wouldn't pass on his request. 'They said there was no point,' Ummad sighs, 'but it still scares me that I don't know how he is doing.' The police took his phone for analysis and a few days later called on Shaiza's phone to say the man was recovering and out of danger. Ummad did not much feel like driving after that.

◆

A row of men sit on plastic chairs staring at a Samsung smartphone propped on a table in Newcastle's St Peter's Church Hall. It is the Friday afternoon after Ummad and Shaiza's wedding. On the miniature screen, a man in a white turban speaks in Urdu. This is Mirza Masroor Ahmad, the caliph of the Ahmadiyya community, and he's delivering his Friday sermon live from Baitul Futuh mosque in Morden, south London. The enormous mosque complex was built in 2003 and is the largest of its kind in western Europe. While the men listen to his tinny words, others around the world tune in on televisions and laptops. The address is translated into eight different languages and broadcast online as well as on a dedicated satellite channel.

'He's the supreme head; he's our pope', a young man called Muhammad explains in deferential tones. 'The religious freedom we find here you can't find anywhere else in the world. We are thankful to your Queen and to your government for giving us that freedom. We think it's our responsibility to serve this nation.'

For Ahmadi Muslims in Newcastle, the nearest purpose-built mosque is more than 30 miles away in Hartlepool. So for the last three years they have taken their Friday prayers here, in a Church of England building that many other Muslims would view as a heretical place of worship. But Tahir Selby, their imam, says this doesn't bother them. 'We try to work hand in hand with churches, it's the same God and the same message of peace.'

The Newcastle chapter of the Ahmadiyya faith was set up in 2009 and the majority of its members are either seeking asylum from Pakistan or have recently been granted it. They are accustomed to worshipping in different buildings and are grateful for the chance to pray anywhere in peace. Faheem, the group's president, works for the same branch of Domino's that employed Ummad. In Pakistan he had his own computer institute and was an IT instructor. He reels off a history of the faith from its origins in 1889 to the fifth caliph of the present day.

As the caliph gives a funeral prayer, the group falls silent. Just after two, his sermon finishes. One of the young men pulls out two long rolls of prayer mats from a Sports Direct bag and lays them on the lino at a slight diagonal towards Mecca. The rolls give the illusion of individual prayer mats, instantly turning the empty hall into a mosque.

The thirteen men take off their shoes, the older ones leaving behind battered leather work slip-ons while the younger men kick off bright Adidas trainers. Many of these men struggle to afford life in Britain. When they sit back on their heels, the holes in their socks face out. A boy young enough to still be in school stands up and sings the call to prayer, enunciating the words Allahu Akbar – God is great – in an exquisite singing voice.

The room is so draughty that most of the men leave their coats on, rustling quietly as they kneel and bend, next to a colourful display of children's sea creature paintings.

As if to confirm their distance from Pakistan, the rain begins to hit the windows hard.

Tahir is the preacher delivering the sermon, a white British Imam who converted to Islam in the Eighties. Dressed in a black suit with a stiff black skull cap and a thick grey beard he speaks in a cockney accent about pride, greed and jealousy, telling the story of Adam taking the apple after being tempted by Shatan – the Islamic name for Satan. He cautions the gathered men not to be tempted by watching too much television, with its sex and violence. 'Everything is trying to pull us away from the worship of Allah,' he says, 'Shatan must be laughing his head off.'

Tahir is more full of hellfire and damnation than his congregants, who look a bit nonplussed by the ascetic lifestyle being promoted. Ahmadiyya is a moderate branch of Islam, one that promotes integration and steers clear of condemnation. But Tahir has the zeal of a convert, saying piously that Muslims don't shake hands with women when a hand is proffered. The other men do so gladly.

After choosing to dedicate his life to Islam in 1984, Tahir went to Pakistan for four years before returning to Britain for an arranged marriage with another English convert. Speaking after the service about his conversion, he recalls: 'They changed

my name which caused problems with my mother. I was Tony
before. I don't know why she minded, she'd wanted to name
me Antonio after an Italian dancer, so Tony wasn't the name
she chose either. She still calls me Tony but everyone else calls
me Tahir.

'I'm from London and I wasn't looking for religion. It was a
group that I was with and I got into conversation with one guy
and asked why Asians didn't mix like other people. He gave
me a book called The Philosophy and Teachings of Islam. I read
the book and it talked about there being three stages of man
and that the lowest was just instincts like eating and drinking.
It took a long time to read it – but by the time I finished it
my understanding of religion had changed. I started reading
more and after about three years I regarded myself as Muslim.
The person who introduced me to Islam was an Ahmadiyya
Muslim. I quickly found out there are very different groups. I
just want to be a good Muslim and it became clear the message
of Ahmadiyya was different to other Islam. The more I read the
more I was certain. As an English person you question a lot of
things and if I hadn't been Ahmadi I would have questioned
things like beheading or Salman Rushdie.'

When it is time to leave the hall, he mentions Ummad
and the week he's had. 'I've just done his marriage,' he says,
smiling. 'I was quite touched that he was marrying her and
looking after the family. I admire him.'

◆

Early the next morning Ummad, Zain and a friend arrive early
for a leafleting session to introduce people to the faith and
improve the reputation of Islam. As well as charity and volunteer work, a key part of being active in the Ahmadiyya faith is

educating people about it and trying to combat Islamophobia. They head into suburban Newcastle and sit in the car, waiting for the others. They chat to make the minutes pass. When Ummad is asked about his wedding, he can't be sure what day it was. 'Was it last Monday?' he asks, genuinely uncertain. Zain laughs 'It's your wedding, you should know.' The brief awkwardness is ended with talk about Pakistan and they laugh bitterly about public figures advocating praying as a means of preparing for an imminent cyclone.

It's so cold their breath hangs in the air inside the car. To pass time Zain starts asking his iPhone questions. Holding down a button to bring up the automated function, he says 'I want to kill myself' and the boys descend into giggles as the computer responds in a robotic voice with information about the Samaritans.

They are still laughing when the phone rings and they are directed to where the others are. Pulling up behind the community president Faheem's Toyota Corolla, the young men get out of the car looking hesitant about the task ahead. 'Not this area,' Zain pleads, looking up the road in embarrassed anticipation. 'There are too many students. They'll shout at us and won't let us in.'

But his entreaties are overruled and each young man is handed a stack of leaflets and a pen to record how many they hand out, how many are put through letter boxes and how many are refused. Strict instructions are given: don't post to anyone with a sign saying no junk mail.

Gathering on the chilly pavement behind the cars, Faheem begins a silent prayer and everyone joins in, covering their faces with their hands. A few moments later they say a quiet Amen together and split into pairs, each taking a long street. Ummad worries: 'It's annoying to come at this time. People have had a good Friday night and they don't want to be bothered.'

The purple leaflet they're giving out has the production values of a Jehovah's Witness' *Lighthouse* magazine, with a purple and grey computer-generated backdrop and the words Loyalty, Freedom, Equality, Respect and Peace in different fonts on the cover. Inside, an article titled 'ISLAM: A Fresh Perspective' gives a brief history of Ahmadis and the group's peace campaigning, alongside a photo of the fifth caliph looking alarmingly stern.

Ummad's leafleting partner is Jalees, who's studying for his A-levels, though his wiry frame means he looks even younger. His family doesn't have asylum yet and their case has been pending for several years. 'I hope it will be OK. I try not to think about it,' he says, looking at his feet. 'I don't know why they're still working on it. It's going to be hard to go to university because we do not yet have status. My older brother is struggling to get into admissions.' His family come from Sialkot in the Pakistani province of Punjab and initially fled to Dubai but could not get nationality there and had to leave. 'That's why there's a problem with the case. You can't claim asylum in Dubai because they have the same attitude that we're not Muslim.'

Jalees has the first leafleting success. A knock on the door is answered swiftly by a nonplussed man and Jalees tumbles out the words 'This-is-a-peace-message-you-can -read-it-in-your-own-time,' and thrusts a leaflet into the man's hand before he has time to close the door.

It's still so cold that mist hangs at the bottom of the road and the brief doorstep waits seem to take forever. Ummad is hesitant before knocking, mortified at the thought of disturbing people resting on their Saturday morning. A guy in joggers

and trendy glasses answers, half awake. 'Hi that's a peace message from our community,' Ummad says. 'Oh ... thanks,' the
man replies, taking the leaflet and retreating inside. About
one in six answer when they knock. 'It's the same delivering
pizza,' Ummad laughs. A white man on a zimmer frame opens
his door and says 'Thank you so much.'

The public does not always respond so well. Once a week
young Ahmadi volunteers run a stall in a shopping centre in
Newcastle, under a proud banner showing their pacifist motto
'Love For All, Hatred For None'. They let people look at the
Quran, answer questions about the faith, give out books and
try to dispel myths about Islam. The previous month the stall
was attacked by English Defence League thugs, with no idea
about the branch of Islam they were targeting. They threw
pamphlets on the floor swearing, and only left when police
arrived.

Giving up weekends to community work is something
instilled into Ahmadis from childhood. The youth branch in
Newcastle arranges monthly charity fundraising events and
helps the local community, giving blood, bagging shopping
and even cleaning up after New Year. The previous weekend
they sold poppies for the Royal British Legion. Standing in
a branch of Morrisons handing out the red paper flowers,
Ummad said he felt proud to do it for the country that helped
him. 'Other Muslims say these soldiers and their families
shouldn't be supported. But I'm living in England and we
need to respect what these soldiers did in the war. I met a guy
at the supermarket who's a security guard. He served in the
Falklands and Northern Ireland and these people who served
their country are not now in good condition. That gives you a
feeling you're doing the right thing.'

Ummad and Jalees have almost covered the length of Addycombe Terrace, the long residential street in the north-east of the city they were sent to work on. 'It's not what we were expecting, people are polite,' Ummad says, incredulous.

Between door-knocks he mulls over Monday's marriage to Shaiza. 'I thought it's better not to think about it and just do it and see what happens. What has to happen happens so I needed to get on with it.' He knocks on another door. 'Hello dear,' an elderly lady says, peering round the frame. Ummad smiles back: 'This is just a peace message.' 'Thank you dear.' She takes the leaflet looking a bit confused.

The wedding preoccupies him as he makes his way down the street. 'Nobody really came, I just wanted to have it in silence. We went for the signing ceremony first and then the religious ceremony was at 1.30 the same day in Hartlepool. We drove there and then came back and had a meal at home and that's how it ended. It was strange but I had to do it. What's the point of dragging it out and delaying it?'

His biggest worry now is whether Shaiza will be willing to stay in Newcastle. 'She's trying to settle down here but she really misses New York. Her office is ready to take her back and she finds it nice over there, so let's see if she succeeds to persuade me. My parents want me to be there too but it will take time to settle and I like living here. My parents would make the baby happy. My dad would take the baby out and he really takes care of her. She thinks that for the baby and for herself it's better being connected to the whole family.' Later, he says more despondently: 'It would be too hard to ask her to stop here. I don't think she'll settle. When she talks about living in America she gets happy and excited and when she talks about here she's not. She's like "OK" but she's not happy.

I don't mind the idea of us living apart in different places but what she's gone through she wants someone to be there emotionally and physically. She'd like to live in London but I lived there for nine months and it didn't feel home really.'

Until now Ummad has spent only a few weeks with Shaiza. There was the week of her wedding to Saad – time in the safe house afterwards – and he visited her twice on holiday in America. 'You get to know a person in that time,' he says, but his words lack conviction.

Jalees and Ummad have come to the end of the street and are ready to stop. They sit on a bench outside Domino's, the designated meeting place for the other volunteers, and eat doughnuts from Greggs. Zain and his partner arrive soon after and want to compare tallies, claiming they gave out 200 leaflets. Ummad and Jalees managed 132.

Climbing onto the top deck of a bus to the centre of town afterwards, Ummad smiles at a shared memory with his new wife. 'Shai had never sat on the top deck of a bus before. She loved it,' he grins, giving a glimpse of the affection he feels for her, even if it is not yet a husband's. For now they sleep in separate bedrooms; Shaiza and Rameen in one and he in another. He looks abashed at this and says he doesn't think they will have children, though he admits his feelings are fluid. 'Perceptions change. When I'm in an argument with my parents I've always got room for the idea that I might be wrong and not mature enough. A year passes and it's good to know that in the future you might think something else.'

'When you're not married you think how it's going to be and ...' He pauses, too kind to express the disappointment written on his face. 'I feel nothing changes. My parents are happy and I'm how I was and everything is OK. When you keep thinking about it, it makes you stressed, but if you don't it's OK. I want things to keep going as they are. It is a big life sacrifice but it's good for my family.' Looking sad, he changes the subject. 'I just finished the season of *Sons of Anarchy*. It's a TV show about a group of biker boys. It's good, there's so much suspense ...' He trails off. The bus reaches Monument in the centre of Newcastle. 'This is her favourite place in the city,' Ummad says. 'She catches the train just to be in this busy part. She'll go window shopping and take the kid around. She enjoys it.' A few shops already have Christmas decorations up and Ummad's excited. 'It feels good at Christmas. I love the lights and the town is full of people. We don't believe Jesus was born but I've got friends and colleagues celebrating, so I always feel happy.'

As the bus nears his stop he mentions hopes of promotion at work. Ummad is fond of speaking in aphorisms, little motivational lines that he returns to when he wants to improve his circumstances. One of his favourites is: 'The one who says he can't and the one who says he can: both are usually right.' He thought of the phrase when he tried to escape the tedium of the Domino's Pizza round and now that his new boss is keen for him to apply for permanent financial jobs at the housing company. 'I told my sister on the phone that I used to dream about how I'd be something in England, in a good job as a chartered accountant. Now I think it can come true.'

◆

A month into his marriage to Shaiza, things begin to improve for Ummad. His fears that the marriage will scupper his dreams of career success are subsiding. Speaking on the phone from Newcastle he says breathlessly, 'I got the job I wanted!'

Eight others were shortlisted, including people who had been there for five years, and Ummad didn't rate his chances. So he set to work. He went to Companies House and got figures from all their newsletters, making graphs with the data he collected, giving concrete examples of how the business could be improved. Ummad describes his boss's reaction: 'He said, 'You blew me away with your presentation. I was satisfied with you but I thought Ummad is a bit of a geeky guy who doesn't speak much. You proved me wrong.'

Ummad is still ecstatic. 'I dreamt about this job in Pakistan and I got it. The next goal is Wall Street and it doesn't seem impossible now. It's the law of attraction.'

Other things have been going Ummad's way too. He has just been voted head of the youth section of Newcastle Ahmadiyya Muslim Association. He even had a chance to travel, booking a last-minute flight direct from Newcastle to New York to see his sister for a long weekend. 'We didn't talk much about the wedding. It was just me and her and we had lovely sibling time.' They drove from Newark to Washington DC and then to Niagara Falls to meet their uncle Mansoor, who lives in Canada. On the drive back they made it through eight feet of snow in Buffalo.

Ummad has never been back to the family's house in Karachi since leaving his childhood home for those last Friday prayers together. While he has asylum in Britain, going to Pakistan is not an option. Sometimes he longs to be back in the country where he grew up. If things improve he hopes to return and help educate people about the need for peace between religions. 'Whatever is happening in Pakistan today, it's happening because of a lack of education. You need education to understand that what is being taught about Islam is wrong and if I could play a part in that teaching perhaps I could help these things go away.'

His brother's death and the wedding attack still play on his mind. When Ummad was treated for his bullet wound, the doctor told him he should see a therapist, but he never did. 'I know I'm not going to lose hope or get tired of life,' he says in justification. When he has time alone he likes to write poems and he's written one for Saad in Urdu. He is thinking of setting up a counselling department within the Newcastle Ahmadi chapter to help new arrivals recover from the trauma of their experiences in Pakistan.

Zain is still studying hard. He hopes to go to Charles University in Prague and Ummad has already volunteered to take him for an open day. He is working so hard that he periodically swaps bedrooms with Ummad and the others, desperate to find the quietest spot in the house to work from. Zain's parents – Ummad's uncle and aunt – stay at home mostly and study English. They live off savings and some income from a beauty parlour Ummad's aunt set up in Karachi. Soon they hope to start a business in Britain.

In December Ummad felt Shaiza and Rameen were beginning to settle. Shaiza was even talking of applying to upgrade her visitor's visa. 'Shaiza says she likes England now,' he said, audibly smiling down the phone. 'Maybe we can stay.' But a month later Shaiza has had enough. Unable to work ever since the attack, she wants her old life in New York back. The health company she used to work for has offered her the same job – and with better pay. She couldn't resist. Ummad drove her to Manchester airport and before they said goodbye, he told her she could come back any time. He wants her to be happy and can see she has a better chance of that in the country which feels like home. Back in Newcastle, the house seems quiet without Rameen running round, and with Zain shut away studying. One day, Ummad says, he may go and join his wife, but he's not in any hurry. He loves his work and his friends – and he loves Britain.

◆

CHAPTER 3

Harley

Like Ummad, Harley Miller has grown to love Britain – though her journey to Europe was more circuitous. It began at a nightclub in Sydney. She was 21 and in a grump about a recent break-up when she stomped back from the bar and saw what she would later describe as a 'male vision' in front of her. 'It was love at first sight,' she says, smiling lasciviously at the memory. 'He just looked so different to anyone else there, with a luminescent white shirt on and great jeans, jet black hair, dark eyes and a chiselled face. I just thought "wow".'

Harley's friend was convinced the dark stranger was speaking French and elbowed Harley in the ribs. 'Go on Harley, go up to him and say something in French,' she cajoled. When Harley demurred, the friend went up instead. After saying something which Harley couldn't hear over the music, the man's eyebrows went straight up. And then, when she pointed at Harley and said 'her not me!' he began nodding. After her friend returned to the bar beaming, Harley asked what she said. 'Voulez vous couchez avec moi,' the friend giggled. The strange man was called James and he had been speaking Catalan not French, but he had no trouble understanding the come-on.

A few months later James moved in with Harley and a couple of months after that he proposed and she said yes. As an only child of immigrant parents, Harley's family in Australia consisted of her mum and dad. Her mum was Iranian and her dad was a Kiwi but neither wanted to live in the other's home country, so they had settled on Australia. Their relocation from Iran to Australia when Harley was three meant that she had no other close family. Since James had an enormous family in Barcelona they decided it made more sense to go there and marry, rather than bring all his relations down under.

They married in Barcelona when Harley was just 23. After the wedding, Harley began a new life in the city. She could speak no Spanish and even as she began to pick up a few words, it was not much help. It was the late Eighties and the Catalan separatist movement was in full voice, putting everyone in the city under increasing pressure to speak Catalan. As well as two languages to deal with there was a completely differ- ent culture. She realised Sydney was like a big country town compared to a European city – she had never lived in a block of flats before and now she was sharing one with James and his elderly mother.

Living with James' doting – and often jealous – mother was claustrophobic and eventually they moved out into a vil- lage in the Catalan countryside. She taught English to children and adults, shocked by how many women of a similar age to her had never learnt to read or write properly. Being in rural Catalonia gave her the first real taste of what it feels like to be considered really foreign. 'Their concept of Australia was from documentaries about the Outback. They asked weird questions like did we have any running water and electricity? Did kan- garoos jump down the street? And did we have any clothes, because they had seen Aboriginal people. It was so weird being seen that way.'

It was the first time she had lived in a place where so few people spoke English. She tried her best to pick up the language, asking people at the shop to teach her the words to ask for simple things, like *pollo*, meaning chicken. But sometimes something as simple as one vowel could fell her. One day she went into the grocers asking for what she thought was a big chicken. She delivered the request loudly and clearly and suddenly everyone in the shop dissolved into giggles. Gesturing at a large chicken, she got what she wanted and took her package feeling puzzled. At home she asked her husband James what was so funny, delivering the lines again: 'un polla grande por favor'. Once he had stopped laughing he told her what had gone wrong. Sniggering, he said: 'you just asked for a really big dick'.

After nearly two years in the village she built up her confidence with the language and longed to get back to a big city. Back in Barcelona she worked with an agency teaching English while James did a series of poorly paid sales jobs. They were on zero hours contracts and it was often very tough.

Then suddenly James got very sick. It started slowly: he was dizzy all the time; forgot where he parked his car and kept having pounding headaches. When the headaches reached excruciating proportions he went for a scan. He had a brain tumour and it quickly became clear it was inoperable. It was the early Nineties and much of the technological developments in treating brain tumours had not yet happened. In her mid-twenties Harley was forced to become a carer, coping with looking after a man who was bed-bound, incontinent and unable to think properly. By the time he went into a hospice he did not recognise her. He died soon afterwards.

Harley and James had been together for five years and when

he died she turned to a mutual friend for support. Fabio was an Italian hairdresser who had become friends with Harley and James after they bought his flat from him. He was kind to Harley as she navigated the grief of losing a husband at such a young age – and soon the friendship turned into a relationship. Harley moved in with Fabio not long afterwards. She had a five-year visa in Spain and when it ran out Fabio asked her to marry him. It was a bit early in their relationship but he wanted them to stay together and knew if they married she would be able to stay in the country.

At the same time, Harley was desperate to find a career that used her head. She was already working part-time in a drug rehabilitation centre and had an Open University qualification in treating drug dependency. She applied to university in Barcelona and passed the entrance exam easily, despite taking it in a second language. She began a degree in psychology, keeping up her rehabilitation work part-time as well as her job as an English teacher. She loved helping patients with addictions and became passionate about different kinds of treatment. Along the way she became so interested in family therapy that she was allowed onto a post-graduate course in it before she finished her five-year degree, working on both at the same time as well as two jobs. 'I was sleeping four hours a day. I was just working and studying, trying to get two jobs and two degrees done.' In the third year of her master's course she began teaching the first years, already building a reputation as one of the rising stars in the field of family therapy.

Fabio supported Harley while she put herself through her studies and they were both happy and in love. When Harley's studies finished she hit a problem. Despite being one of the strongest graduates in her class, with several years' practical experience, she found it impossible to get a full-time job in Barcelona. As part of its assertion of its Catalan identity, therapy practices and hospitals in the city were giving priority to applicants with Catalan names. When she finally did get work as a therapist it was terribly paid; she would have earned almost double as a cleaner. At the same time, Fabio was forced to sell his hairdressing business as part of a protracted separation of assets with a former partner. It seemed the perfect excuse to go travelling.

By this time it was 2002 and Harley was in her thirties, having lived in Spain for more than a decade. She had only ever intended to come to Barcelona temporarily to get married to James – then they had planned to explore Europe together, but somehow she had ended up staying. Now she was finally getting the chance to see the continent. She and Fabio bought a white VW campervan with a pop-up roof, packed up their belongings, as well as a dog and two cats, and went all around northern Europe. In Norway being a foreigner was an unpleasant experience. Fabio had very dark skin and dark hair – and they were both tanned from the travelling and were speaking in foreign languages. In one little village they were so 'foreign-looking' that none of the villagers would serve them. 'That was a taste of racism and discrimination – I was no longer seen as white and I started realising how protected and privileged I'd been. In Spain the way you were treated as an immigrant was a racial thing; if you were Moroccan or black you had lots of difficulties but if you were white you were fine.'

The experience soured the end of their adventures and they decided to drive to Italy and try life there. Fabio had not been home for years and was enjoying his family making a fuss of him. Harley struggled to get permits to work and ended up working in a pillow factory in Portofino. Fabio did not want to work more than part-time so they were in a town full of millionaires but had no money.

Eventually Harley managed to set up a private therapy practice. She would have preferred to work within the public healthcare system but it was impossible to break in as a foreigner. She had taught herself Italian by reading the papers and the dictionary and her practice built up quickly. Soon she had a steady client list which supplemented her pillow factory income, but she hated working in the private sector and wanted a chance to work full-time in her own language. She was also fed up with Italy and the racism she saw there. She spoke Italian with a Spanish accent and her tan, dark hair and shabby clothes meant people assumed she was South American. At that time South Americans largely worked as home helps and were looked down on by many Italians. Once, in a chemist, Harley was asked to use the service door so that she wouldn't be seen and lower the reputation of the establishment.

Around the same time she went back to Australia to visit her dying father. She returned with a renewed determination to pursue her career properly – and to leave Italy.

In Barcelona she had translated for British therapists at conferences and knew that family therapy was widely used in the NHS and that her expertise would be needed. She looked online and was flabbergasted at the number of jobs being advertised. She put in up to 30 job applications a week in the UK and was soon getting shortlisted.

◆

Harley's first British job interview was in Eastleigh. She flew over with Fabio and they were unimpressed by the small

Hampshire town. 'The clinic was on a bus depot site and I thought 'Oh God, this wasn't what I thought the UK would be like'. It was very bleak and very ordinary.' There was a job centre across the road and they went in to ask what help Fabio would get while he looked for a job if they moved there. 'None,' they replied. 'He can't get benefits until he has been here six months.'

They were not fans of Eastleigh but Harley was determined that they would move to Britain, where she felt both of their prospects would be better. Since Fabio had no visa restrictions, he decided to go ahead of Harley, living in a B&B in Watford and applying for work. Harley got another interview, this time in Wolverhampton. 'I thought Eastleigh was bleak until I went there,' she recalls. The interview was even worse than the city. Tony Blair's government had just released a consultation paper into public services' ineptitude in the wake of the death of Victoria Climbie. The interviewer asked: 'Given the consultation paper and the current situation, how should services improve so this doesn't happen again?' Harley lost it. 'I just turned around and said, "Let me see if I got this straight. The system failed this girl who died and because of that a whole body of people came together in a committee to make recommendations, and you're asking me, someone who has never lived here and does not know the case, what I think?" I said, "I think we're wasting our time, don't you?"' And with that, she left. She is still unsure whether it was the grimness of Wolverhampton or the stupidity of asking such a specific question to a foreigner that made her walk out of the door.

Finally she got a call asking her to an interview for a job in St Albans, not far from London. After a day-long interview (with no silly questions) she got the job straight away.

It was 2005 and her new life had to begin quickly. She and Fabio arrived in St Albans on a Friday, found a flat that would accept a dog and a cat and bought a car. Three days later she started work.

Meanwhile Fabio was fed up of hairdressing. With Harley's encouragement he had been to a couple of hairdressing interviews and was insulted when people asked to see how he washed hair and did a cut, colour and perm. He had owned his own salon and now he was just another immigrant. Harley having a proper job meant he wanted to try out other things. 'I supported you all those years you studied,' he said to Harley 'I don't want to cut hair any more. I want to be an artist, I want to paint'. She decided not to bring up the two jobs she had worked at while studying and offered to support him. As the months went on their relationship became increasingly strained.

'There wasn't much happening in terms of painting,' Harley recalls, 'There was a bit of doodling but also a lot of watching *Flog It* and *Antiques Road Show*. The sofa started taking his form.' Harley was losing patience. She was paying the rent, buying his cigarettes, clothes and paying all the bills. She even bought him a car and insured it. Next Fabio decided to retrain as a tiler. For his course project, while others tiled a mock kitchen or bathroom, he made a mock-up Mondrian painting in three-dimensional tiles that was taller than Harley. The creation was beautiful and the college was impressed but he was already bored of tiles. With plumbing it was similar. For that project he made a sculpture out of pipes that he bent, but he did not work as a plumber.

Harley could see he was depressed and unhappy. One day he went for a walk with the dog and someone threw a meat pie at him from a bus window. They were living in deepest whitest Hertfordshire and there were not many people with dark skin. Sometimes he had racist abuse shouted at him in the street. In Spain and Italy his neighbours had said hello, but here when he said hello they just blanked him. He felt angry and lonely, fed up of relying on Harley but too proud to take menial work. Worried at his deterioration, Harley bought him a flight home to Italy. She said: 'Take it, go and spend a week with family and you'll feel better'.

While he was away he called and texted Harley, saying he loved her and how grateful he was for the ticket; that he had really needed the break. But when he came back early in the morning a week later that all seemed to have changed. Harley was just back from taking the dog for a walk and he said 'I've got something to tell you. I'm going back to Italy; it's over between us'. Recalling the conversation, Harley says: 'He couldn't take it any more, he said he was sick of being a nobody. 'Here I'm just one more immigrant, why should I live here when in Italy I'm a somebody?' he asked me. His family is well-known in his home town and they have been hairdressers for generations. He said: 'Why do I have to struggle for a job here when there I don't have to and I'm respected? I'm not treated as a 'wog' there. Here I'm just your husband.' It was a total reversal, because in Italy I was the wife of him and people didn't acknowledge me or even learn my name. I said: 'I don't want to live in Italy, because what you're complaining about was my situation there'.

In a last-ditch attempt to save the marriage Harley asked him to come to Australia with her for Christmas. It was 2007 and her father was dying of cancer. She thought this might be the last Christmas they spent together and wanted to pretend for her parents' sake that everything was OK, so they had one less thing to worry about. They drove to the airport, where the plan had been to leave the car in the long-stay car park. Fabio parked, turned off the engine and said 'I'm not coming. I'm going to Italy now. I'm dropping you off at the airport and I'm going home'.

Harley cried all the way to Sydney. She watched sad films in the hope that the other passengers would think that was the reason for her tears. When her parents met her at the airport, they asked 'Where's Fabio?' and she cried all over again.

For the next few months the relationship limped on. They spoke every few days and decided that maybe they could make it work long-distance and give each other space. He would live in Italy, she would live in England and they would visit each other. Fabio told her how much he missed her and on her first visit to Italy it felt brilliant; they seemed more in love than ever.

Back in Britain Harley was sick. She had undiagnosed endometriosis and was exhausted and vomiting all the time. Fabio had always said she could just call if she needed him, so she did. He was happy to come – he was about to enrol on a cruise ship hairdressing course in Watford anyway, he said, and he would come and stay. Harley had been desperate to see him but when he arrived she suddenly saw things differently. 'I was sick in my dressing gown and all he did was yack about himself; he didn't even ask how I was. He said: "You always criticise everything I do". I said "I'm too sick for this. Just leave." So he left.'

Gradually Harley picked herself up. The doctor diagnosed her endometriosis and with treatment she recovered. She called the Home Office to ask what she should do about a visa now she and Fabio had separated. Their advice was that for now the remainder of her five-year spousal visa was still valid and she would need to apply for permanent residence once it expired in 2012. A couple of months later she received a letter explaining some of the requirements for her continued spousal visa. It suggested she was fine, making no mention of the need for her European husband to have been living in Britain at the time of the separation.

With her immigration worries gone, Harley happily began to establish a new, independent life for herself. Her career was going well and she moved to London for an exciting new job setting up a programme to treat young people displaying sexually harmful behaviour in two major London boroughs. Her psychotherapy expertise was being recognised and she loved the challenge of using her skills properly. She bought a beautiful Victorian flat in south London. It was her own, and its high ceilings and large windows opened out onto a wide tree-lined street. It was late 2009 and she was finally happy again.

◆

Working as a family therapist you get used to having bad days. But Harley had never had one like this. The NHS clinic where she worked was chronically understaffed and Harley was one of the few senior clinicians who had not left, leaving her with an enormous pile of complex cases. It had also just been taken over by a new trust and staff were under increasing pressure to be faultless automatons. Her first meeting of the day was a very complex child protection case. As soon as she walked into the building the receptionist told her there was a problem: the family she had issued child protection proceedings against were there and they were angry. Before she reached her office the father was shouting at her in the corridor. Harley had given her professional opinion that things were not going well enough for the child and the father was livid. Other people who were sitting and waiting for their appointments gawped in horror. The yelling only stopped once Harley's boss and a social worker intervened to calm the situation. They later investigated and agreed with Harley's assessment.

The evening before, Harley had come home to a letter from the Home Office. It was June 2013 and she had been waiting more than a year to hear back from them after applying for permanent residency in Britain. The letter said that not only was her application denied – but that she should never have stayed on after the marriage to Fabio disintegrated. The news seemed to come out of nowhere: it was the Home Office who had told her the visa was valid, how could they now say she had stayed illegally?

Now she was in an NHS waiting room having just been screamed at for protecting a child in a country that only the day before had informed her she was not wanted. There had been more stressful work situations in her line of work; she was familiar with armchairs being thrown at her by troubled kids and was once even accidentally locked in a room with a murderer. But those incidents did not come close to affecting her like this one. She ran into her office, slammed the door and began to cry. The sobs were hiccoughing out and she could not think what to do next. 'It was the strangest sensation', she recalled later, 'It felt like my brain had melted and was just fizzling out. I thought it's not good for my clients if I can't think straight; psychotherapists can't take care of kids if they're falling apart.' The stress of everything going wrong at once – the visa, the new management, and now being screamed at – was too much. She picked up her bag and went home.

There was another big reason that the timing of the visa refusal was terrible. Three months earlier, after four years of being single, she had finally met someone who made her happy. She had been sitting in the British Film Institute bar on London's Southbank, waiting for her date to show up. She was dressed in her most glamorous date outfit: a white dress and white pearls with a flash of bright lipstick. She was 48 but she could easily have passed for a decade younger. Chris Morris noticed her straight away. A year older than Harley, the Hackney schoolteacher-turned-property developer, was quickly entranced. Harley was beautiful, friendly and flirtatious.

She had also been stood up.

They had already been chatting for a while, talking about jazz and their love of old movies, when it became clear that Harley's blind date had failed to materialise. So Harley invited Chris to join her in the cinema. When the old black and white movie finished, the impromptu date continued – and within a few weeks they were spending more and more time together. Chris was kind and thoughtful and they shared lots of the same interests (even if he was wrong about modern jazz being better than the old stuff).

When Harley went off work with stress in June, Chris was there to help her put herself back together again. He dedicated himself to cheering her up – and even though she was beginning to worry that she faced being hoofed out of the country, she could not help falling in love. In the meantime she hired a solicitor to question the Home Office's decision. There was an error in their argument and her lawyer was confident that it could be sorted out with a few letters.

It was another six months before Harley heard any more about her immigration status. At that point she was still signed off with stress from the NHS clinic and was beginning to despair of her employers. The work was stressful but she hoped to continue it part-time when she recovered, while being her own boss the rest of the week. Though a staunch supporter of public healthcare she could see why some patients preferred to go private on mental health issues in order to keep their treatment out of any official records.

By this time she and Chris were closer than ever. Harley had been saving money for a while, hoping to open her own clinic using her different specialties, including speech and language and autism. She still got rent from the home she had shared with Fabio in Hertfordshire and had saved up enough to put down a deposit on her own premises. Since Chris was a property developer, they planned to go into the venture together. He would do the finance and administration – and help her find an office – and she would do the clinical work.

They searched for several months before they found anywhere suitable. Then in November they were looking round a building in the City. They both loved it. The location was brilliantly central and the rooms just felt right; they had found their clinic. Then Harley's phone bleeped. She looked down to see a message from her lawyer and her face drained. The message was stark. The Home Office had sent a letter rejecting the argument he had made and she had 28 days to leave the country or she would be forcibly removed. They made their excuses with the estate agent and left him standing there, shutting the door behind them.

Having lived outside Australia for almost a quarter of a century – and in Britain for almost a decade – the prospect of being forced to go back was shattering. All her close friends were in Britain and her only family left in Australia was her mum.

Not wanting to get her employers into trouble, Harley showed them the letter from the immigration authorities. Three days later she was ignominiously sacked. Her lawyer rallied, gathering material to put in an appeal to the Home Office on the grounds that she had been misled into thinking she could stay in Britain – as well as a human rights argument centring on the close friendships she had formed. The moment was like a political awakening for Harley. She was upset by the government's scapegoating of migrants and Ukip's growing popularity on the back of criticising Britain's newest residents. Still in a rage, she wrote down her thoughts and posted them on Facebook in a lengthy public message. After a friend shared what she wrote, it was suddenly being reposted on computers across Britain.

This is what it said:

Hello my friends,

You may have noticed that recently I have been posting up lots of political articles, some of which you may agree with, others not. Many of those articles have been about immigration. Some of you may even know why I've been putting those posts up – out of protest.

You see, as an Australian living in the UK, I am an immigrant. In recent times, I have seen how there has been an increasing political campaign by a particular party which very much scapegoats immigrants for what is going on in this country. Sadly, the other parties, afraid of losing votes, have followed suit.

The point of this post is not to get into a political debate with you. Quite frankly, I'm not interested in a debate. The reason why? It's very simple. It has affected me directly.

I have been in this country for 9 years. In the whole of that time I have worked for the NHS, in the Child and Adolescent Mental Health sector, helping young people of this country through sometimes quite severe mental health problems. Some of those young people still contact me to this day, to let me know of their achievements and well-being.

I have also contributed in taxes that whole time. I have never been unemployed, I don't have children and I don't have a disability. In other words, I have paid my taxes but have never required, thankfully, to draw on benefits for anything. Ever.

I am considered as 'highly skilled'. Without going into my CV, suffice to say, I have two Masters degrees and various lesser qualifications.

I own my own property.

I do not have a criminal record.

Yet, with all of that, on Friday UKBA/Home Office decided not to renew my visa and I have no right to appeal. As of Friday, I was given just 28 days to pack up my house, my home, my life and leave.

As of Friday, I am no longer allowed to work. Yesterday, I was formally dismissed from my job without notice or severance pay, after 9 years dedicated to the UK National Health Service, reaching a senior position in which I was held in high esteem. I should also point out that that meeting was called a 'hearing', in which there were 'allegations' and an 'investigation', as though having my visa renewal rejected was a crime. (Admittedly, they later apologised for this but only after I made it clear that it was a disgrace).

Ironically, I am no longer entitled to health care. The very same health care that I have contributed to in terms of work and taxes.

In fact, as of Friday, I have no rights in the UK whatsoever, despite owning properties and my years of contribution here.

The only way around this for me now is to demand my removal papers (and risk arrest), which then grants me a right to appeal. A day in court with legal representation costs several thousands of pounds.

I wanted to tell you all this because I want you to know, as UK citizens, what the REALITY of the immigration situation is.

So when you read in the papers or hear in the media that the government has reduced the number of immigrants in this country, think of me and say to yourself 'now I know how they do it!'

Thanks for your time.

It got more than 1,700 'likes' in a single weekend. Shortly afterwards her story was covered in *The Independent* and other online news outlets. *The Times* followed suit and soon television channels wanted to interview her and her name was all over the internet. Her situation united outrage on the left and right. *Telegraph* journalist Allison Pearson wrote in a sarcastic column that Ms Miller's was a 'tricky case' since she was not 'an unemployed Latvian claiming benefits, she also has the disadvantage of speaking English, paying taxes and being highly qualified.'

Soon that original Facebook post had been shared more than 30,000 times and a petition started by the same friend who had reposted her Facebook message had more than 10,000 signatures. Harley was pleased with the response, though troubled at being a poster girl for right-wing opposition to the government's stance on immigration. As a white, middle-class, English-speaking NHS worker from the Commonwealth, she had a lot of support from fans of Ukip. But Harley herself was increasingly angry at the treatment of migrants from around the world, going on Twitter to berate ministers on immigration issues.

'I hate this whole divisive thing of good immigrant and bad immigrant', she said. 'The government say they want the ones that work hard and are educated. They can't even stick to their own propaganda. That's why people have been so shocked at what happened to me because they say they want this type of person yet they gave me the boot.' Her partner Chris felt similarly outraged. 'If you look at some of the comments on Harley's petition they're absolutely abhorrent,' he said later. 'She fits into the narrative that what the British public want is a good white immigrant. I taught in Hackney for twenty years and spent time with different ethnic groups, so I find that narrative repulsive, but unfortunately it's the one that's holding sway at the moment.'

Harley embraced her new role as migrant provocateur – it helped to fill the time while she waited to hear what would happen next. She took to Twitter and Facebook to highlight other peoples' cases and followed the news more than ever before; it distracted her from the very real fear that her life in Britain was over. 'The public think that all immigrants are sitting on corners smoking, drinking and scrounging; or that they're animals,' she would say to friends in impassioned speeches. 'The nurse in the hospital, the person serving you coffee: all these people are affected by that.'

Her lawyer successfully persuaded the immigration tribunal that there was an appeal case to be heard, though the first available court date was not until the following summer.

In the meantime Harley tried to readjust to a new life at home. Chris's job as a self-employed property developer meant he had plenty of spare time and soon they were spending almost every day together at Harley's flat. After two failed marriages, Harley was in no hurry for them to move in together even though she knew it would help her immigration case. She liked them having their own homes to retreat to when they needed space.

Finding ways to kill time became crucial as she adjusted to the gear change of being a senior – and very busy – psychotherapist to being an unwanted migrant with no rights to work or learn in Britain. She could not be deported with a court date pending, but nor could she do anything. She already loved the London swing dancing scene, enjoying the Fifties outfits and upbeat music. She went along to dances and caught up with friends. Each meeting was tinged with the sadness that it might be their last.

After a while her criticism of the immigration authorities became more muted – she was advised it might damage her case. And as she used up her savings she was forced to spend more time just sitting at home. She taught herself to hula-hoop as a way to kill time, learning all the moves watching YouTube. By the end of the summer she could even hula with her feet. Her seed money for a clinic was soon all but gone. Worse than the financial worry was the state of constant anxiety that her life in Britain was about to be pulled apart. Friends hated to see what was happening to her. 'But you're not a criminal,' they said, in disbelief.

♦

The frontline in the legal battle between the Home Office and London's migrants sits on an industrial estate opposite the deliveries entrance to a Tesco superstore. This is York House, an immigration tribunal not far from Heathrow Airport – its charmless location presumably chosen to make it convenient for swift deportations.

It is here that Harley has come to appeal against the decision to send her back to Australia after almost a decade of specialist therapy work with vulnerable children for the NHS. It is a sunny day in August, more than nine months after receiving the letter that abruptly ended her working life in Britain.

There is one small problem. Harley hasn't arrived yet. Her barrister, Colin Yeo, one of the country's top immigration specialists is there, sitting in the bland waiting area along with a gaggle of ten friends and supporters. With just five minutes to spare until the court opens, Harley arrives with Chris in a state of serious fluster. Having left with plenty of time to spare they relied on a sat-nav to get them from south to northwest London and the journey ended in panic. As it turns out, they needn't have worried. When the court begins sitting at 9.30 the wait has only just begun. Although twenty judges were sitting, the tribunal was so oversubscribed that hers is one of half a dozen or so cases on something called the float list. This means your case is given no specific time – you simply wait, all day if necessary, for a gap in the schedule.

Her collection of friends, all ready to bear witness to Harley's life in Britain, show not only the strength of her personal roots in the country, but cultural ones too. These are people she first met in swing dancing class, or on trips to the theatre or to see obscure black and white films. She cannot imagine recreating this in Australia. After 25 years away, she says 'you can't compare the two countries; only one of them is home'.

Andrew Hall has been one of Harley's dance partners for the last two years. He is resident DJ at a south London dance club called Hula Boogey and has 1930s tattoos of hula girls under palm trees on his arms. It was Andrew who first reposted Harley's Facebook status and set up the petition. He is carrying a brick-thick wad of paper with all the supportive comments and signatories printed out, ready to show the judge. 'Perhaps I could smack him over the head with it,' he jokes.

The morning drags on in the 'snack bar' – really a bare room with a couple of vending machines. This is immigration purgatory, where people wait to discover if a life in Britain is won or lost. The room is full of people, all sitting in huddles round Formica tables on plastic chairs, but it is almost silent, its inhabitants too anxious to chat.

In court, all the documents and listings refer to Harley as Mariam – her recorded first name. The formal title adds to the surreal air of the occasion. Aside from work, she has always gone by her middle name, Harley. She goes outside for a smoke to calm her nerves and when she returns, her partner Chris tries to break the tension playing videos of *Father Ted* on his iPad. He manages to raise a laugh in the grim surroundings as he shows a clip of the bungling priests stuck in a lingerie department.

Chris is trying to stay pragmatic as the case drags on. 'We've got contingency plans,' he says. 'The worst case scenario is that she has to leave the country but the good news is it looks like that would be removal not deportation, so she wouldn't face a ten year ban from the UK. I'm trying not to get overly emotional. My view is that's the best way because there's not a lot we can do now.'

Others struggle to contain their feelings at the thought of Harley being banished to the other side of the world. One close friend, Rebecca Turner, a firefighter who first made friends with Harley in a library in Hertfordshire when she was living there nearly ten years ago, said 'It'd be like a part of me being ripped out if she was sent back. You discover a lot about your own country when things like this happen. You'd think the UK was better than this and had more heart. There's a certain integrity you'd expect in the system and what you find is quite shocking.'

Though many of Harley's ten witnesses are close personal friends, others are people ready to testify to her skills at work. Katriona, a manager of one of the sexual exploitation services she worked at is effusive in her praise. Though Katriona represented the victims and Harley typically counselled the perpetrators, she was impressed with her colleague. 'She's very professional and knows her stuff. Sexually harmful behaviour is just one small part of her knowledge base. She's got all sorts of knowledge, including lots that's quite specialist. I haven't come across another professional with that range of expertise.'

The ultimate testament to Harley's accomplishment at work comes from former patients and their parents, many of whom have written witness statements describing the difference she made in their lives. Among those waiting with Harley in the court's drab anteroom is a middle-aged mother who first realised that her daughter's therapist was facing deportation when she read about it in *The Independent*. 'I just thought it was outrageous,' she says. 'Mariam was someone who helped my family really tangibly within mental health services. We've seen lots of therapists because my sixteen-year-old daughter has Asperger's and anorexia, but Mariam was looking at the whole picture. It enabled us to chip away at things that gave me the knowledge and power to help make progress.' She says she would be 'horrified politically anyway' at the idea of Harley being deported, but also 'on the level of someone in the NHS making a difference I was embarrassed and horrified that we were treating her like that as a nation. The idea that there isn't someone available for families in that turmoil is terrible. If you think how pushed the service is, it's a disaster.'

As it approaches lunchtime, a hearing slot has still not materialised. A clerk appears and tells everyone that no judges will be sitting for the next hour. Colin the barrister tells everyone to leave the building if they can, adding ominously 'we could be waiting a long time'. The only real option in this windswept development is the oversized Tesco opposite. Everyone troops over to sit in the supermarket cafe, prodding plates of industrial lasagne.

Back in the waiting room, Colin talks quietly about his thoughts on the case. 'I think it's 50/50', he says. 'Human rights are really hard to win. The idea of a good or bad immigrant isn't something that Harley or I buy into – I don't like this undeserving migrant dialogue – but it does run that there are positive attitudes to white migrants from Commonwealth countries. Her relationship with Chris will not help her case particularly because they're not married and they don't live together, so it won't carry much weight with the judge. These are judges who split families and deprive children of their parents day in, day out.'

Colin is still hopeful the case will be heard – in fourteen years he has only needed to come back on another day once. The hearing only needs 40 minutes of the judge's time; typically how long it takes to decide if someone's life in Britain is over or not.

The afternoon drags on and when nothing has happened by 3.15, the clerk returns. Anyone still waiting to see a judge will now have to have their cases adjourned until another date can be found. The next slots will be in a month, at the earliest. Harley is mortified – all ten of these people have had to take a day off work, some leaving early that morning to make it for the 9.30 start. She is also distraught at the thought of the wait ahead. 'Of all the scenarios I went through in my head, this wasn't one of them,' she says, blinking back tears between puffs of a much-needed cigarette. 'It's unbelievable to sit in that room for six hours and now have to go through it all again. There's also the financial strain and the added legal fees which is a huge burden now. But it's the whole sitting and fretting all over again for another month that will be the worst. It feels like pulling my fingernails out one by one would be easier than this.'

According to Colin, the delay is further evidence of chronic under-resourcing in the immigration courts. 'The Home Office does an estimate of how many cases are likely and communicates it to the tribunal service. Every year they're miles out. The tribunal is hugely under-resourced and the waiting times are four or five or six months to get an appeal.'

Chris, finally showing a chink after staying positive all day, looks crushed. 'You wouldn't put up with that from any other service; you wouldn't *get away with it* in any other public service', he says angrily, as they get into the car and begin the drive home.

◆

The week after the hearing that never was, Harley and Chris go on holiday. With no visa or passport Harley can't leave the country, but she can explore Britain. Desperate for a break, they drive to Bude in Cornwall, spend a week at a jazz festival and enjoy time outdoors trying to forget about immigration.

When they return to York House a month later it is like Groundhog Day. Only this time Harley is early. She meets the same group of friends, most of whom have been able to get another day off work, and they sit drinking the same cups of metallic machine coffee.

After their nightmare on the float list, this time they have a slot in front of a judge. It is his first appointment of the day and Harley is jittery. 'Before it was the waiting that was the problem; now it's the jumping straight in,' she jokes, fidgeting with her handbag.

Upstairs, outside the court room, is a small, windowless consultation room that Harley and all her witnesses pile into. Outside, a small panicked Afro-Caribbean family with a teen-age son are being helped by a harassed-looking lawyer. 'Look, were you convicted of GBH or not? We have to know,' she says, in urgent tones. He looks at the floor impassively.

After a brief wait, Harley's case is called. The court is not much bigger than the airless consultation cubicle they have just been waiting in. The only indication that this is not an airport waiting room is the crest above the judge's wheeled office chair saying *'Dieu et Mon Droit'*. There is not enough room for all Harley's witnesses in the cramped space, so some are forced to wait outside.

The lawyer for the Home Office looks flustered and unprepared. She opens up a battered suitcase and begins to read Harley's case, making hasty biro notes in the margins. The room has all the gravitas of a stationery cupboard but when the judge enters, everyone still stands.

The Home Office's lawyer tries to buy time. 'They only faxed this through at the weekend, so I'm having to read it now,' she says. 'Give me another ten minutes and I'll be ready.' When the case is finally ready to begin, Judge Raymond explains what's happening to Harley. 'Judges are independent in this process; they're not part of the Home Office,' he says, before introducing Ms Bell, the Home Office lawyer and laying out the order in which everyone will speak. He seems kind, telling Harley 'coming to court is a stressful thing and we understand.'

Ms Bell, the Home Office's counsel, begins proceedings. Racing through the chronology of Harley's life, she confirms the dates for her early life in Australia, her time in Spain from 1989 to 2002 and her two years in Italy. Once Harley has agreed to it all, Ms Bell says briskly, 'So, Australia is where you spent the most part of your life then?' Harley left when she was 23. Struggling to keep her emotions in check, Harley says, 'Well, about half my life. I'm 49 now.'

Ms Bell next brings up the difficulties Harley said she would face in finding the same psychotherapy work in Australia. Harley tries to defend her position. 'The hospital situation is completely different, they don't have an association of family therapists like we do here and the hospitals and clinics don't have a specific role for child therapists. It's not as easy to get a job there,' she says, attempting to keep the panic from her voice.

After grilling Harley on her career, she moves to her personal life. 'In relation to Chris Morris, you're still living in separate accommodation and not married?' she asks, pointedly. Harley concurs, her hands shaking.

They rattle through the next few witnesses. The mum of one of Harley's patients is asked about her daughter's new therapist. 'So she's receiving good treatment then,' Ms Bell says, to make it seem Harley is surplus to requirements. When she moves onto Harley's partner, Chris, she asks the same incredulous question she put to Harley: 'You've been in a relationship for eighteen months now and you have separate addresses?'

Using the same hard-ball tactic, she interrogates Harley's old friend from Hertfordshire, Becky Turner. Once she has established they see each other once a month, she asks, 'Well, couldn't you just talk on Skype?' The question prompts an impassioned speech that backfires on the lawyer. 'I know we have a lot of means in the modern world to communicate with each other,' Becky says with a wobbling voice, 'but there's nothing like sitting in the same room as someone you love to get the warmth of that friendship, to get the subtlety of a situation. To be physically affectionate. For the modern world, once a month is quite a regular meet up.'

By now Harley is crying and even the judge looks moved. The tactic has been an own goal. 'No further questions,' Ms Bell says, backing off.

Next up is Katriona, the manager of a sexual exploitation service who previously worked with Harley. Ms Bell again tries to use the witness to show that Harley's expertise could just as easily be deployed in Australia. Once she has cornered Katriona into saying that children are sexually exploited around the world, it seems she has proved her point. But the train of thought prompts Judge Raymond to bring up the recent high-profile case of abuse in Rotherham. The scandal has prompted government promises to do more to tackle exploitation. 'Would this field in which you both work be the field that's going to be of importance with what's been going on?' he asks. Katriona and Harley nod vigorously.

Andrew Hall is the next witness, the swing dancing friend who launched Harley's Facebook appeal and online petition. He slams the heavy wad of printed signatures and comments onto the table. The judge by this point is in a jovial mood. 'Morning Mr Hall, lovely shirt you've got on,' he says, smirking at its red and white Hawaiian print. As Andrew goes through the levels of public sympathy, showing screen grabs and the thousands of messages of support, the judge looks impressed. As the interview wears on, the judge's mood becomes downright silly. He asks about Andrew's job at the Hula Boogey club, where his DJ name was Reverend Boogie. 'Are you a man of the cloth then?' the judge teases.

In her closing argument Ms Bell says that Harley's skills could easily be taken to Australia and that her friendships – and relationship with Chris – could be continued 'through modern communication'.

Harley's barrister Colin gets the last word. He details how the phone call and letter from the Home Office reassured her she could legally stay in the UK. He points out her 'only real arguable tie to Australia is her mother in her 80s' and that part of the reason for having maintained so few friendships in Australia was the fact that the Home Office led her to believe she had a future in Britain. 'We can see on a human level she's been misled by the Home Office,' he says. He points out her unique and valued skill set and the public interest argument for her to stay. In conclusion he gestures at the gathered witnesses, explaining that her network of friends in Britain is so strong that they have all taken another day off work to come to court for a second time.

The judge looks kindly at Harley, thanking her and her friends for coming. Afterwards Colin is buoyant. 'Everything went right, it went really well,' he says, 'the judge seemed to appreciate what you were saying'. But before Harley begins celebrating, he adds: 'A word of caution though, some judges can be very friendly and still come back with a negative decision.' The judge has delayed his decision so he can deliberate further. Harley leaves feeling cautiously hopeful but still bruised by the way the Home Office lawyer had questioned her. Colin tries to be reassuring: 'It's not personal. They're not out to get you, they're out to get all migrants.'

♦

It is early November 2014 before the postman rings the doorbell with the package Harley has been waiting for. It is now a year since she was forced to stop working and begin in earnest her battle to stay in Britain. As the weeks wore on after her hearing in September and no verdict materialised, she had begun to lose hope. She became convinced that the judge would be under pressure to reject appeals and that, even if he did sympathise with her, the legal case might not have been strong enough.

The doorbell rings again and the downstairs neighbour answers. By the time Harley makes it to the entrance hall, the neighbour is clutching an official-looking envelope. Seeing from the outside it is from the Home Office, her stomach lurches. The neighbour, an old friend, runs to get a bottle of wine. At the same time another friend who was coming for coffee anyway arrives and the three of them stare at the envelope. They decide that even though it is not yet eleven in the morning, they will only open it together once they are all sitting down with an open bottle and some very full glasses.

It takes several minutes before Harley has laid out the glasses and positioned her friends either side of her. She carefully tears open the envelope and peers inside. Then she loses her nerve. The first page is just a cover letter saying that the court's decision is enclosed, a thirteen-page document. Unable to take in all the information, Harley hands it to one of her friends, who skims through the case summary, reaches the decision and begins to read aloud. The wording is unequivocal. 'It seems palpably evident,' she reads excitedly, 'that her removal would be detrimental to the investment of the British public at large'. Harley can hardly believe what she is hearing. The judge argues that Harley's contributions to Britain and the NHS 'amount to compelling and exceptional circumstances warranting consideration outside of the rules' and her job had brought her 'the highest accolades and appreciation from numerous colleagues'. He also says that she should be allowed to stay on human rights grounds, because of her extensive network of friendships and community links in the UK, particularly citing the 50,000 people who pledged support on Facebook and in the petition.

When she hears Judge Raymond's concluding sentences, Harley is almost in tears. She had not dared to hope he would side so resoundingly against the Home Office. 'It would be disproportionate in all the circumstances,' he says, 'and not justified by any legitimate public interest in the maintenance of immigration controls, if the appellant were removed to the considerable detriment of the professional and community at large within which the appellant has made such a large practical and emotional investment.'

An hour later Harley is drunk with excitement at the news. She is also just drunk. The surprise win has created an impromptu party and the wine at such an early hour has made her giddy. 'It still hasn't sunk in; I just feel really, really privileged,' she says on the phone, the disbelief still in her voice. She called Chris and she called her mum in Australia. Her mother was so shocked and excited at the news that she hyperventilated and had to call back ten minutes later.

She was getting ready to put her exciting news on Twitter and Facebook – where tens of thousands of people had offered support and were asking her daily for news of a verdict – when she noticed an extra message after the ruling. It was an anonymity order so strictly worded that she could not publish any information about her victory at all. Telling her close friends had probably been fine – but anything else would put her in contempt of court. She called her solicitor who explained the gagging order was rare but occasionally used to protect vulnerable witnesses. In this case, several of Harley's young patients and their parents had submitted detailed accounts of how her treatment had helped them. The odd thing was that neither they – nor Harley's lawyer – had asked for anonymity and certainly not if it meant a blackout on all reporting of her case. It felt strange to have succeeded on the back of public support and not be able to tell anyone.

♦

Harley waited for a month to see if the Home Office would appeal the decision. She did not want to challenge the anonymity order until she was sure they would not – reasoning that if they thought there would be no publicity around the case they were less likely to contest it. Then in December a package arrived at her lawyer's office. It was her passport, finally returned after more than two years in the Home Office's drawers. And inside was a visa, giving her two and a half years' leave to remain in the country.

'I just feel like I've been let out of prison,' she said later that day. 'It felt like I was under house arrest for a year and a half and now it feels like I've been released. For a year and a half of my life I couldn't do a single thing: I couldn't enrol on a course; I couldn't progress my career; I couldn't even travel.'

As soon as her passport was in her hand she borrowed some money and booked a flight to Sydney to see her mother. Now 81, Harley's mother was frail and it had been one of Harley's biggest fears that she would die before her battle with the Home Office was over, forcing her to choose between seeing her mother a last time and securing a future in Britain. Meanwhile, her lawyer began work with *The Independent*'s legal team to put in formal challenges to the anonymity order.

Harley wanted to surprise her mother, who she had not told about the passport delivery. She also wanted to make sure she'd be in when she arrived, so she phoned ahead and told her to expect delivery of a parcel on 23 December.

It was early morning on the day before Christmas Eve when Harley landed in Sydney. By the time a taxi pulled up outside her mum's house in the suburb of Brighton-Le-Sands it was 8.30 but the house looked shut up. She rang the doorbell and put on her strongest Aussie accent to pretend to be a courier delivering a parcel. Her mum was still in her nightie with a toothbrush in her hand when she walked to the door and saw a suitcase through the screened porch. She thought 'Why has Harley sent me a suitcase for Christmas? I've got a perfectly good one.' It was only once she stepped outside that she realised who it was. She could not believe her eyes. For the next three weeks she drank in every moment of having her daughter in the house. They talked and talked and talked, filling in the detail of the last three years of Harley's life. Most days she went to the beach at the end of her mum's street and for long walks on the nearby wetlands. She had missed the sunshine and the clean air – and most of all she had missed her mum.

But being back in Sydney was strange. The area around her mum's house looked exactly the same, but elsewhere there were huge developments springing up. The city had become almost unrecognisable and she kept getting lost, walking a few blocks before realising she had no idea where she was. She had lived here for twenty years but finding her way around once familiar parts of Sydney now meant using a sat-nav.

It was not long before Harley began missing London. The buses and trains seemed so infrequent here and when she went to the opening of the 2015 Sydney Festival she couldn't help feeling underwhelmed. 'Is this it?' she found herself thinking guiltily, imagining the scale of a capital-wide arts celebration in London.

Saying goodbye to her mum after three weeks of intense time together was a wrench. She felt guilty for having stayed away so long and sad at the separation. But as she settled into her seat on the plane to Heathrow she knew she had made the right decision. She was coming home.

Back in London she has begun seeing patients privately again, meeting them in a rented room in Liverpool Street. She enjoys being back at work though she is not in a rush to pick up her old work in public health. 'I'm not going back to the NHS unless something really interesting comes up,' she explains. 'Going back the way it is now doesn't fill me with excitement.' Instead, she is wondering about combining her new obsession with Britain's immigration system with her existing psychotherapy expertise. 'I might try working for an NGO now,' she says. 'I feel very sorry for the kids here but there are services for them. What about people without access to the NHS, like kids in detention or asylum-seeking children who've been through the trauma of war and aren't getting any help?'

A few days after arriving back in London there is more good news. The gagging order on her case has been lifted and at last she can thank her friends – and strangers – for their support. She logs onto Facebook and Twitter to spread the good news to the thousands who followed her case. For the next 24 hours her phone bleeps constantly with updates, as messages of congratulation stream in from across the UK. Soon Harley will apply for permanent residency in Britain. If it is granted, the Home Office will acknowledge what more than 30,000 people in the country knew already: Britain is Harley's home.

◆

CHAPTER 4

Clive

Clive has wanted to go home to Zimbabwe for more than four years now. It's a cold November morning in Glasgow and Harare seems a long way away as he tries to stay warm beneath a clattering fan heater in a night shelter kitchen. This is Anderston Kelvingrove church, the only reliable place for destitute male asylum seekers to sleep indoors in the city. In a room behind him, other men are packing away their sleeping bags and putting on layers of clothes, readying themselves for another day outside. Clive zips up his coat and watches the television from one of the blue waiting room chairs, as the others begin to file in. The weather forecast comes on and everyone's eyes turn to it. The announcement of temperatures just one or two degrees above freezing does little to cheer the mood.

Shortly before eight, a female volunteer in a bright knitted jumper arrives and when the BBC newsreader announces 'It's eight o'clock,' she suggests to the men that they think about going. The Church of Scotland allows them to sleep there only at night and it's her job to make sure they leave. But it's still dark outside and nobody moves. Clive gets up and hastily starts to make coffee, grabbing a piece of white bread which he rolls in one hand and dips into his cup. At five past eight, five people are still sitting eating breakfast, slowly, prolonging these precious last seconds inside.

At ten past, when they sense they are pushing their luck, they head out of the glass doors, angling forward against the cold. It's almost another hour until they'll be allowed into the library, the best place to while away warm hours with an empty pocket.

Clive walks up the hill from the church in the morning darkness, sticking closely to the inside edge of the left hand pavement. 'There's a primary school on the right side and they say we can't walk on that side,' he explains matter-of-factly. 'There used to be a hostel by the school and a Polish woman was killed. Now they don't want people from the shelter to walk by. I don't know what they think we'll do to the children, but we have to stay on this side.'

Now 31, Clive first came to Britain in January 2008. He says he grew up in Mufakose One in Harare, but he has no way to prove it. He left the city in a hurry with no passport – until then he had never needed one. Clive's father was an accountant for British American Tobacco and they lived comfortably in a nice home and sent Clive to a good school. Then politics intervened. 'My parents were [opposition party] MDC activists and so was I. Both my mother and father were beaten up,' he says. 'My father died a normal death but I think it was a lot to do with the political pressure. It was just illness like you got a headache and then that was it – but it happened after the beating from [ruling party] Zanu–PF boys.'

His father's death prompted Clive to leave the country. The money left in his will was enough to get out of Zimbabwe and Clive barely hesitated before handing most of it to smugglers. With no passport and no visa, these gangsters offered the quickest route out. He says they helped him get to South Africa without a travel document. 'The man I met told me to give him 5,000 US dollars. I asked: "So what do I get for that?" And he replied, "You get to England. Don't worry, everything is sorted".'

The smuggler put Clive on a cargo ship headed for France. With no way to keep track of the days, he soon lost count, but he believes it took more than a month. 'I didn't like being on the sea,' he recalls, 'the waves were scary and it was cold.' He was held, along with fourteen others, deep in the bowels of the ship. They were kept next to the cargo and given almost no food and only a small amount of water. They came out on deck only twice during the journey. The visits came out of nowhere – the smuggler appeared and said brusquely 'Come for some fresh air'. The first time, Clive tried to drink it in, knowing he might not get another chance. 'I stood on the deck and I could see nothing, just clear water that way and that way,' he says, gesturing in all directions. 'I stood for maybe half an hour and then they took me back down. It was very dangerous with no food in the hold and when they put us in they said: "You're on your own." I'm not sure even the captain knew we were there.'

When the ship arrived in Calais another man collected them. He had a picture of Clive and some of the others and took them to 'a shack in an empty place' saying that he would come back with something to eat. He left them at eleven in the morning and didn't return until evening. 'I was scared; I wasn't sure if he would come back but he told me not to leave so I stayed,' Clive recalls. When the man eventually returned with tea and bread he told Clive to start by drinking the tea slowly to warm his intestines. 'I was very thin and it had been so long since I'd eaten that the first food could have made me sick,' Clive recalls. He did as he was told and it felt fantastic to have something in his stomach again. Clive and two others were hidden in the back of a truck among boxes and pallets. The lorry drove onto the ferry from Calais to Dover, and then on to London.

It was January 2008 and when the truck pulled up in the capital, the driver opened the back, said 'You're in London now', and sent them all out into the cold. Clive had £600 in his pocket and nowhere to go. He was afraid to try a hotel or hostel because he worried they would ask for a passport. On his first night he slept in a church with some guys from Ukraine. Within a week of arriving it began to snow and he was spending most of his time with the same bad crowd, knowing they might help him find shelter. He squatted with them in a church and was shocked by how many seemed to do drugs. Clive was homeless in London for two months before deciding to escape on a coach to Leicester. 'London was not good, it was very hard to live there. I felt if I was to survive I'd end up doing bad stuff. The people I was around were doing bad stuff and I thought: "I don't want to end up like that."' One night he was stabbed in the back by a gang of three English men who thought he might have money. It was so cold that he didn't realise what had happened at first, but then he felt the heat of gathering blood between his shoulder blades. It was the sign he needed to get out.

Someone had told Clive that Leicester was nice – and it seemed as good a place as any to start a new life. On his first night in the city he walked a few minutes from the coach station before stumbling across a nightclub called Liquid. He went inside. He learnt this trick in London – nightclubs and casinos are open all hours and once you've paid the entrance fee you can stay in the warm for most of the night. They have the added bonus of offering opportunities to meet women. That night he was sitting in the corner when a British girl who had been drinking heavily came over and asked him to dance. Her name was Sioned, she was very pretty and Clive couldn't think of a reason to say no. She was a single mother with a young boy and girl, surviving on benefits. They had a great time dancing and when the evening ended she asked where he lived. 'Nowhere,' was all Clive could say. She thought he was joking and they spent the night in a hotel together.

The next morning Sioned went home and Clive wandered out to spend the day on the street. It was not until she called him on his mobile later in the day that she realised he hadn't been joking. 'I told you, I'm on the street,' Clive explained. That was all the prompting she needed. 'If you're on the street you can stay here with us.' Within minutes she picked him up in the car and brought him home to stay with her. Their relationship lasted three years, with Clive living there on and off.

In 2009, when he had been with Sioned a year, Clive summoned the courage to claim asylum. He wanted a chance to set down roots in Britain and to start working. While the Home Office considered his case, Clive was given accommodation in Coventry but within a couple of months his application was rejected. With no passport and no way of proving his identity, officials refused to believe he was Zimbabwean. 'They didn't have anyone from my country to interview me, or ask experts to meet me. My lawyers just said "Sorry, they don't believe you".' Clive wanted to stay but was also fed up of being without a job or a home, reliant on handouts. 'When they refused me I didn't appeal. I just said: "OK, I'll go back". The way I grew up if someone says no you take that as no.' He had recently learnt that his mother had died.

Living in Britain without a visa or asylum was much harder than he had anticipated. 'I thought my life would be easier and I'd have freedom. I thought I'd have a good life,' he says. But he couldn't work and had nowhere to live. When his asylum claim was rejected, the Home Office told him he had to go back. 'I said "How can I when I don't have a passport? I came in illegally. Can you get me out?"' The Home Office seemed puzzled by his request. A month later they told him he must apply to the Zimbabwean embassy for a passport. This seemed ironic to Clive since they had previously said they didn't believe he was Zimbabwean. On all his subsequent Home Office documents it says 'Zimbabwean' in the nationality section. If they really thought he had made up his past why was it on all their paperwork?

Returning home was a drastic measure – particularly because intimidation of anti-government activists continued – but anything was preferable to the indignity of being denied a job, a home – a life. Clive applied to the International Organization for Migration, which helps people to return home. They paid him a grant of £2,500 to go back but when he went to the Zimbabwean embassy to apply for a passport, officials refused to give him any travel document. They weren't interested in helping someone who had tried and failed to get political asylum from their country.

Since Clive had not left and there was no asylum case pending, his accommodation and financial support was stopped. This was late 2009 and he was homeless and destitute in a foreign country with no obvious means of escape. He stayed briefly at a shelter in Coventry and again with Sioned. When, in 2011, Sioned said she wanted a break in the relationship, Clive decided to try his luck in Scotland. He wanted to get legal advice on solving his case. In England he would have to pay for a lawyer, but he heard that in Scotland he was more likely to find one who would work for free. The Coventry shelter told him of a place in Glasgow for failed asylum seekers and he boarded a coach to the city. In all he applied three times to be relocated back to Zimbabwe; every time he was thwarted by the embassy. On his last attempt in 2012 he was given proper housing while he waited for the outcome. But when relocation failed for a third time, he was out on the streets again.

There are routines for coping with homelessness that break up the tedium and stretch out hours in the warm. Clive has been relaying his story while walking along Glasgow's frigid pavements, the cold seeping up from the concrete through thin shoes until feeling has disappeared from all extremities. After leaving the night shelter there is almost an hour to kill until the first stop of the morning inside the grand stone pillars of the city's Mitchell library. A large hub of computers and comfortable office chairs can be used for free there, near the back entrance on the ground floor. It is a popular spot among the city's underclass, offering a potent combination of entertainment and warmth at no cost.

Clive goes to the desk and shows his library card to receive a log-in voucher for a computer. 'When your hour runs out you can usually just ask for more,' he explains. 'The thing with the library is you can sit there all day if you don't want to go anywhere.' Once online he browses through his favourite Zimbabwean news sites and catches up with friends on Facebook. He starts chat sessions with a friend from Leicester and scrolls down the news feed showing friends in Zimbabwe settled with wives and families. 'I miss my friends. When I first came I used to have contact with people back there but I don't any more. The people that used to be my friends are all married and have their own families. We don't say anything much to each other on Facebook. They don't know what's happening to me here.'

Time seems to slow to a halt when you have twelve hours to kill and a finite number of warm places to kill them in. Clive cannot return to the shelter until eight at night, when he can finally relax, watch some television, go to sleep and wait for the cycle to begin again. Until then he browses the web, watching the seconds of his hour-long internet pass count down until it's time to beg for another one. At busy times this is flatly refused. On Sundays and on Christmas Day, this only source of respite from the cold is closed. 'I hate Sundays,' Clive says. 'The library shuts and there's nowhere to go. I just leave the shelter waiting for any place to open.' On those days he tries his luck wandering in the shopping mall and sitting in bookies'. But when paying customers are expected, he can't stay long.

Clive negotiates a second hour on the library computer and uses it to play free online poker before heading back outside. Somehow the air feels even colder. 'In Zimbabwe you just wear a T-shirt,' he says, his hands shaking with cold as he lights a discarded cigarette butt.

Walking alongside a busy road, he picks over his meagre hopes. 'I'd love to work and look after myself, rather than wait for charity and go from place to place. One day I want to have my own house so I can say 'I'm going back to my house'. I haven't had a proper home since 2012. I'm just stuck like this.' When he catches glimpses of people in their cars or homes it compounds his isolation. 'Every day I look at people and I think of all those days I'm wasting just sitting down or walking. I would love to settle down but how can I do it? How can I have a family when I'm on the street? I've thought of killing myself so many times and I've tried three times now. I'm on antidepressants and all I want is to sleep. Every day, 365 days a year I do this. I just walk around. Every day it's the same.'

Clive heads down a dank cobbled bin alley with broken glass that smells strongly of piss. On the far side is a Radisson Blu hotel and on the other, a slick car hire company. He walks towards a huddle of scraggly drunk men leaning against bins by a doorway. They're waiting to go into the Marie Trust, a Catholic charity that serves up free showers and meals.

A woman at the door signs Clive in and gives him a fluffy peach towel and a bottle of hotel shampoo. He has lunch first – soup and cake – and then a shower. Climbing the steep stairs to the dining room he passes laminated signs saying 'No football colours inside' and a picture of a caged bottle of beer covered in the words 'Escape the trap'. Everything is run by religious volunteers; mostly kindly older ladies in purple pinnies.

Anyone without money can come for one free meal a day. If you arrive in the morning that's porridge and beans on toast. At lunch it's soup, or, for £1.20 you can get chips and maca-roni. In the canteen, 30 guys and a handful of women sit eat-ing hungrily. One lets out a loud belch and nobody reacts; sobriety eludes most of them. Few here are migrants; almost all are Glaswegians who no longer have a home. Some read copies of free papers left on tables, though the Glasgow tourist brochure and leaflets about the Pope go untouched. Listening to the heavily accented chatter around him, Clive says: 'The English I grew up hearing was not like this. I'm always saying "pardon?" It happens less now but I do still struggle. People on the street here say hoose not house.'

Clive comes to the Marie Centre almost every day to eat and wash. 'A lot of people expect me to look dirty because I'm homeless but why should I? I don't see it that way. People often don't believe I'm homeless. I went down to the Clyde river one day when I was waiting for the shelter to open. I had £2 and bought a cider and started to drink it. A group of teenagers looked at me and I asked them for £2 so I could drink more. They said 'No, you don't look like you're on the street'. People want homeless people to look rough.' It's understandable that someone could assume he had a perfectly good home. He is clean shaven, dressed in fresh cords, a thick jumper and a new-looking black body warmer, topped off with a red beanie hat. He says the clothes were all donated to the night shelter and he takes pride in keeping them in good condition.

When he's finished his shower he begins walking again. Pacing through the centre of Glasgow. His route takes him past a branch of Ladbrokes near Central Station. He has £1 in his pocket and wants to spend it there, 'Maybe I could make it £5,' he says. He perches on a stool on the fixed odds roulette machine and pushes the single coin into the slot. Tapping the screen with the speed and precision of a practised expert, he places 5p bets on red and black tiles. The first round is won and he double taps on the 25, making a new bet. This time he loses. The entertainment is over in less than a minute and, with few people sitting in the shop, staying on would be too conspicuous.

Back out in the cold he keeps walking, looking in shop windows and smoking half-cigarettes down to the nub. He gets ill often, he says. Colds, toothaches, headaches, fever. And most of all, depression. There is a GP for homeless people on Hunter Street who sees him regularly.

Clive's only income is from a Glasgow charity called Positive Action in Housing. They give him – and many other destitute migrants – £15 a fortnight to subsist on. Clive remembers explaining his situation to the charity's director, Robina Qureshi, and her shocked response. 'I told her my story and she said "Are you serious? This is your case? I've never heard of anything like this." But that's my situation.'

Sunny Singh, a project officer at the same charity, has helped Clive and others in similarly tricky situations. From his desk in a busy open plan office he phones a network of volunteers who give up bedrooms in their homes to make sure the city's most vulnerable migrants have a place to sleep. 'Men can stay at the night shelter but there's no equivalent for women. They're not given a place to stay even if they're pregnant. The Home Office only provides housing to pregnant immigrants at 34 weeks if their case has been turned down. We had a situation last night that a pregnant woman who was facing a night on the street was sent to stay with a volunteer.'

As Scotland's only asylum city, Glasgow has received thousands of asylum seekers, mostly redistributed there after arriving in London as part of a programme to reduce pressure on overcrowded south-east England. Recently, Scotland has taken pride in having a more welcoming attitude to migrants of all kinds than its southern neighbours. This is particularly the case among the younger generation, a phenomenon reflected in the story of the *Glasgow Girls*. First a documentary, then a stage play and finally a BBC drama, *Glasgow Girls* told the true story of a group of teenagers who successfully campaigned for their asylum-seeking friends to be released from detention and allowed to stay in the country. Ahead of the referendum on Scottish independence, charities noticed a surge in people crossing the border to seek help. A rumour went around that it would be easier to get asylum in the new Scotland – so people headed north ahead of the poll, only to be disappointed when the country voted No.

Charities like Positive Action in Housing are increasingly relied on to help with all aspects of migrants' cases. The Refugee Council used to be the first place asylum seekers turned to when navigating the system, but it has fewer resources to help since losing a government contract for providing this advice. Now seeing someone for initial guidance in person is rarely an option provided by the government. Instead there's an expensive phone line called Asylum Help that Sunny says often goes unanswered for up to an hour. Destitute asylum seekers with meagre resources, hoping to find out what's happening with their housing or food, end up running out of phone credit before they've got through to a human being. Sunny often makes the calls for them. 'After 40 minutes, once they get through they're not given an appointment straight away. They're told to call back after a few days. I always call the English line because the foreign language ones are too busy.'

The charity is still trying to help Clive find a way to resolve his case, but in the meantime he has found his own informal housing arrangement for the coldest days. He made a friend in the city called Victor, a fellow Zimbabwean whose asylum case is still undecided, meaning he is provided with accommodation. 'Victor is a year older than me and he says I'm his only friend. I like to visit in the afternoon and watch television with him. We sit and talk about our situation. He's got a Chinese flatmate who knows me so, if Victor is not in he lets me in to sit on the sofa.' On the worst wintry days Clive walks straight from the shelter to Victor's house, hoping he can spend the day inside.

Sometimes he daydreams about careers. He was good at English and Maths at school and aspired to be an engineer or something in IT. 'I want to learn and get qualifications but the only courses I can do would be English language ones and my English is already good,' he says.

Drinking is one way Clive has tried to make time pass – and anaesthetise his worst feelings. In summer 2014 his drinking reached a dangerous level; he drank so much he had fits and the doctor gave him five years to live. In the midst of all this he was seeing a British girl who also had a booze problem – as well as being bipolar. He met her when he was out drinking in the park with his friends. Their days mostly consisted of drinking and fighting; fighting and drinking. She had a flat, gave him a key and let him stay most nights. One evening he went there early; he'd already drunk too much and was desperate for bed. 'She came home and started hitting me on the face in bed,' Clive recalls. 'I woke up and fought back because I'd been sleeping. I was asleep and then she was kicking me with her legs and hitting me in the face. Next thing I'm hitting her and then the next thing I know she's not in the house. When she came back she was with the police.' The officers arrested Clive and charged him with common assault. 'She wasn't injured really. She had bruises on her face, that's what my solicitor said.'

In court he was sentenced to twelve weeks in Hewell Prison but was released the next day as he had already served half. 'Since I came out of jail I haven't been drinking that much because I don't want to go back. A lot of bad things can happen because of this situation but I want to try my best not to do anything bad.'

The United Nations estimates there are 10 million state-less people living around the world. It is not known exactly how many are living in Britain, but Asylum Aid believes the number grows by around 100 every year. In the UK, many end up stuck in immigration detention for years; sentenced to a life behind bars for the crime of having no identity. Clive envies their incarceration. He is so desperate now that he wants to be taken into detention. At least there he could sleep, stay warm and have regular meals, he reasons.

'Every time I go to the Home Office now they say "Sit down there" and for 30 minutes I wait and then ask, "Are you guys thinking of taking me into detention? Because I'm happy to do that, I'm happy." But they don't. I was hoping they would put me in the detention centre after I was released from prison because I stayed for two years without checking in with the Home Office. I did it because I was told if you do that you'll be detained.' But when the day of his prison release came, nothing happened. Clive said: 'Please, is it say-ing anything about detention on my paperwork because I really want to go?' They were astonished. 'I've never heard anyone who says they want to go there,' one officer said incredulously. Clive was despondent. 'But I do wish to go there; I'd love to go there.'

It's now early 2015 and nothing has changed. Clive is wait-ing, hoping an opportunity to create a real home – in either country – will present itself. The Home Office is looking at his case again but their previous form suggests little will change. If he can hang on another thirteen years there's a small chance he could persuade a judge to give him a right to remain: those living in Britain for twenty years or more without resolution are sometimes given clemency. But it would mean spending his best working years in limbo, and with his criminal record there's no guarantee of success.

Clive's attempt to put the last six years of his life into words is simple. 'I came in the hope of a better life than I had. I just thought I'd have something better, but I've got this.'

◆

CHAPTER 5

Hristina

A short bus ride northwest from the Ladbrokes betting shop where Clive spent his last pound is Maryhill Integration Centre. When Hristina Lazhovska arrived in Glasgow from Bulgaria three years ago, this was the place that pulled her from the grasp of depression. Faced with a choice of working for their future or having a life together in poverty, she and her husband Georgi had decided to leave their five-month-old baby Pepe in Bulgaria with her in-laws. The separation was like a bereavement and the women at the centre picked her up again.

'It was so strange for me not to have him there,' Hristina recalls, blinking away tears. 'I would push the trolley out of Tesco thinking it was a baby pram because I was so used to it. I was a mum yet not a mum because my baby was so far'.

The decision to tear apart their family was not taken lightly. 'I didn't emigrate, I evacuated,' she says of their move. 'I'm not embarrassed to say it; that was the way I felt it. It was an evacuation. It was a moment in our life when we had to get out.'

Her husband's roadside recovery business, which ran two small trucks, collapsed. Then he lost another two jobs in quick succession thanks to the businesses imploding and suddenly they were left with a small baby and almost no money. 'It was a situation where we had to choose between nappies and milk. We had £10 and no milk or nappies. I had to choose between feeding my son or giving him nappies. If we hadn't had parents to send money we would have been totally lost.'

Before Pepe was born, Hristina had been working as a physiotherapist. It took her four years to train up at university, yet the pay as a highly qualified clinician was just £100 a month, with living costs not dissimilar to Britain. After two years' experience, the pay was still less than £200. 'I love my country but I hate the government. It's not normal that young people in good health who are ready to work hard should be in poverty.'

Hristina and Georgi were living in the small city of Burgas on the Black Sea coast. It was where they had grown up and they loved its pleasant nineteenth-century architecture and fresh sea air. Britain had not been their first choice of an evacuation route. They were originally planning to go to Benghazi in Libya. Georgi's parents had already been living out there in a pleasant villa in the sunshine for twenty years. His dad worked in the local oil industry and had a much better quality of life than he could ever hope for back home. When Hristina found out she was pregnant they thought it would be the ideal moment to relocate and join them for a few years. Her mother-in-law had shown her the lovely accommodation that came free with the job by moving her laptop's webcam around the room when they were chatting. Sunshine and a better quality of life seemed within reach. Then the war started. It was a few months into her pregnancy when the protests started getting more vociferous and they had a Skype conversation with Hristina's in-laws in Benghazi. 'They said life was very calm and peaceful and they didn't expect war,' she recalls. 'People were going out to protest in Tripoli but it didn't seem violent.' The next day security forces were firing on crowds of protest- ers in Benghazi and footage of the civil war breaking out was beamed across the world. Hristina and Georgi could not get through to his parents all day. They had dropped everything to flee on the first available ship for Turkey, leaving almost all of their possessions behind, including a car and all their furniture. When they arrived safely home in Bulgaria, they decided to stay put. They had been on enough adventures and decided to retire with the modest savings they had made from life in Benghazi.

But Hristina and Georgi were still keen to try life else- where. There had to be an alternative to the daily struggle to make enough money to feed themselves. Hristina had made friends with a Scottish woman called Angelina ten years earl- ier. Angelina regularly came on holiday to their seaside city; they first met when she stayed in a summer resort where Hristina was working. They got on well and had stayed in touch on Facebook with Angelina sending Christmas cards every year and regularly encouraging Hristina to visit her in Glasgow. When Georgi lost his third job in a year, Hristina told Angelina of their desperate finances and Angelina sug- gested that they try life in the UK. Hristina recalls: 'She said: "Come here and I can help you" and that's why I came.'

In 2011 Bulgaria was a member of the EU but – as in Romania – working rights had been delayed so that its citi- zens did not yet have the right to take employment in Britain. However, with a free rein to travel to the UK, many came and were self-employed or worked illegally. Hristina and Georgi sold a small house in the countryside that was left to them by Georgi's grandmother, giving them £2,000 for flights and seed money in Britain. They were too scared to bring Pepe. They had no idea if they would find work and knew there was a chance they could be homeless and have to go without food. The idea of putting a child through that was too much. They also reasoned that if they both worked they could save more money. Since Pepe's grandparents were now back from Benghazi and loved spending time with him, it seemed an easy solution to leave him with them. They were also leaving behind Georgi's son from his first marriage, who by then was in school.

As they were preparing to leave, Hristina had a Facebook message from Angelina. 'She had originally said she would be there to meet us at the airport. But a week before we were flying out she said: "I'm going to Turkey, leave it for another time". I said: "How can we leave it when we've spent all our money on flights and told our landlord we're going?"' Hristina heard nothing more from Angelina and they decided to fly anyway, hoping she would be there as promised. With so much of their savings blown on the tickets it seemed they had no choice. 'When we landed I thought she probably wouldn't be there but I had a plan B. I reserved a room in a hotel because I knew 99 per cent that she wouldn't be there, even though Georgi was still dreaming that she would be.' As Hristina guessed, there was no sign of Angelina. It would be several months before they heard from her again, and with no explanation for the silence. They got a taxi to the hotel, which was an enormous tower. 'It was a culture shock to see the size of everything. Glasgow is bigger even than the capital of our country and everything was huge. Even the hotel reception was on the fifth floor of the building.'

The next morning, Georgi woke up and went straight onto

Gumtree, the classifieds website. Within a short while he had found a studio flat on Maryhill Road. Hristina had the better English, so she called the landlord and they went round that same day. 'The room was strange, there were no straight walls,' she recalls. 'The landlord was called Vinod and he was in his 60s with adult children. He was Indian and I'd never met anyone Indian before. He wanted bank account details or recommendations and we had neither. We had nothing; just our word. I said: 'We just landed yesterday and we have nothing, will you give us a chance?' He looked unsure but he agreed to let them stay. 'He was from abroad and knew what it was like to come here and struggle to survive,' Hristina says of his decision to take the risk.

A few small acts of kindness in the days that followed made their first month bearable. The previous tenant was a man from Kazhakstan. He had struggled when he first arrived and knowing that they would not be able to get the internet without a bank account, he offered to give them his contract. 'He was kind because while the landlord was making a decision on whether to take us he heard our story and knew that Skype was our only opportunity to talk to family. He said, "You're good people and I know you won't run anywhere without paying, because I know where you live. Keep my internet and just pay me in cash for it when you can."'

On that first night in their new flat they called home on Georgi's ancient laptop. When Hristina saw their five-month-old Pepe in her in-laws' arms she blinked back tears. She was desperate not to make things harder by crying in front of her husband, so she waited until she could lock herself in the bathroom. Once inside, she turned on the shower to muffle the sound and stood beneath it, weeping uncontrollably.

As the days continued, her yearning for her baby boy did not lessen. Their flat was opposite a park and as she became more enveloped by depression the view seemed to taunt her. 'It made me so sad to see the park because I could see ladies with prams,' she remembers. 'I felt totally lost and alone. It was strange to be just me and my husband. I feel it sometimes in my heart what I did leaving Pepe behind. I did it for him but he's too young to explain it to. He would smile at us on Skype and we would play peekaboo and that's all. My mother-in-law would always point at the screen and say, 'That's mummy and daddy'. I watched him grow up on Skype. There were things I saw only in pictures: his first steps, his first words, his first birthday. All on Skype.'

Reliving the separation, Hristina blinks back tears. 'I didn't used to be able to talk about it without crying,' she says, making a valiant attempt to stem the torrent of emotion.

They paid a £600 flat deposit and £300 rent, leaving them with enough money to survive for a handful of weeks without work. On that first day, they knew they had limited money and went to Tesco to buy a loaf of tiger bread and some ham. When they left Bulgaria they had packed just one knife, a plate, two cups, two forks and two spoons. They made the bread and ham last for three days, eating it from a shared plate.

Their upstairs neighbour was friendly and introduced himself. He gave Georgi tips on finding work and he told Hristina about a community group that met up the road from her flat. 'I didn't know what this was,' Hristina says, 'In my country we don't have places like that.' He introduced Hristina to Rema (Remzije) Sherifi, who ran the Maryhill Integration Network. A former radio journalist from Kosovo, Rema arrived in Britain as a refugee in 1998 and knew what it was like to leave behind a home you loved. Her warmth was a lifeline to Hristina. Recalling their first meeting, Hristina says: 'Me and my husband were speaking quietly together in Bulgarian and Rema smiled a cheeky smile. When I asked her where she was from, she said: "The Balkans as well." She had understood what we were saying. She asked me if we had children and I said, "Yes but we left them with their grandparents". She said, "You probably miss them a lot". When I started to cry I could see her eyes fill up too. It's not very often a stranger feels your feelings and takes your drama to heart. I was unknown to her but she cried with me. She said, "Come to the Oasis group, it's a social group for women and you'll enjoy it as there's a lot of people in the same position."' The group met every Thursday lunchtime and it quickly became the focal point of Hristina's life in Britain. 'I was waiting all week just for Thursday to come round. At the beginning there was no reason for me to get up with no baby and no work.'

It was December 2011 when Hristina and Georgi arrived in Glasgow. Within a week Georgi had found work in a car wash making £2.50 an hour, working twelve hours a day. 'We knew about the minimum wage, but he didn't speak English and he couldn't work anywhere as an employee,' Hristina explains. 'The car wash saved our life. Without it we would have been living under the bridge by the end of the month.' He had been told about the job by a man from Bulgaria called Neno, who he met on Facebook. Neno had worked there when he first arrived in Britain and offered to stay on in Scotland so he could take Georgi there and introduce him to the boss. 'There are not a lot of Bulgarians that would do that for someone else in trouble,' Hristina says of the favour. According to Hristina, Georgi had an uphill battle getting taken on, even at near slave wages. 'The boss was a Pakistani man. At the beginning he didn't want to take my husband on because he had no experience and he was slow. Neno was there and said, 'Take him on and try him and teach him'. So they did. They took him for one week unpaid but at least it was something.'

Georgi passed the probation and after a week was getting a wage, albeit a tiny one. It was not the first time Facebook had helped them. Hristina and Georgi met indirectly thanks to the site. A mutual friend was on Hristina's Facebook page and when Georgi saw her profile, he said, 'That's my wife'. The photo showed a young woman with alabaster skin, a kind round face and sleek dark hair. Hristina says proudly: 'He felt love just from seeing my picture.'

While Georgi slogged it out at the carwash, Hristina was desperately trying to find her own work online and struggling to stay positive. She wanted to work legally, which she could do as long as she was technically self-employed. For four months she searched and searched. 'It was terrible. I looked on Gumtree and indeed.com and applied for so many jobs. At the beginning I loved weekends because I knew at the weekends if I applied for a job no-one would reply, so it was relaxing because I couldn't worry about it. But on Sunday everything would feel stressful again because of the waiting and waiting to hear. It made me feel so tired.'

The car wash was in the south of Glasgow, far away from their flat. Georgi would walk four miles to the site, work for twelve hours and trudge home again, all for £2.50 an hour. With little food and endless work, his body turned to a skeleton. He is 1.8 metres tall and when he arrived in Glasgow he weighed around 90 kilos.

After a few months at the car wash he weighed just 60 kilos. Speaking three years later, Hristina says: 'He can't wear the clothes we bought him at that time. We threw them out and hope he will never be that thin again.' Eventually the pay went up to £3 an hour – still less than half the minimum wage. 'Some people believe it's hard to be paid this little,' Hristina says, 'but for people like us it was the only way to survive until I found a job. The horrible thing is there are a lot of people in the car wash earning that money and they don't mind because they haven't got any choice.'

Two months after they arrived, when Hristina had still not found a job, Georgi saw an advert on Gumtree looking for drivers for a fizzy drink company. Desperate to escape the car wash, he applied and was told to pay £60 for a criminal records check. He paid the money and never heard from them, but since they had said to come the following Monday, he turned up at the company's headquarters. The company were upset at what had happened but told him they had never advertised for a job. He had been scammed of the last of their savings. Georgi was crushed by the setback. Hristina recalls: 'He wasn't disappointed that they took £60, he was disappointed because he believed too much that he would find a better job than car washing.'

After four months, Hristina finally found minimum wage work as a self-employed cleaner, wiping down the toilets in Gala Bingo and Paddy Power. It was hardly physiotherapy but at least it was legal and she could earn a decent wage and pay taxes. In time she got more clients, mostly private flats, and they gradually saved the money to fetch their son from Bulgaria.

In December 2012, a year after they first arrived, Hristina and Georgi flew back to Bulgaria to pick up Pepe. Hristina had hoped he would toddle into her arms, but instead he flinched. 'When we went to take him he didn't recognise Mummy and Daddy, he turned away. It took me two weeks to win him back.' She worries that he has been scarred by the separation. 'Sometimes, especially when we visit my parents-in-law, he doesn't let me go out alone without him. When me and my husband go to the shop I can hear him shout "Mama", so I think he can probably remember.'

At the airport after Christmas, her in-laws waved them off. Hristina felt for them – she knew herself what having thousands of miles between her and Pepe had felt like. She could see Pepe's grandmother turn scarlet as they said goodbye. 'She was trying so hard not to cry but she couldn't stop.'

◆

It is almost two years since Hristina and Georgi collected Pepe and brought him to Britain. Hristina is in the kitchen of a comfortable two bedroom flat on the top floor of a concrete block overlooking thousands of cars streaking across the raised M8 motorway. A desolate playground, some scrubland and several underpasses separate the estate from the centre of the city. The kitchen overlooks the block's outdoor walkway, and she is standing by the window baking traditional Bulgarian food for a meeting of Rema's Oasis women's group. The Banitsa – layers of flaky puff pastry with eggs, milk and feta cheese – smells delicious but she cannot have any. It is the start of her Advent fast and she will eat vegan now from 15 November until 24 December. She still observes the traditions of the Orthodox Church even though she goes less regularly. Her nearest Orthodox church is a Greek one near the centre of Glasgow and she says: 'I don't understand what the priest is saying but I go at Easter and Christmas. I made the distinction a long time ago between church and religion. I think if you believe in God you can pray anywhere.'

Her son Pepe, now three, is showing off his toy animal collection in the living room. In crisp English he says: 'mouse, lion, dog,' before handing over assorted toys. A laptop on the floor plays a DVD of a penguin cartoon in Bulgarian sent over by his grandparents. On a television next to it an Australian reality show about animal cops blares out for Hristina's benefit.

The bleep of an incoming call on Skype sounds from the laptop speakers, interrupting the cartoon. Pepe looks up and tries to get Hristina to answer it. When she says 'Not now,' he begins to cry, desperate to speak to the granny who brought him up like a son. Hristina acquiesces and calls back. Within seconds a kindly-looking middle-aged woman in glasses comes onto the screen. Hristina knows too well the pain of separation to make either of them suffer: 'She calls on Skype two or three times a day sometimes. It's very hard for her and I don't mind.'

After a year in Britain, Hristina gave Georgi a pep talk about the car wash. 'I told my husband "Your child is worth more than this, you need to learn more than this." In my country he was a professional driver and he was wasting his skills.' Georgi took in the speech and began applying for all the driving jobs he could. Within a few months he was delivering cars for a rental company and was finally in legal work.

It took Georgi a while to get used to the strict driving regulations. When he and Hristina returned from Bulgaria with Pepe they could hardly open the front door. Behind it was a mountain of letters from the council – all final warnings on penalties for driving in a bus lane. Georgi was shocked – he had seen a sign saying the bus lane was only enforced at certain peak times and thought it applied across the city. It did not. There were 23 letters and they were all final warnings, meaning the charge was £90 not £30, yet they had never received a first letter. Here they were, in Scotland with their son for the first time, with very limited funds and a bill of more than £2,000 for an honest mistake. Hristina was distraught and went to the council. Their reaction made her feel more than ever that she had made the right decision to move. 'I spoke to a lady and explained we never got the first letters. She was kind and said, "Sit and write it down for an appeal letter". They understood and sent us the original letter for all of them, meaning we paid only £30 fines and it came to around £700. They started from the beginning again and gave us a chance to explain. People helped us and believed us; in my country that would never happen.'

They have not always been given such fair treatment in Britain. Georgi's job at a major car hire company had been going well: he even got a Christmas bonus of £800 in 2013 for being one of the best employees (the only Eastern European in the workforce to be given one). But by the following autumn things soured. He was on a zero hours contract and when his boss discovered damage to one of the cars Georgi drove, he fired him on the spot. 'He made one mistake and they said "bye bye,"' Hristina explains. 'They didn't give him his last paycheck because they said they would keep it for repairing the car. He had paid insurance but that didn't seem to help. I think they believe that if no-one is looking for their rights they won't challenge it. They were trying to say that he lied to them because he didn't say there was damage on the car but he didn't notice it. He just hadn't seen it. He's not a conflict person. I wanted to see Citizens Advice about it but Georgi didn't want any trouble. I like to look for my rights but Georgi wanted to move on.'

It took him almost another month to find work again, this time in a food factory. 'He wakes at 4am to go to work at 6am near Edinburgh. I thank God that I have that kind of man as a husband,' Hristina says. The job cutting potatoes and packing food does not use his driving skills but at least it is a fixed contract with guaranteed hours. Hristina is now 32 and still does cleaning when she can get the childcare for Pepe but she longs to return to physiotherapy. On a bookcase next to her favourite novels – *Jane Eyre*, *One Hundred Years of Solitude* and *Harry Potter* – are her physiotherapy textbooks. 'The first thing I put in my suitcase when I left Bulgaria was Gabriel García Márquez. The second was my text books because I thought "one day I want to do this again".'

She is proud of her and Georgi's work ethic and the tax they pay. After years of struggling in tiny flats they now have a council home. 'My husband's tax return for last year is £2,000. We don't take benefits but we're not earning enough for a two bedroom flat. Rema recommended that we apply for one and it has been a big help.' She is acutely aware of the reputation of Eastern Europeans in Britain and desperate to show what her family contributes.

'On the TV and the newspapers there are bad things about Romanian and Bulgarian people. Sometimes I feel embarrassed saying I'm from Bulgaria. Even though I've worked so hard and paid taxes and never been on benefits. When we went to the job centre after Georgi lost his job it was strange. The first question was: "What nationality are you?" and when we said Bulgarian I could see their face change. Then we said, "We came here two years ago and this is our first time applying for

benefits because we really need them." They were really surprised and then they were nice. I noticed they were cold and
suspicious at first when we said Bulgarian but I think I can
prove I'm not that kind of Bulgarian. I know some people who
came here four or five months ago and they said: "I applied
for council tax benefit and I didn't get it yet." That made me
cross. I said, "Oh, you don't want to pay council tax? Go back
to our country if you don't want to pay." They make money
but they don't pay tax and they're still taking money. I stopped
talking to them because to me they're thieves. I don't mind
British people cheating the system because they're British and
they live here. But someone to come over and cheat the system
that's not OK. Go to our country and cheat the system. Most
people come because they want to work but there are a lot who
come for an easy life. They don't see that if you work hard and
get more work then life will be more easy.'

On the wall above her sofa is a small oil painting showing the beautiful old architecture in her home town, with
wrought iron lanterns and elegant balconies looking over cobbled streets. She looks at it with pride. 'That's the main street
that goes directly to the sea. There's a huge sea garden full of
green trees that we go to at weekends and these are the old
buildings from the Victorian times.'

The view from her window in Glasgow is rather different
but she knows what she left behind is less idyllic than it looks.
'If I could live a normal life there, like I do here, I'd be there
immediately: it's beautiful. But it's too hard. Friends who have
stayed in Bulgaria are suffering. I have a friend who studied
physio with me. His sister is a language teacher and he is a
physio but they are both living with their parents because they
can't afford to live alone. The income they receive in these

highly qualified jobs isn't enough. It's hard to pay the bills. The prices are the same as the rest of the EU but the salaries are not the same. We've been too long under communism for 45 years and after that when things changed and democracy came the mafia started to control things and now the government is just stealing. They'll get money from the EU but the money doesn't go to the normal people. They have bank accounts in Switzerland and big houses everywhere but the normal people are suffering a lot.'

She looks at Pepe in their living room surrounded by puzzles, toys and games – and a laptop playing a cartoon – and the contrast is stark. 'It's hard to describe how much harder life is there. When my father grew up in a small village where everyone was poor, he was six before he got his first toy, a wooden truck. He says he will never forget it because he had been dreaming about it for so many years. Glasgow gave me opportunities for a much better life. I live in a two bedroom flat, which would never happen in my country. When I was growing up my parents, grandparents and brothers were in two rooms and only one of those was a bedroom – most of us slept in the living room. My child will not live like that.'

The physical closeness of her upbringing makes her miss family and the security that closeness offered. 'My biggest fear here is that something will happen to me or my husband and our child will be alone. In our country it's just a phone call distance and someone is trying to help you. Here it's stressful because we're alone. It's me, my child, my husband and that's it.'

Hristina has also struggled to recreate the close friendships she had in Bulgaria. 'I think it's harder to make good friendships when you're older because you always compare with friends from your childhood. My closest friends are still in my country. I enjoy solitude but at times it has been too much.' When loneliness threatened to engulf her in her second year in Britain she discovered a Facebook group for Bulgarian mums in the UK. It was through this she met Radina, a fellow Bulgarian in Glasgow who is now one of her closest friends outside of Bulgaria. The group has more than 6,000 women in it, all living in Britain or about to move over and looking for tips. It has proved so popular with newly arrived mothers that it is increasingly Bulgarian parents' answer to Mumsnet. 'People ask everything on there, like what to do if you hate your mother-in-law, what to do if your child has a temperature, how to get a British passport or where to go for good food. It's where you go for life and I enjoy using it. There are different characters on it and sometimes people fight. Most people in my country want to say what they think; they argue about everything.'

She scrolls down the group's news feed and pauses at the more interesting posts. 'In the evening it gets really busy. In this post it's about how much better you'll feel if you stop drinking milk. This one says they have children that are two and three years old and are asking if they should teach them English or Bulgarian. People are saying Bulgarian because it's the mother language. This lady here is asking for help because she knows a Bulgarian mother with three wee children and the father just left and he doesn't want to confirm that the children are his and she's suffering because the twins are just one year old and the older one is two. So mums are coming together and collecting clothes so that they can package and send clothes to her.'

The most dramatic example of the group helping out a mum in trouble happened earlier in 2014. 'There was a post

from a lady who was left by her fiancé. She was homeless in
the park and nine months pregnant. She was in London somewhere. And this group came together and helped her. She
heard someone talking in her language in the park and she
asked for help. It was the person who saw her that posted on
Facebook. They found her a place as well through Facebook
and someone gave her a home and lots of women sent clothes.
Her name was Ina and she called the baby Victoria because she
came into this world and won.'

As she finishes the story she closes the laptop and begins
to get Pepe ready for an afternoon at nursery school. 'I want a
better education for my son and a better life,' she says, helping him into the royal blue sweatshirt of his school uniform.
Its logo is a brightly stitched planet earth with children of all
colours holding hands around the edge. 'I love that symbol,'
Hristina says, gesturing to Pepe's chest. 'We're not born rac-
ists; we're all brothers and sisters no matter what the colour
of our skins.

She leans down to put on his yellow digger wellies and a
Thomas the Tank Engine coat. As he steps across a heart-shaped
doormat that reads 'Home is Where The Heart is', he looks
like all the other young children filing through the estate to
class. But Hristina doesn't want him to be exactly the same.
'I think Pepe will feel part of the Scottish community but he
won't be Scottish,' she says firmly.

She takes Pepe's hand and they walk through the drizzle
to his nursery on the edge of the estate. Inside, the word 'welcome' is written in a cacophony of languages and a long wall of
knee-high coat pegs shows names from every culture: Fatima
next to Lydia; Yullen next to Oliver. Pepe waves goodbye and
goes inside and Hristina leaves to get the bus to the Maryhill

Integration Centre, clutching her special Banitsa pastry. The centre is no longer that near her home but she still goes every week; it has become the closest thing she has to family in Britain.

When she arrives at the unprepossessing block that houses the centre, the sounds and smells of people enjoying the community's annual lunch waft down the stairs. Stacks of buggies sit in the hallway as new mums abandon them to get inside. At the top of the stairs, inside an otherwise small and sterile room is a joyful scene. More than 40 people from all over the world – as well as a handful of Scots – are sitting around tables crammed into the space, tucking into dishes from each others' home countries. Hristina adds her Banitsa to the banquet on the food table and starts chatting to Rema. She may never live in the same country as her family again, she thinks, as she stacks her plate with vegan food. But this is a pretty good second best.

◆

Emad

Emad's council flat off the King's Road, Chelsea, is not as salubrious as the address suggests. The World's End estate is a series of redbrick blocks behind a Co-op supermarket, a mottled damp mattress and other detritus abandoned outside. Emad's home is a single room with a mattress and a sofa, plus a small bathroom off one end and compact kitchen at the other. The flat is clean but messy, all his clothes and immigration documents shoved into a teetering pile on top of a suitcase in a small built-in cupboard. His doormat is the Syrian regime flag – 'I like wiping my feet on it,' he grins mischievously.

Growing up in Damascus, Emad had always been more aware than his friends of his country's political failings. His father Tyseer was a property developer and a prominent opponent of the Syrian regime since the 1970s. At home, Emad heard stories of how dissenting voices were crushed; the way some groups were denied an education; how the rights of Kurdish people were ignored. Tyseer was Sunni, but Emad's mother Nawal was Shia and came from an influential Alawite family. The marriage was a rare one: the minority Alawites have dominated Syria's political elite for decades, ruling over the country's Sunni majority. Unions between the two factions are relatively uncommon.

Nawal's family was not happy with the match, which happened not through careful arrangement but, quite literally, by accident. Nawal was riding her bicycle in Damascus one summer's day in 1975 when a beautiful man stepped out into the road. Before she had time to brake she careered into him. Recalling the moment decades later, she would give a girlish giggle and say, with a lascivious glint in her eyes, 'Elvis Presley'. Tyseer's lustrous dark sideburns, high apple cheeks, thick quiff and smoky eyes earned him the nickname.

Nawal was only sixteen and she was quickly infatuated. They got talking and soon the two were meeting in secret, walking together and sharing the stories of their young lives. After a fortnight Tyseer took Nawal home and introduced her to his mother; to everyone's relief they got on well.

The problem came with Nawal's family. When she told them she had fallen in love with a Sunni Elvis-lookalike they were so furious that they beat her and – between the punches and kicks – ordered that she stop seeing him. When she refused, they threw her out of the house, excised her from their wills and warned she would never hear from them again. A month later, Tyseer and Nawal married. Nawal's family wouldn't speak to her for more than a year – and remained distant.

Nawal became pregnant almost immediately. Emad was born in June 1976 and for a brief time their life seemed charmed – they were in love and had a beautiful baby boy. Tyseer's property development business grew. He won a contract with the Cham Palace chain, which ran a fleet of Syria's five-star hotels, and soon the small family was wealthy. Tyseer always drove the latest Mercedes and they lived in a grand house in the old city at the heart of Damascus. The home was in the traditional Old Damascene style, built around a court-yard with fountains and trees.

When Emad was nine the government took control of the area and they were forced to move to a flat elsewhere in the city. It was around this time that Tyseer's criticism of the government became less private. He would speak out and then disappear to prison for days, weeks, even months at a stretch. Tyseer had been careful to protect his family from his political activities. Perhaps thinking that ignorance might keep them safer, he made sure Nawal and Emad never knew much more than that he was opposed to the government and not afraid to be public about it. Nawal would plead with him to tell her what was happening but he gave half-hearted explanations, 'It's a political thing and it's not your business'. She would later wonder if his reticence was thanks to her own family connections: her uncles and cousins, though they had largely disowned her, were high-ranking officers in the army and intelligence. Perhaps, she reasoned, he feared his activities would get back to them and make things worse for everyone.

◆

The year before Emad left to study in Britain, his father Tyseer disappeared. It was 2004 and his uncle and other close relatives had already left for Canada after getting into trouble with the government. Emad recently discovered that his father had a secret second family, another wife that he took without permission from Nawal, as well as four other children. On the last night they spent together, Emad quarrelled with his father after witnessing his mother prepare to leave the house to defuse a fight. Emad fumed: 'Why don't *you* leave? If you have to fight, why must she leave? It's more dangerous for her.'

Tyseer took the hint and left. He never came back. Emad can still remember every word of the argument though he hates to relive it. It plays on his mind that he never had a chance to say sorry.

After a few days Emad began to worry. He called his uncles and Tyseer's other wife, but they hadn't seen him. He tried hotels, thinking his father may have checked himself in to take a break from them. This time there was no trace of him. As more days went by, Emad began to check hospitals, police stations and prisons but nobody had seen him. He paid a solicitor to help Nawal with the search and she tried to go with her to all the prisons in the country. Eventually after four years (and countless bribes to officials), Emad's family discovered Tyseer was being held in Sednaya prison, which, as the civil war progressed, gained global notoriety for its torture and mistreatment of prisoners. When riots broke out at Sednaya in 2008 and dozens of political inmates were slaughtered, the family gave up hope that he would make it out alive.

◆

When Emad had sat in Damascus picturing his future life as a student in Britain, he imagined the nightlife would be incredible. He wasn't after drink or wild parties but he was sociable and loved to stay out all evening chatting in cafes. Late nights were not Portsmouth's speciality. It took two weeks before Emad was thoroughly bored of the coastal town he had come to study in. 'That is a totally dead town,' he would say later. 'Damascus is really alive, but in Portsmouth at 4 o'clock in the afternoon there is nothing there.'

He was supposed to stay for two months to complete an intensive business course, but couldn't face it. He was also shocked at how bad his English was. 'I thought I was quite good at English, but when I started that course I realised it was zero. I was just sitting there with an open mouth.' Most of the English he knew was from American movies and television. He listened to a few Longman language tapes, but his small selection of well enunciated words, like 'burrrglar' and 'nonsense', did not exactly make him a winning conversationalist.

It was December 2005 and Britain seemed to be dark all the time. With no friends or family nearby, a course he could barely understand and a desperation to live in a busier city, Emad decided to move to London. He had paid an agent £7,000 for the Portsmouth course but he said later, 'I'd have died if I'd stayed'. He rented a flat in Harlesden, north-west London and looked for a new course, living off savings from several years earning good wages working for a courier company in Dubai and Damascus.

After Portsmouth, Harlesden felt dangerous and Emad's friends scared him, warning 'Don't carry anything with you'. Accustomed to needing official identification everywhere in Syria, he was walking around with his passport in his pocket and was now terrified of losing it. When he called the Home Office to see if he could get an ID card to use instead, the woman on the line was bemused. 'Nobody will stop you for not having ID,' she explained. 'The police won't stop you at all if you don't make any trouble.' Emad couldn't believe it. In Syria, police would even stop people for having a dirty number plate – and wouldn't leave without a bribe. 'That's why they call Britain a free country; it's amazing,' he enthused. Years later he would say that feeling of freedom from arbitrary police interference in Britain had lessened. 'The last few years things have changed. Stop and search is getting really annoying for people. It's happened to a lot of friends and it's not good.'

Being a student meant having a visa to stay in Britain and Emad wanted more qualifications. He started taking English lessons at William Shakespeare College, a private college in Deptford Bridge. He remembers the course being a bit shambolic – sometimes there were teachers there, often not.

Emad's lessons took around twenty hours a week, the rest of the time he worked as a sales assistant in the Kingston branch of TK Maxx. He won best associate several times for his customer service and took pride in knowing answers to any questions about the shop. He even caught a few shoplifters. But standing on his feet all day became more difficult. He was diagnosed with SAPHO syndrome, a rare inflammatory bone disorder that causes extreme pain in the joints and requires seven different kinds of daily medication. He began arriving late, something he blamed on the difficulty moving his limbs first thing in the morning.

While Emad studied in London, back in Syria his family prepared an engagement party for his girlfriend Amani. She was beautiful and Emad was excited about their future; they had been meeting in secret for several years before, in 2008, they were engaged at an enormous party with 400 guests. Emad's mother was happy to see him settle down.

Emad came back to Britain excited about what lay ahead. He could bring his fiancée to join him once he had a six-month resident's permit, so he sent off his passport to what is now the Home Office, along with information about a new business administration course he had enrolled on at William Shakespeare College. The degree was not as it seemed. That year the government introduced a licensing system aimed at closing bogus colleges which were offering overpriced, poor quality (or non-existent) courses – effectively as a way of selling visas to Britain. A clampdown saw hundreds of colleges close, booting out legitimate students hoping to achieve, as well as those taking advantage of a scam.

Emad hadn't finished the first year of what he thought was a three year degree course when the college demanded the full fees and told him to stop attending. Soon afterwards it was shut down. 'It was a waste of time and money. At the end you find you're a victim of a trick. There was chaos in the education system at that time and you'd pay a lot of money and then find the course was not accredited by the British Council. I thought I was studying in the UK not Africa; I thought I was studying in the best place in the world for education.'

Emad had spent more than £20,000 on student fees for various courses, not including living expenses. He had savings and sold property in Syria but the money began to run out.

Months went by and Emad's passport had still not been returned, leaving him unable to work. He called the government's immigration helpline every day trying to find out what had happened, but it was a premium number and he was low on funds, so he cut down his calls to once a month. On the first day of every month he rang, after up to an hour waiting, they would just say the file was 'in progress'. He grew to hate the term almost as much as the 0870 number, which he can still reel off the top of his head eight years later.

When Emad had no passport and no visa after a year, his fiancée Amani lost patience. With such a public engagement, everyone expected them at least to be living in the same country by then. The gossip in Damascus began in earnest. People told Amani they were sure Emad must have girlfriends in Britain and just wanted a wife for holidays in Syria. She did not know whom to believe but it hurt that she still hadn't seen Emad after all this time.

Once the whispering reached a crescendo, Amani's parents called Emad demanding an explanation. He had none to give them – the Home Office only ever told him it was 'in progress'. Then her father gave Emad an ultimatum: 'You have until December. Either come here and take her, or bring her to Britain, or it's over'. With no passport, Emad could do neither and when December came and he was stuck in London, the wedding was called off.

Emad was in limbo with no job and no wife, but he still had to pay rent. Within a couple of years he had run up debts of £15,000. On his last call to the Home Office, almost two years after he first sent them his passport, he lost his temper. Normally the call centre gave the usual 'in progress' response or 'there's nothing on my screen,' but this time the woman at the other end of the line took a closer look. She said their records showed they twice tried to send the documents in a package two months ago, but it was returned to sender. Emad couldn't understand: the address had been right, he had hardly gone out, and there had been no failed delivery note. He said 'OK fine, send me the documents now, I'm at home and you have my address'. A few days later a letter arrived from the Home Office, titled 'Untraceable Passport'. The department had lost his passport. Years later, long after his immigration status had been sorted, a package with no accompanying letter arrived at his house. It was his missing Syrian passport.

◆

Emad realised in spring 2011 that he might never return to Syria. He had lived in Britain for six years but it had always felt temporary. A place to study, make money and new friends, yes, but not a home. Forbidden from working or studying until his visa was sorted, he was glued to Al Jazeera, following the rumblings of a political revolution back home. Finally it looked like the Arab Spring was coming to Syria.

When police opened fire at protesters demanding Bashar Al Assad's resignation in Daraa, in March 2011, the Syrian uprising began in earnest. Emad conducted his own London demonstrations, in tandem with peaceful protesters on the streets of Damascus. He would stand outside the Syrian Embassy in Belgrave Square calling for democracy and the overthrow of Assad's regime. All those political chats with his dad as a child were finally coming to fruition and he wanted to use his time in Britain to help. Soon he was not alone outside the embassy, and a small coterie of democracy campaigners came to stand alongside him. They waved Syrian flags, chanted 'Assad Out' and carried placards saying '40 years of fear'.

The longer his passport was missing, the less money Emad had. Soon he was forced to sleep on friends' sofas. The Syrian embassy refused to give him a new passport – saying they were conducting 'security checks'. Though his statelessness was due to an error by the Home Office, he was given no government support, leaving him homeless, jobless and heavy with debt. The revolution gave him new purpose. In March he was one of the founder members of the Free Syrian League, helping to organise opposition to Assad from afar. He would coordinate help for the Free Syrian Army and with his links with dissidents across the country became a go-to person for up to date information on government resistance. Soon he was spending every Saturday and Sunday outside the embassy in Belgrave Square, Tuesdays outside 10 Downing Street, and most days in a small basement coffee shop on the Harrow Road in west London. The informal cafe became a popular hang-out for exiled Syrians, a place to discuss the latest news of the revolution and swap tips on life in Britain.

As the protests outside the embassy became more vociferous, embassy officials began to take action. Sometimes they could be seen standing at the windows filming the people below, taking a record of all the faces. That was when the phone calls began. At first they were rude but not frightening. People who Emad assumed were working for Syria's secret service would call him and demand that he stop protesting. When he asked how they got his phone number they hung up. But once he formed the Free Syrian League in March the calls became more aggressive. 'Now the real trouble starts,' they said. 'We know your family in Syria'.

In Damascus, Emad's mother Nawal started receiving calls too. Initially they just said 'You must call your son and tell him to stop, otherwise you'll be in a lot of trouble. You know what we can do.' Then they came to her flat. There were about ten of them and she guessed they were military intelligence, dressed in civilian clothes. Around a week later, Emad was on one of the Arabic television channels still being broadcast in Syria. He was being interviewed in a cafe on the Edgware Road in London and he criticised the government, talked about how he was organising the protests and why he wanted the overthrow of the Assad regime.

The interview was broadcast in Syria at about 3pm. At 6pm the interrogators arrived at Nawal's flat in Damascus. This time there were far more of them – she could not count the number, but they filled the flat. They took all Emad's documents from his old bedroom, seized a desktop computer he had left behind and broke a lot of furniture as they gutted the rooms for clues. Then they started pushing Nawal and slapped her hard on the face. All the time they were gleefully filming the scene on a mobile phone. They said 'Who does he work with in Syria? What do you know? Are you helping him? Or any other activists?' Nawal kept saying that she had no idea and that he was outside the country so how could she know? Then they made their final threat: 'You see all this,' they said, gesturing at the gang of thugs rifling through her stuff, 'It will stop if you tell your son to stop doing what he's doing in the UK. Then we won't do anything and we will stop coming here. But if you don't ask him to stop we will send you to join your husband.'

That evening she packed all the papers and valuables she needed into a handbag to keep with her at all times. She knew she might have to leave quickly. The next day she was at a neighbour's house when a friend came running to tell her she had seen a gang of officials breaking down the door of her house. She did not need any more warnings. She got in a taxi and fled to Jordan.

Back in London Emad claimed asylum. He now knew that he would never be safe in Syria while the Assad regime remained. Even if he had wanted to return it would have been impossible; the Syrian embassy had been refusing to give him a new passport ever since the British government lost his. Being classified as a refugee would solve the problem of his statelessness.

The asylum interview was straightforward. The Home Office official asked him about the Free Syrian League, his role in setting it up, and his harassment by embassy officials. A Scotland Yard investigation into his treatment in Britain helped evidence his claims – and within weeks he was given refugee status and allowed to stay in the country. He still had no official passport but was given a special blue travel document for refugees.

✦

Three years after those first embassy protests, Emad is sipping orange juice in a cafe in Knightsbridge, looking as if he has aged two decades. He is just 38 but his hair, once black and worn in a quiff not unlike his dad's Elvis cut, is now in a straggly grey ponytail, and his eyes have dark circles around them. The war has crushed him. In the early days of the revolution he was full of optimism for a new Syria, but now it is early 2014 and the picture looks very different. Factions within the Syrian resistance have started fighting each other and what had seemed to Emad to be a cause of democracy and freedom has largely been overtaken by Muslim extremists.

'Look at my hair, it's totally white,' he says, pulling a grey strand out of his hairband. 'The last years have been bad. Revolution. People being killed every day and when you see how people have been shot and slaughtered you can't do anything. You want to do everything for them but you can't.' He is cynical about Britain and other powers' involvement in the war. After opposing Assad's brutal crushing of the democratic uprising, Britain and its allies U-turned, now seeing the greater threat as Islamic extremism.

'Extremists in Syria didn't create themselves,' Emad says. 'Isis, they are not really Islamic people. Someone created them. I believe France, Britain, Saudi and Iran have all supported them at some time. We didn't have Sunni-Shia problems like this before. Unfortunately Western intelligence had to get involved and after that everything burned. How many countries got involved in Syria? And each had a group they were helping. They say there are up to four million refugees now but I think it's even more and 150 people are dying every day.'

On his more maudlin days, he blames himself for his part in that death toll. 'You do something for the Syrian people's freedom but you feel you brought them more suffering. I'm part of it. I'm one of the first people who stood outside the embassy and said no.'

Preoccupied with the war and hampered by the often excruciating pain of SAPHO syndrome, which makes physical work or early starts difficult, a job has proved elusive. His condition is exacerbated by stress and cold weather and at times he can hardly move. He is on benefits, receiving £100 a week and living in a council flat in Chelsea. Half of that £100 he sends back to his mum Nawal, who is now living as a refugee in Turkey. His main sustenance is £1 or £2 portions of fried chicken from Chicken Cottage – 'it cuts your stomach but it's cheap'. Mostly he does not bother to leave his flat at all.

He has seen others fare even worse. A Syrian friend called Baha who had been living below the radar in London after smuggling himself into the country illegally, found the pressure too much. He had a gambling problem and he had lost much of his family back in Syria. With no money, he had asked Emad for help two years earlier. Emad did what he could, lending him a chunk of cash and telling him to pay him back when he got the chance. Not long afterwards Baha called Emad when he was busy and he forgot to call him back. He did not hear from him again. Some eighteen months later, someone came to check the gas meter in Baha's flat and found his body. He had been dead for about three days. At the end he was so thin that he weighed just 45 kilos; he had an immunity disorder and had tried to kill himself before. Just a few months earlier Baha was granted refugee status but it had not been enough to curb the feeling that he had lost everything he cared about.

Emad knows he has teetered close to the same feelings. He has been given medication for depression but stopped after a few days when it didn't seem to work. Now he feels the only way to make things better is to improve things for his mum Nawal, whose hardship plays on his mind. He feels responsible for her abrupt departure from Syria and worries constantly about her.

After Nawal arrived in Amman, Jordan, she stayed at a hotel for a couple of days before reporting to the UN, telling of her harassment in Damascus and getting a certificate of her refugee status in Jordan. The office was empty then; relatively few people had yet claimed asylum in the city. Her money was running low. After paying for the taxi across the border she had just 400 Syrian pounds in her pocket, worth less than ten British pounds. She had been working as a dressmaker in Syria, doing small amounts of sewing and tailoring, but she had not had much income. After Emad's father went to prison, she had given Emad much of the money from the sale of family property to spend on his education in Britain. She had six thick gold bangles, a chain bracelet and two necklaces that she had brought with her and sold one by one whenever things got desperate. Without a receipt she had to accept below market prices, but it kept her alive. Emad was able to wire some money via a credit card and for a couple of months the UN gave her a stipend to help with living costs. As more Syrians arrived, the price of everything went up. She found a room in a shared student flat and made friends quickly. She was old enough to be their mother – perhaps even their grandmother – but the young women warmed to her considerate nature and wicked sense of humour. Her new Jordanian friends made her feel young again. Photos on her smartphone show them trying on oversized sunglasses in shops together and giggling at shared jokes in the flat. They called her 'Om Emad', mother of Emad, and they heard all about her only child, who she spoke to every day on Viber or Skype.

Outside this friendship circle, the welcome in Jordan was distinctly cooler. As more refugees arrived, many in Amman began to turn against them and there were protests on the streets calling for all Syrians to be kicked out. Shopkeepers would refuse to serve Nawal just for being Syrian, and she heard her fellow people being referred to as dogs. Desperate for money and a roof, Syrians would work for lower wages and pay higher rents, fostering resentment among working class Jordanian families.

After a failed knee operation years ago, Nawal struggled to walk far, her left leg stuck in a stiff straight line. When she needed to travel any distance and could afford it, she would take a taxi. One day she was in a cab going a relatively short distance into town. The meter said 0.85 Dinar – less than a pound – but the driver said he wanted 4.5 Dinars. When she argued, he said 'It's good Assad is kicking you because you deserve to be killed'. He tried to grab her money, but she handed him a one Dinar coin and scrambled out of the car. It was still more than the meter said and she hoped it would be enough to end the argument. As she walked in front of the car to leave he drove it into her, knocking her into the road. While she was lying on the floor he took a 10 Dinar note from her purse and drove off, leaving her too bruised to move properly for a week.

Once his mother had arrived in Amman, Emad began work on bringing her to Britain to join him. It is not possible to apply to be a refugee from outside the country, so instead he applied for a settlement visa, where family members of someone living legally in Britain can be brought over if you can prove that they are dependent on you. Just applying for the visa cost £470 (by 2015 this cost had risen to £600). Twice Emad found the money to apply, using credit cards and borrowing from friends. Twice he was rejected. The Home Office argued that because she was not over 65 she could not be classed as dependent, even though she had no other close relatives besides her imprisoned husband. They also said that since their surnames were different – something very common in Arabic families – he could not prove he was her son. In their second rejection they cited inconsistencies between the two applications. There was no option on the form to put that her husband had disappeared and was probably in prison, so the first time round she ticked 'divorced.' She thought this was most accurate because under Sharia law she was considered divorced since he had now been gone without a trace for almost a decade. The second time she ticked 'widowed.' She had given up hope that Tyseer was alive and thought it might help her case to make it clear he was not there for her.

The rejections have only added to Emad's feeling of helplessness. It is January 2014 and David Cameron has just announced in pious tones that Britain will accept a limited number of the most vulnerable refugees from Syria. Emad knows his mother will not be among them. He is also bitter that it has taken an intervention from Ukip for the Prime Minister to act. 'Even Nigel Farage said "I'm against immigration but Syrian refugees are exceptions; you can't just leave

them like this being slaughtered". Even the most racist polit-
ician ever is saying this! David Cameron didn't want to keep
quiet after that so he had to do something but I don't see any
refugees arriving.'

Emad's scepticism at Cameron's announcement is later
proved right. Journalists were briefed to expect around 500
refugees to arrive and wrote articles accordingly. Six months on
it emerged that just 50 had been given a new home in Britain
under the scheme. In Sweden, whose population is a sixth of
the size of Britain's, almost 60,000 Syrian refugees had been
given shelter by the end of 2014. In Germany the number
was 80,000. Britain accepted asylum applications from those
in the country illegally – or already living here – but in 2014
this amounted to just 2,081 people.

Emad's frustration at not having his mother with him is
further piqued when he begins to meet and hear of fake 'Syrian'
refugees getting into Britain. A friend was attending English
classes, supposedly with other Syrians, when he discovered
that several had faked their identities. They were Egyptian,
Lebanese, Palestinian or Iraqi. They had smuggled themselves
into the country, destroyed their documents and claimed to be
arrivals from Syria, a place they knew would guarantee them
a stay in Britain at least until the end of the war. Emad heard
a valid Syrian passport was worth around £6,000 on the black
market. An Egyptian man even asked to buy Emad's expired
(and void) Syrian passport for 3,600 euros to help with his
asylum claim. Emad declined. His safety in Britain was not
for sale.

Discovering so many bogus Syrian refugees angered Emad,
who felt they were taking places much-needed for his people.
He was also dumbfounded by the incompetence of the Home

Office: these men did not even have Syrian accents and had little knowledge of the country, yet they had not been found out. But he did not want to report them to the police; he understood how difficult their journey to Britain had been and that the countries they came from had their own problems.

When Emad heard about the taxi incident in Amman he was furious. He felt helpless knowing his mother was suffering and was desperate to move her somewhere safer. Between them they scraped together the money for a flight to Turkey. He hoped he might be able to go and meet her there – or have a chance of bringing her nearer still.

The one piece of good news that Emad had not been expecting came from his father. In December 2013 Emad's uncle in Canada paid top officials to learn what had happened to Tyseer. He discovered he had not died in the 2008 massacre at Sednaya prison but was still being held there. It did not bring Emad any closer to being reunited with his father – and many people said death would be better than a decade in Sednaya – but it was a relief to know where he was.

♦

It is September 2014, more than three years since his mum Nawal was forced to flee Syria. Now she is on the move again but this time, her journey could be fatal. Without a visa, Nawal would not be allowed even to set foot on a flight to Europe, so Emad found another way. After years of struggling to resettle her in Europe legally he decided to try boat smugglers. The last he heard from his mum was two days earlier, when she called him from a smuggler's satellite phone while bobbing around in the middle of the Mediterranean. She was about to transfer to a smaller boat, ready to head into Italian waters. She had sounded frightened so Emad had made an effort to keep the conversation light. Nawal had told him, her voice cracking on the line: 'If I drown you have to keep going on with your life.' Trying to make her laugh, Emad replied, 'Don't worry, if you drown I'll pick up another mum from the Sunday market.' With no word since, he is now haunted by the idea that he could have sent his mother to her death.

The plan had been for Nawal to call as soon as she arrived in Italy. She had a smartphone so even if the phone signal didn't work she would log onto wifi and send a message on a messaging app like Viber or WhatsApp. When it had been 24 hours with no news Emad called the Italian coastguard. The man who answered spoke in Italian but when Emad said 'English?' he replied almost fluently. Emad told him he was calling from the UK and before he had a chance to finish the sentence the man at the other end of the line said, 'You want to know where your family are don't you?' When Emad said yes, he was friendly but explained they got a lot of similar calls and with an enormous ocean it was not easy to trace the ramshackle boats carrying refugees. Emad gave him the number of the satellite phone Nawal had called from but the coastguard could not get through on it.

Another day has passed since that call and Emad is so restless in his flat that he cannot keep his hands still, his mind racing faster than he can type words into Google. He has not slept and sitting on his sofa in a rumpled t-shirt and jeans he is chain-smoking roll-up cigarettes with one hand and typing into a keyboard with the other, his web browser up on his television screen. He is looking up ferries to France, hire cars and hotels. If she does make it to Europe alive, he expects her to arrive in Italy within days and he wants to be there to help.

He keeps looking at online maps, zooming in and out of the Mediterranean, looking at what port might be a logical arrival place after sailing from Turkey.

His plan is to leave in a few hours on a ferry with a Syrian friend, Mohammed, who wants to go to Milan to see the refugees arriving there. A confirmation email from MyFerryLink pings into his inbox for an evening crossing. Beneath it is an automated message from the Syrian Network for Human Rights; its subject line reads: '2,591 people were killed in August'.

The money for the smugglers and his own journey to Italy had to be found quickly and Emad had little time to think it through. He managed to get a credit card after being economical with the truth about his employment situation. He also sold his car for £4,000 and his motorbike for £2,500 – something he realised he should have done long ago. When this still did not raise enough, he worked afternoons under the radar in a friend's second-hand car shop. The friend gave him £50 a day, plus £50 for every car sold. In less than a month he had sold more than 60 cars and he finally had enough to help his mum. 'If I put my head in sales, nobody can stop me,' he said later of the burst of activity.

At the car rental company he is relieved when his economy booking is upgraded for free to a comfortable SUV. Glancing at the boot, he sizes it up as a hiding place. 'Why not? I could bring her back that way. If they catch me what are they going to do? It's my mother.'

At Dover, Emad and Mohammed's car is stopped and searched. When they hand over their refugee travel documents they are asked scores of questions. 'Where are you going? How long for? Where are you staying? Have you got a hotel booking? What do you do for a living? Where did you get the money from? Whose car is this?' Emad explains it is a rental car and that he got the money by selling his car – which is partly true, he had sold his car to fund the trip. Then the immigration officer opens the boot, finding stacks of bottled mineral water and food for the long journey ahead. 'What are you going to do, make a swimming pool with it?!' he asks, getting more suspicious. Emad tries to stay calm and says he is just holidaying in France. But eventually he waves them onto the ferry.

After driving a short way in France, they stop at a hotel not far from the Swiss border. Emad has still heard nothing from his mum and he gets up early the next morning, desperate for news. They are just crossing into Italy when Emad's phone rings. He does not recognise the number but when he hears the voice at the other end of the line the relief that floods through him is physical. 'Habibi, Habibi – my love, my love – I'm in Italy,' Nawal says, crying with joy. She is on a friend's phone and texts him a virtual pin of her location, showing she is in Crotone, in the far south of the country. He still has no idea how she survived the journey – she sounds exhausted and says she has a lot to tell him. Given she is almost a twenty-hour drive away, they decide it will be quicker – and cheaper – for Emad to wait in Milan while she comes by train to the city.

A few hours later Emad and Mohammed reach Milan. Now that he knows Nawal has made it across safely Emad begins to relax. He is excited and nervous about their meeting and kills time looking around the city. 'I feel like I'm on holiday' he laughs. He sits in cafes with Mohammed, eating pizza and admiring the city's old buildings.

The next day Emad learns his mother has been held up – the men who promised to buy her a train ticket have not kept their word and he kicks himself for not driving straight down there. To kill time, he and Mohammed go to Milan Central station to meet some of the other refugees arriving from Syria and hear their stories. The city's elegant 1930s station has become a hub for Syrians beginning their journey across Europe, with thousands passing through every week. Following the Lampedusa disaster the previous October, when 366 people drowned after their boat caught fire near the southern Italian island, the country softened its policy to immigrants. It became the first EU country to decriminalise 'illegal' immigration and the change made it a beacon for those fleeing conflict in Syria and across the Middle East. For a year afterwards Italy also sent Navy ships out daily to patrol the Mediterranean in search of those stranded in boats. In an unfortunate twist of fate, the slackened rules and improved rescue services only increased people smuggling, as those fleeing conflict took the calculated risk that they were more likely to make it across. The Navy patrols had been a source of comfort to Emad and Nawal – and were one of the reasons they felt prepared to risk the perilous boat trip.

More than 170,000 refugees arrived in Italy in 2014 after being rescued at sea, mostly by the Italian Navy. The figure is more than double the total number of refugees that arrived the previous year by boat in Italy, Greece, Spain and Malta combined. As more and more people took the perilous journey in the hope of a new life in Europe, the death toll soared too. Around 600 refugees perished in the Mediterranean after their boats sank in 2013. A year later, a record 3,400 people died or disappeared after attempting a crossing.

The first person Emad meets is Khaloon Spenati, who is perched on a polished marble wall inside the main concourse, bouncing his baby son on his knee. He hardly notices the sharp suits and clacky shoes of the afternoon rush hour stream by. Less than a week ago he and his family were among 300 men, women and children certain they would die in the Mediterranean in a boat designed for less than half its human cargo. 'The boat we went on was a mini Titanic', he jokes to Emad, though from his fleeting smile he is clearly only just able to laugh about their perilous journey from Tripoli. 'The Libyan smugglers treated us like sheep, like animals. It was a deadly journey. It was a very small boat that kept swerving right and left. The boat was designed to hold a maximum of 150 people, but there were 300 of us on board. It was only fourteen metres long and four metres wide so it was sitting very low in the water.'

Khaloon tells Emad he plans to get his family across to Sweden to try to make a fresh start. A heavy chunk of his remaining savings – which are now around 2,000 US dollars – will go on rail fares as he gets his family across Italy, France, Germany and Denmark to reach Sweden where they want to claim asylum. Like many families they refused to give their name or fingerprints when they arrived in Italy to make it easier to claim asylum elsewhere in Europe. Under the Schengen Agreement, those seeking asylum in the EU must do it in the first European country they arrive in. But if no record is ever made of their arrival they can try their luck elsewhere.

The scale of new arrivals is overwhelming for the Italian authorities. Police sources told the national paper *Il Giornale* at around the same time, 'we cannot control them any more. We cannot even identify them.' A week earlier, the Interior minister Angelino Alfano went to Brussels and persuaded the Commission that Europe would do more to help Italy. There are reports of coach-loads of refugees being dropped at Milan station to disperse them from the south and encourage them to leave the country. But most people seem to be middle-class families who had already saved enough for a fare to get straight on the train there and buy onward tickets elsewhere in Europe.

The majority of people that Emad speaks to in the station say they are heading for Sweden, Holland and Germany. Nobody wants to stay in Italy with its reputation for offering scant help to refugees once they arrive on land. Recent headlines about the unrest at Calais and the challenge of crossing the Channel mean only a hardier minority – mostly single men – are aiming for Calais and Britain.

Milan's increasing role as a jumping off point for asylum across Europe has transformed parts of the station into an unlikely refugee camp. Emergency water is handed out by aid workers beneath two-storey screens advertising Dolce & Gabbana couture. A humanitarian help desk offering advice and a shuttle service to a nearby camp is so swamped that yellow roadwork barriers have been erected to allow staff space to work.

Outside a newsagent's selling overpriced snacks and magazines, a Save The Children play area has been erected, its young charges sprawled out on foam mats doing colouring. Around the edges families sit on their meagre luggage looking on. One skinny young teenager lies splayed out on his bag, his last reserves of energy being used up on a rattling cough that doubles him over. Over the course of the day several hundred people are ferried in minibuses to a camp on the outskirts of the city. But most want to stay and wait for onward trains.

Before he heads back to his guest house for the night, Emad speaks to a 23-year-old student who has been trying to get to England for the last seven months. The man, who did not want his name published, left his home in Nabek, near Damascus on New Year's Day 2014, heading first to Lebanon and then into Turkey. He paid smugglers for a fake passport but the only one they could get was Algerian, which cost him 3,500 US dollars. He flew to Rome where they discovered it was a fake and arrested him. He explained he was Syrian and would not go back but they insisted he must return to Istanbul. After 48 hours of resisting getting on the plane he was taken to a back room by Italian security staff – he could not tell from their uniform if they were military or police – and badly beaten. Photos on his phone show large purple bruising on his forehead just after the attack. He got a medical report of his injuries once he reached Turkey and hopes to press charges against the Italian authorities when he finally reaches safety.

Not put off by the experience – or the risks of breaking the law – he travelled by sea to Greece where he paid 3,000 euros for a fake Italian identity card and bought a flight to Venice. He's light skinned and could easily pass for a native European, even dressed like an Italian backpacker with a cap, a large hiking rucksack and faded jeans. At the airport in Athens he was questioned by immigration to test if he was Italian. In Italian they asked his name and if he could count to ten – both of which he had taught himself just in case. After a moment's hesitation they let him through.

Before now he had never broken any laws. A fourth year civil engineering student, he left Syria with just a year to go on his course because it was becoming too dangerous. Waiting for the first train headed towards Calais he explains he is desperate to reach England and pick up his studies. 'I'm a smart guy and I'll prove it,' he says in accomplished English. From the bottom of his rucksack he digs out a dog-eared envelope full of papers showing his outstanding grades at Damascus University. Shaking the wad of paper he says: 'I just want to complete my studies. I want to complete my life. Is that too much to ask?' A month later Emad learns the young man finally made it to England after paying smugglers to get him across at Calais.

Emad goes back to his hotel room with his head full of the stories he's heard. His mother has finally got a ticket to Milan and will be arriving on a train from Crotone at seven the next morning. He wonders what changes she will see in him – and he in her. They last saw each other six years earlier in 2008, when Emad was in Damascus for his own engagement party. Then he had been happy and optimistic, about to start a new life and train in business in London. Now he is unemployed, sick and single, eking out a life in a capital city designed for the wealthy. She is 58, has diabetes, a bad leg and a heart condition and has been running from her home for three years. But for the moment he is not thinking of that. He gets out his phone and looks at a recent photo she has sent him of her smiling with new friends she made in Turkey. The idea of seeing her after all this time still does not feel real. As an only child whose father was often absent for long stretches, Emad was always very close to his mother. At times their relationship was more like two friends than mother and son, and he likes to call her by her first name, Nawal, unlike most of his school friends, who called their mothers Ummah or Mama.

◆

Emad wakes up late the next morning after a terrible night's sleep, his joints so stiff with stress that he cannot walk down the stairs without a crutch. The back window of his hire car has been smashed by thieves and by the time he has picked the glass off the seats he is even later, haring up the road to the station. Just under the marble pillars of its entrance he spots Nawal waiting. She looks stooped, wearing a black hijab and long black dress and clutching an oversized yellow carrier bag, but her whole face is transformed by a smile when she spots him. He half hops, half tumbles forward on his stiff legs, desperate to reach her – she shuffles towards him, her left leg jammed in a straight line. And then they are hugging. It is a long time before either can let go. Nawal sobs into his shoulder, sometimes smiling, sometimes almost howling. 'Alhamdulillah, Alhamdulillah' she says over and over, thanking God for the reunion she had begun to think might never happen. 'Six years, six years' she whispers in Arabic and then cries again, her tears gathering in puddles on the shoulder of his leather motorbike jacket.

When they finally let go of each other they look around shyly, unsure what to do next. Emad suggests breakfast and drives them back to the place he has been staying, a threadbare hotel that resents its guests even more than its bedbugs. The man on reception looks aghast when Emad asks if he can have an extra person for breakfast, but when he sees frail-looking Nawal hobble in behind him, he acquiesces. As she goes to sit down in the basement restaurant, she pulls a heavy brass pestle and mortar from a small shoulder bag. 'What's this?' asks Emad. She has brought it all the way from Turkey as a present. Emad smiles his thanks and tries not to laugh. He is grateful but amused too at the idea of her carting something so heavy and of so little use to her across the Mediterranean. As the smell of coffee brewing reaches her nostrils, Nawal gets excited. 'I haven't had a proper cup for fifteen days,' she says, her eyes glistening. When the strong espresso arrives, she gulps it down like much-needed medicine and soon drinks another. Seated around a small table, Emad has a chance to look at her closely. 'Look at your face, it's black', he teases. Nawal had always prided herself on her alabaster skin, but after almost two weeks with no cover on a boat, it is scorched by the sun and peeling.

All through breakfast Nawal cannot stop looking at Emad, reaching out to touch the top of his hand and stroking the side of his face. Whenever they laugh or smile, the family resemblance is striking. Emad suggests she uses his room to sleep before they try to travel any further, but she will not hear of it. 'I don't want to sleep,' she says, her eyes alert with caffeine and the thrill of seeing him. 'If I close my eyes and sleep I can't see you!'

They go to a garage to replace the glass in the car window and say goodbye to Mohammed, who will stay on in Milan. With a mended car they begin the long drive across Europe. Seeing Nawal has hardened Emad's resolve to get her to Britain. He had been wondering about taking her to Holland or France where she would be safe and nearby without needing to break the law. Now he is next to her, the idea of leaving her behind is inconceivable. 'What was the point after all that, otherwise?' he says. 'Nearly dying and all that hardship over the sea to come to a strange country and be alone. She risked it to be with me. Now I have no choice; I have to get her in illegally.'

As the drive gets underway in the September sunshine Nawal unwraps her passport from several layers of clear plastic that had been protecting it during her sea voyage. Settling sideways into the back seat, her stiff left leg propped up across it, she finally feels ready to fill Emad in on the journey that brought her here.

Nawal was in Turkey for four months before she managed to get a passage to Europe. She met up with other Syrians and by texting friends of friends of friends she got recommendations of smugglers to go with. If you bring a new customer to a smuggler you get commission, so people were keen to make recommendations. She met a lot of gangsters offering different routes at vastly differing prices. One man said he could fly her to Europe for 12,000 euros, with documents included, but the route was risky and not guaranteed. As she lists the different methods she considered, she scrolls through the contacts in her phone, pointing out all the smugglers' numbers still saved there. She did not mind the meetings – she saw them as a necessity for her escape – but the characters she met were often frightening. They would give her one name on the phone and when she used it at their meeting would say 'Who's that?' She wanted to find the cheapest option and knew many would claim to be smugglers but turn out simply to be cheats and liars.

Eventually she was recommended a man calling himself Abu Kasim – father of Kasim – who said he could get her to Europe by boat for 6,000 euros. The first 3,000 would be paid in advance and the full amount would not be given until she arrived safely. Abu Kasim told Nawal to get on an internal flight from Istanbul to Adana airport in the south and then call him again. When she arrived at the airport, he directed her towards a bus to Mersin, a large port city on Turkey's southern Mediterranean coast. She got off the bus at an agreed stop and called Abu Kasim again. 'Wait for me,' he said. And then, after a while, he said 'Are you wearing black?' When Nawal said yes, he gave instructions. 'You see the cars in front of you, a white one and a dark red one? Walk towards them'. She did as he asked, feeling frightened. She had never dealt with criminals before and the idea terrified her. As she reached the cars she saw a man about her age sitting hidden behind some trees, smoking. He had been testing her; making sure she was not being followed or working with the police. Nawal did not trust him but she knew he was her only hope of getting to Emad.

Once Abu Kasim had dropped Nawal at a hotel in Mersin, she did not see him much again; it was his son, Kasim, who handled the practical arrangements. Kasim looked much meaner than his father. He was about twenty and at the hotel he was always with women. His arms had fresh track marks from heroin use. He told Nawal that he supported Isis and that the money raised from each boat trip went to funding their munitions. She had no idea if it was true but he certainly looked crazy enough to make it believable. The others working with him were Shia and it did not seem likely they would support Isis but Kasim was always boasting of his role in the terror group, even saying he was smuggling weapons for them.

It was Kasim who arranged cars to take everyone to the ship. When Nawal asked his father whether Kasim would be coming on the boat too, he said 'I'm not crazy. I wouldn't send my son on that death trip!' Nawal would not let the ominous response lie. 'So are we going to die then?' she asked him. His reply was not reassuring. 'It's a deadly trip,' he said. 'Nobody knows what will happen; you might die; you might not. Nobody knows and nothing is guaranteed.'

Smuggling more than 200 people out of a country by sea is difficult to do in daylight. Kasim waited until nightfall before he collected Nawal. He went to her hotel room to get a code that would release the first instalment of her payment for the journey. Each person with a place on the boat had deposited their money in an account accessed by a four number pin. The pin for the final payment is given to the smugglers only once they are safely off the boat. But Kasim was greedy. He knew that she would now be desperate not to lose her place so he demanded jewellery and other valuables before he would take her with him. Reluctantly, she handed over what she had, including a gold bracelet that had been a present from Emad.

Kasim dropped her and fifteen others off at a deserted beach. It was 4am when they arrived and they were terrified. Dogs ran around, frightening them, and there were flies and mosquitos everywhere. They waited and waited in the darkness but by eight in the morning they realised nobody was coming. They found a bus that would take them more than two hours back to Mersin and had to pay more than 200 US dollars for the privilege. That evening they saw Kasim and demanded an explanation. He said they had been waiting for a small boat but that it had been seen by the coastguard and taken to the police. When the same happened in a different location the next night, she realised he was lying. She later learnt that using the passengers as bait was a common way to test whether an area was safe and unmonitored.

◆

The night Nawal finally made her escape came four days later. A driver arrived at her hotel and asked for five people: two in the front and three in the back. Like the drivers on the previous nights, his car was Syrian, with number plates registered to Damascus. He drove for around quarter of an hour until he slowed almost to a stop and a man came out of the darkness on the verge, hissing 'quickly, quickly, hurry, hurry'. Next to the car was a high bank and he ushered all five to crawl up it as quickly as they could. Every time a car passed they had to pin themselves flat to the ground. Nawal's knee was stabbing with pain; she was unfit and overweight, her body feeling heavier still as she tried to drag it uphill. After half an hour of walking, crawling and scurrying they were told to wait in a scrubby wilderness of sand and rock.

While their guide left to get another car-load they were forbidden from using cigarettes, phones or anything that might shine a light. Too afraid to protest, they all sat in perfect darkness and silence.

Throughout the night more and more people were delivered until there were around 60 of them. After trudging to a second assembly point, they joined another twenty people, this time including young children and babies. All 80 were then taken onto a small wooden motorboat. The boat was so cramped that people had to sit on top of each other. Every surface was covered with bodies and people perched on the side and sat cross-legged on the floor. The babies and young children were given biscuits – nobody wanted their screams to draw attention to the tiny vessel as it pulled out into the Mediterranean.

As Nawal continues telling her story, the Italian mountains either side of the car get higher and higher, their peaks snow-capped even in the warm late summer sun. Engrossed in hearing his mother's adventures, Emad has hardly noticed the miles go by. Now, with a jolt, he sees signs for France and realises how close to the border he is. On the way to Milan with Mohammed, his car had been stopped at the Swiss border and they were asked a lot of questions. Then it did not matter and they were ushered on, but since his mum has no visa to be in Europe, he is afraid of checks. This time he is avoiding Switzerland altogether but he is worried about encountering the same problem at the French border. Whatever happens, he does not want to cross over in daylight.

'These are nice roads, I never dreamed to come to these countries,' Nawal says, looking at the crisp asphalt stretching out on the horizon and the foothills of the Alps passing the windows. Emad pulls off at a spaghetti junction and eventually they are driving through the small mountain town of Aosta. It is mid-afternoon and the sun is out in a clear blue sky. It feels again as though they are on holiday. This is an off-season alpine resort and they get a room easily at a faded (and very empty) log cabin hotel. The owner looks somewhat surprised by his new arrivals, but tries to disguise it. They are not serving food so Emad walks to the supermarket coming back with his arms laden for a picnic of fresh bread, cheese and fruit. The sight of the food makes Nawal smile. She had so little to eat on her boat journey that she cannot readjust to this plentiful supply, taking handfuls of complimentary chocolates whenever she passes the reception desk and secreting them into her pockets. They take the food onto the flat roof of the hotel, where some rickety tables and chairs have been left out. 'I never dreamed I would come somewhere like this; it's heaven,' says Nawal, kicking her legs back in the chair and smiling at the view of the mountain above. She takes off her headscarf to feel the fresh air on her hair, revealing the white edges of her face where her hijab has protected them from the scorching sun.

The holiday feeling does not last long. She looks worried as they discuss the best way to cross the border, eventually deciding to sleep for a couple of hours and leave during the night. The hotel owners are confused when Emad offers to pay just a few hours after arriving. As night falls, Emad is thoughtful, looking out over the mountain and smoking a cigarette. He is nervous about attempting to cross the Channel the next day – but he is hopeful the British authorities will understand. 'She gave me everything; I have to give her everything I can. When the government lost my documents I never tried to get any money or anything but I lost a really important part of my life – my engagement. Now I'm not asking for much – we can live on the money I get already. I just want them to let her in.'

Waking at 3am, the town is fast asleep when they climb into the car. Nobody says much but Nawal is too nervous to sleep, looking out of the window and wondering where the border will come. Driving through the Mont Blanc tunnel, Emad does not even realise he has crossed the border until he emerges on the other side and French police stand in the road ushering him to stop. His palms sweat and he gets ready to get out their passports. But when he rolls down the window, the policeman says 'Do you know what speed you were doing?'

In his nervousness Emad had driven at 79kmh through the strictly 70kmh tunnel. The fine is 45 euros, cash only. Relieved it is a fine and not the abrupt end of their journey Emad drives into Chamonix in search of a cash point. After paying the gendarme he drives on, the sun beginning to cast an orange tinge at the foot of the purple sky.

His nerves shot after the border – and jangling at the

thought of the next crossing – Emad lights cigarette after cigarette, his hands shaking. Nawal teases him and reminds him of the day he persuaded her to give up what had been her three packet-a-day habit. Emad had been fifteen and he told Nawal, 'If you quit smoking, I'll get married.' Emad laughs: 'You did quit, but now I smoke and I'm not married!'

The two reminisce about life in Damascus. 'The whole world doesn't compare to Syrian soil,' Nawal says, playing a music video of Syria on Emad's phone. She starts crying, looking at the scenes of people smoking sheesha in peaceful squares with elegant fountains. Emad keeps his eyes on the road but reaches back to hold her hand. Nawal has always been very sociable and in Damascus she had a huge network of friends and neighbours who she would cook and eat with. 'The street was like one family,' she recalls. Whenever there is a lull in conversation, the bleeps and chirps of Nawal's phone become more insistent as she connects back to the world she's left behind – to friends in Damascus, Amman and Istanbul who already miss her. They are elated she has arrived safely and not contributed to the gruesome Mediterranean statistics.

As Emad struggles to stay awake at the wheel, he asks Nawal to carry on the story of her journey to Europe. She takes him back to the moment their little motorboat with 60 people on board reached the ship that would take them across the Mediterranean. 'When we reached the big main boat there were people inside who had been waiting for two days already,' she says. 'They had no food. There were cockroaches in the boat and it had a fetid smell. There was only one toilet for everybody and it was dirty and old. They were locking their mineral water in the cabin so there was nothing but a small tank of water that was very dirty. The tank hadn't been cleaned for a long time and the water was yellow with a bad smell. I got stomach problems and diarrhoea. I was passing it like water and everyone was vomiting over the side.'

By the time everyone was on board, there were more than 230 people, plus the captain and crew, Nawal remembers. The crew seized everyone's Turkish money, saying they did not want it to be discovered that anyone was using Turkey as a smuggling route. By the time they had emptied everyone's wallets they had around 4,000 Turkish lira – more than £1,100. The fishermen who ran the boat later said they had not been paid yet by the smugglers. Each passenger was made to promise that they would tell anyone who asked that they had fled Syria via Lebanon and caught the boat from Egypt. What little international policing efforts there had been were focused on Egyptian vessels – and they wanted to keep it that way.

The women were separated from the men, taking the upper deck of the large fishing boat, while the men were sent down below. At the beginning the women were under an awning which protected them from the sun, but then the captain became paranoid and asked them to remove it in case it attracted attention. Even so, they had it better than the men, who were locked downstairs, only allowed to come up for air in small groups of twenty that were rotated every hour. 'There were a lot of young men and it looked like Guantanamo prison in there,' Nawal recalls. 'You could see from their lips they were thirsty; they were dry and caked in white.'

As the days wore on, the lack of food or clean water became unbearable in the heat. On the first day they were given foul smelling fish and Nawal could not eat it. She did not realise that would be the last proper meal she would be offered. When she had asked Kasim if she should bring food, he had promised it would be provided on the journey – and the people she knew who had been smuggled on the same route had said there was plenty. But over the next few days at sea she was given only a piece of mouldy bread – and, on another day, a small portion of soup. Everyone begged the captain for water and food. After an hour of begging the crew would fill up a small bottle of dirty water and give it to ten people to share a sip each. But they almost never gave out food. As more people fell ill, the queues for the single toilet became enormous and fights broke out.

On the boat Nawal heard horrific stories from the country she left almost three years ago. There were children under ten whose mother had died in an explosion. One woman was a solicitor whose right arm had been blackened and melted by a bomb blast. It was leaking pus and was almost down to the bone; it would soon have to be amputated.

On the second morning of their voyage the clattering roar of the boat's engine came to an abrupt stop. It quickly became apparent from the panic on the fishermen's faces that this was not planned. One woman screamed 'That's the end of us!' and fell unconscious at the news. Nawal tried her hardest to hold back the panic. She thought: 'I'm in the middle of the sea and there's no-one around; there are no options. Only God.' At that point she began to pray as hard as she could, muttering lines from the Quran under her breath. Eventually another boat was called to help. By around midnight, the engine was fixed and they began to drive again.

The next day, just when people were beginning to relax again, an aircraft was spotted above them. 'Get down!' the captain shouted and everyone was made to lie still on the deck so they would not be spotted. For a while the boat then changed course, heading towards Egypt, before doubling back on itself. It took another day's sailing before they reached the edge of Italian waters – and it was at this point she had her satellite call to Emad. Many smugglers transfer their human cargo to a smaller boat at the edge of international waters to avoid being detected and receiving a human trafficking prosecution. The idea then is that the passengers steer themselves into Italian waters in a smaller boat and hope to be rescued by passing Navy ships. The risks are high.

As they waited on the edge of Italian waters, a small motorboat pulled up alongside them. The tiny vessel was narrow, about 20 metres long and looked ancient. The cockroaches on this one were even bigger – and much harder to escape. To Nawal it seemed big enough to hold maybe 30 people at a stretch and the five men who had driven it to fetch them looked frightened when they saw the crowds of people. The captain of the fishing boat told all 230 passengers to climb onto it. Everyone had to sit on top of each other. One of the crew of the smaller boat was only fifteen. He looked terrified and, like the others, kissed the hands of the people climbing aboard and begged them not to tell anyone in the Navy that they were any different from them. Another of the crew was weeping and trying to conceal his tears. 'We're refugees like you,' they said. And from their scared, innocent faces, Nawal believed them. It is quite common for smugglers to make refugees who cannot pay the fee work for them for a few journeys before earning their freedom. These young men were probably not refugees exactly – they were Egyptian. But they may well have been on the boat for similar reasons as the others.

There was a small amount of food on board the smaller ship, but a group of tough young men were guarding it.

They were quick to show their knives and even the boat crew looked afraid of them. The small wooden boat had a little cabin with a storage room attached, which is where the food was kept. Nawal thinks it had been intended for everyone but that this gang of thugs had kept it for themselves when they realised how little there was. They asked Nawal and a couple of other women to prepare a meal from the food inside. In two boxes were potatoes, aubergines and tomatoes, along with two dirty black cooking pans and a gas cylinder. They chopped and prepared carefully, their mouths watering after nearly five days without proper food or drink. When she and the others had finished their work the gang of young men devoured what they had made, giving each of the chefs a single spoonful of it and a tiny piece of bread. She felt like a prisoner, scared of what the men might do and still unsure if she would get out alive. The rest of the boat's occupants were given nothing and began to shout 'We're hungry, we're hungry, you can't eat it all!' but as the gang flashed their knives they soon quietened down.

Later that day their journey took a further turn for the worse. Nawal was sitting on the floor at the back of the boat and she noticed that water seemed to be leaking in next to the engine. It had begun as a slight puddle, but by the next morning there was a steady flow and she could see the hole it was coming from. She kept quiet, not wanting to frighten the other passengers, but she began saying Quranic passages again. One of the boatmen had seen the hole too. 'The boat is sinking,' he said to the man next to him, 'let's save them quickly'. He called the original smuggler, Abu Kasim, and asked him in urgent tones to send another boat. They had no idea where they were and he was unwilling to help. When they tried to call the Italian coastguard they realised they had used all their credit on the call to Abu Kasim.

Almost everyone on board seemed to be crying but though Nawal knew the danger, she did not care as much as she had when they had hit trouble earlier in the journey. Exhausted and hungry, with her diabetes making her plummeting blood sugar all the more debilitating, she was beginning to give up hope. 'Maybe this is meant to be the end,' she thought. Then she saw the bird again. As far as she knew they were hundreds of miles from any land but she had seen a little bird fly over them the previous evening and there it still was. It had followed them through the night and Nawal became convinced it was a good omen.

Not long afterwards, an enormous boat passed by, not too far away. They waved frantically at it and one of the women shouted out 'we're sinking,' but it didn't stop. Thinking they had missed their only chance, their resolve began to falter. But within an hour the same ship was back, this time with two others. The enormous ships surrounded the decrepit little boat and signalled for it to stop. The crew could see that none of the vessels belonged to the Italian Navy and began to panic that they would be brought ashore in Greece. They had no way of telling whether they were in Greek or Italian waters but they knew that nobody wanted to end up there. Refugees have a terror of being sent to Greece; it is so inhospitable to them that in 2013 the European court ruled it would be against an Iranian man's human rights to be sent back there from Germany – because of a 'real risk of inhuman or degrading treatment.'

It was around eleven at night and as the enormous ships circled them, one shone a spotlight on the little boat and began to film on a video zoom. They wanted to be sure that there were no pirates on board before they helped. The ships looked like they were commercial or industrial – the people on board did not have naval or coastguard uniforms.

Soon one of the ships, probably an oil tanker, was closer and sent a dinghy to fetch two English speakers from the sinking boat. It seemed like they were gone for an eternity – and in that time Nawal could not stop thinking that they might be taking them to Greece, or worse, refuse to help. Eventually when the dinghy returned it was to tell them they would all be saved. They lowered a crane and began to load on passengers. Nawal was so unwell, and her leg so immovable, that she was among the first to be taken, along with children and another disabled woman who was normally a wheelchair user but had instead been laid out prone on the floor. As the rescue got underway, one of the small boat's crew, the one who had wept when the passengers first came aboard, was crying again – this time with relief. He told them the reason he had been so upset when he first picked them up was because he knew the boat was sinking and he was aghast at the volume of passengers he would be responsible for, especially given that they included children, the disabled and the elderly. He thought he would have all their deaths on his hands.

Once around 85 people were on board the oil tanker they said 'OK, that's enough,' and they began to load up the other vessels. The crew of the tanker brought three deckchairs for Nawal, the other woman with a disability and a pregnant woman. They confiscated everyone's mobile phones, keeping them in the hold for two hours and made a makeshift toilet on deck out of an enormous plastic container with a hole in it.

Before leaving Turkey, Abu Kasim had told Nawal to leave almost everything, not even allowing her to bring her insulin supplies with her or her blood pressure drugs. She was desperate for sugar and was exhausted. Nobody spoke Arabic – the crew seemed to be a mix of American, Japanese and Russian men. But Nawal managed to communicate to the captain and he came back with a pile of chocolate and sweets – as well as a machine to test her blood pressure. The pressure was healthy and he gave her the thumbs up.

After around an hour, the captain and some of the crew came back with food. They had plates of tuna sandwiches and more than 100 boiled eggs with sweet sauce. People were ushered inside one by one to use proper toilets, showers and beds. As she was taken through the hold, Nawal saw a canteen and saw a picture of coffee. She knew the English word and had been desperate for a cup. 'Coffee! Coffee!' she said grinning hopefully. They laughed at her excitement and let her have one, with strict instructions not to tell the others.

The ship was organised and the crew made sure everyone had a chance to rest in a room and have a shower, drawing up a careful rota. They took everybody's clothes to be washed and dried and gave them meals every two hours. They had fried eggs in the morning, Spanish rice with fish, as well as chicken and soup. Nawal was in heaven, her only fear that she might inadvertently ingest some forbidden pork.

As they neared the shore they radioed to the Italian coastguard who sent two boats out from the port. When they climbed out onto the dock at what Nawal would later discover was Crotone, there were groups of journalists and film crews watching them intently. Female officers from the Navy who spoke Arabic and were originally from Morocco and Algeria sidled up to Nawal and some of the other women. 'Who's the captain?' they whispered, 'is he still with you?' Nawal was not actually sure where the crew had gone – they had not been among those rescued with her on the first boat – but she also felt protective of them because they had begged her not to tell. She shook her head. Nawal could see their original little boat on the side of the dock smashed into pieces and turned upside down. This was a relatively new practice by the Italian authorities. In previous cases, smugglers' ships were just left in the port, enabling their owners to sneak off with them later and carry on their work.

After a twenty-minute coach journey, Nawal and the others were taken to a large building like a hangar by lots of men in uniforms that looked like the Army. Then the Red Cross arrived and siphoned off the elderly and the disabled – Nawal among them – taking them to a separate facility. They took down names and illnesses and gave them clothes. Like many others, Nawal had managed not to show her passport or have her fingerprints taken, which would have ended her hope of settling in another European country, since the Schengen Agreement requires refugees to stay in the first EU country with a record of them arriving. After two days of empty promises from the men staying at the camp with her that they would go and get her train ticket to Milan, Nawal organised it herself. With a bag full of medical kit and food from the Red Cross, she boarded the train to Milan.

◆

As Nawal's story tumbles out along the French motorway, Emad looks more and more upset. 'I think I'm crazy. I had no idea the danger I was putting you in. If the Home Office had just given you permission to come to the UK none of this would have happened.' Telling what happened has been cathartic, but now Nawal is desperate to get to Calais and find out if she will be getting into Britain 'Can't we go faster?' she asks Emad, anxiously leaning forward to him in the front seat. But with one fine already and his emotions everywhere, he is keen to keep a steady pace.

When the car reaches a service station, Emad gingerly lays down a thick jumper on a bench before his mum sits on it. 'You've been sitting on hard boats for a long time,' he says, his face still taut with emotion from hearing her story. Back in the car again, Nawal's mood lifts, as if telling the story has exorcised some of the memories. She plays with Emad's phone, looking up music from singers they used to listen to and playing it loudly through the car stereo. One singer is interrupted mid-flow and ignominiously skipped because she is Alawite and has spoken in support of the regime. Nawal is enjoying being DJ, grinning as she seeks out new songs to remind Emad of home. She asks him if he has anything by a singer she remembers from Homs but he shakes his head firmly. Emad deleted all his songs when he learnt that he was supporting Assad. Every so often she grabs Emad's shoulder and leans forward to rest her head on it 'When I was away I felt depressed and helpless but now life has a real taste because my son is next to me,' she says, smiling. 'Everywhere I go I think of nothing else but Emad. The girls who used to live with me even loved Emad without meeting him because I had said so much about him. I have no money, no house, no husband, but having Emad is a gift from God.'

At another service station, this time just outside Calais, they stop for another meal. After being away from food for a while, now it seems Nawal cannot stop eating it. Sitting down in a canteen, she marvels when a sprightly elderly couple with white hair walk past. 'Look they're so healthy but they're really old,' she says, pointing in disbelief. She is not the only one staring at strangers. As Nawal walks back to the car, most people seem to be staring at her, their faces pinched in disgust. A few even mutter disapprovingly at her hijab as they walk past. They cannot see the dimples, the mischievous smile or the kindness in her face – just a black headscarf and a long black robe.

A few minutes into the short drive towards Calais ferry port, the car falls silent. The joy of Nawal's DJ session has vanished and now she looks scared again, tears starting to well up in her eyes. Emad is unsure what to do when he gets to the border. A friend in London with British citizenship who is of a similar age to Nawal and also wears a headscarf has lent him her passport. It was a brave and generous gesture but now Emad is worried that being caught with it risks not only getting his friend in trouble, but jeopardising his and Nawal's chances of a life in Britain. He had only brought it with him as a back-up plan but he is beginning to panic that if they are turned down at the border and the car is searched, he could be found out. After a quick discussion he presses the button on his electric window. It seems to go down in slow motion as he drives along the inside lane of the motorway. Then, with a flick of the wrist, he throws out the passport, its pages flapping manically like a bird in a hurricane.

In the seconds afterwards, Nawal looks back at her Plan B sitting face down in the road with cars streaming over it. And then the real tears come. This time they are not silent but wracking sobs, her whole body rising and falling as the fear grips her. 'I don't want to be on my own any more,' she howls to Emad, closing her eyes tight. Trying to calm herself before she reaches the ferry port she holds onto his shoulder and mutters lines of the Quran, hiccoughing occasionally as the tears subside.

Not wanting to get off on a bad foot with the British authorities, they resolve to ask for asylum directly at the border. They had heard that when 60 Syrians had staged a hunger strike in Calais the previous October, blocking a footbridge and threatening to jump off it if they were not given a passage to Britain, the Home Office had acquiesced and reached a compromise where Syrians who could prove they had family in the UK were allowed to come. Hoping that this was now standard policy they decided they would just tell border officials that Nawal was Emad's mum and he was bringing her to join him as a refugee in Britain.

As the traffic begins to slow and divide into lanes according to ferry bookings, a group of tall North African boys walk down the centre of the motorway. It is September, just days after refugees from Eritrea, Syria and Sudan have tried to storm a ferry bound for Dover. The soaring numbers of migrants arriving via Italy are having a knock-on effect here, where more than 1,000 people are camping out in the hope of coming to Britain. Many spend their days as close to the ferry terminal as they dare, hoping to catch a lift with a passing lorry, preferably without the driver noticing.

It is a sunny Sunday afternoon and the queue for passport control is rammed with late summer holidaymakers in estate cars stuffed to the roof with bags and booze. A Range Rover in the next queue along is packed with a jovial British family who pass around each other's passports to kill time, giggling at the bad photos. Emad is gripping his and Nawal's in his hand, his heart thudding. The boat ahead is tantalisingly close – so near that Emad and Nawal can see its flags gently rippling in the breeze.

Soon it is Emad's turn in the queue. He pulls forward slowly and a bored looking man takes the passport and flicks through the pages. When he gets to Nawal's, the flicking becomes more frantic. He thumbs all the way through one way and then back the other. 'Where's the visa?' he says, exasperation already in his voice. When Emad admits they don't have one and that she is here to claim asylum in Britain, the man's expression darkens. He grabs his radio and barks into it: 'We've got a facilitator here.'

Turning back to Emad he growls: 'Why doesn't she have one?' raising his voice so colleagues can hear. 'WHY? Why haven't you claimed asylum in France as the first safe country?' he says. Emad stutters, and tries to appeal to his sympathy. 'She's disabled, like me, and I'm all she's got. Can't you help?' The man's expression only gets angrier. 'Oh, *you're* disabled are you?' he says, his voice spiked with sarcasm.

He tells them to pull over and a new border official, this time an Asian man called Sabir, listens to their case. Nawal stands on the pavement weeping wretchedly, unable to hide her despair. She cannot understand the words being spoken but she knows the news is not good. Sabir is clearly affected by the scene and listens patiently as Emad explains why he has brought her. Soon the chief on duty, a Geordie guy called Mark, is called over. He too seems sympathetic but repeats the mantra that he can 'only work within the rules.' He won't comment on whether officials used discretion the year before to allow Syrians with families in the UK to cross at Calais. When asked how long it would take for a decision he sighs and says 'Look, it's busy. We've got a bus full of Indians and it's a busy Sunday afternoon.'

As she waits for her interview, Nawal kneels down and kisses one of the officer's hands, still crying and begs him to let her through. He looks bashful and unsure what to do. The afternoon turns to evening and the interviews continue. Mark warns that the wait is likely to be fruitless. Emad tries to stay strong as his mum clings to him and sobs, but his face falters. 'I never expected it to work,' he says, though his crestfallen expression suggests otherwise. In a small waiting room the immigration officers look perplexed. They are used to people trying to sneak through, but this is something different. Holding their heads in their hands, Emad can hear them saying 'We've never come across this before. We don't know what to do.'

It is late at night before officers tell Emad and Nawal they cannot claim asylum. Their argument is that they have applied on French soil, even though they know it had technically been left when they reached the British border post. An officer escorts the two of them back to the French police, who he says will stamp Nawal's passport and make a record that she has arrived in Europe. But when they get inside the compact French police station, the gendarme simply takes her passport out of an envelope, hands it back to her and tells her to go. Just as Italy had turned a blind eye to her arrival, knowing she would go elsewhere and be one less person to look after, so France was ushering her on without making a record.

That night Emad finds them a room in a guest house in Calais. Nawal keeps asking him what will happen next, the clear subtext being a fear that Emad will have to go back to Britain and leave her. But seeing her so vulnerable has only strengthened his resolve to bring her with him. 'It will have to be illegal now,' he tells her. 'They've given me no choice.'

✦

When Emad and Nawal wake in Calais the morning after their ordeal at the ferry's immigration control, they feel hollow. With their Plan B currently flattened under traffic on the northbound A26 and funds running low, they struggle to stay positive. Nawal is tearful and Emad smokes cigarette after cigarette trying to think of a new plan. After a few hours he resolves to go in search of smugglers who might be able to get his mum across the Channel. He scrolls through his phone and calls everyone he knows in London. 'Do you know someone who came through Calais? How did they do it?' he asks over and over. After meeting all the smugglers that were recommended he keeps looking, desperate to find a route more comfortable than the back of a lorry because of Nawal's leg and faltering health. Within four days he finds someone who promises he has a solution. At ten in the evening the smuggler arrives to collect Nawal from her hotel. She hugs Emad goodbye and he sits in their room, waiting to hear she has got to Britain safely. At 4am his phone rings. It is Nawal, but she is not calling from Britain; she is standing outside the hotel.

The men had driven Nawal to a freight port in Dunkirk, half an hour up the coast from Calais. Then they told her – despite their promises to Emad to the contrary – that she would be travelling in the back of a lorry. She was nervous but too desperate to argue. Opening up the back of the truck, they gestured to her to climb up over an enormous pile of wooden pallets that was several metres high. It was freezing inside and her leg seemed stiffer than ever as she made her way slowly to the top, the smugglers pushing her from behind. There were six other young Kuwaiti men in there with her, all hiding among the pellets. They waited inside for around two hours, trying not to make a sound. Then they heard the door open behind them; a policeman had stepped in and was searching inside. He climbed up the pallets and within seconds his face was just a few feet from Nawal's. He began to laugh – not unkindly – and said 'Hello!' in English, giving a silly wave. They had been busted but the policeman did not look upset with them. He counted each illicit passenger off the lorry as they climbed down one by one. Nawal was last – she was stuck high up on the pallets and her locked leg meant it took her half an hour to gingerly ease herself down to the ground. The policeman smiled again when she eventually reached the bottom. He asked why she had picked Dunkirk, saying 'It's too high security here; we have to check all the trucks. Calais is much closer and they don't check all of them. Next time try Calais. Tonight sleep; tomorrow Calais.' This was not the first time a French gendarme had helped Nawal and she was grateful – though she knew it was in their interest to have fewer asylum seekers stay in France.

By the time Emad lets her back into the hotel, Nawal is cold and shivering. He helps her up to their room and begins to argue with the smuggler 'You said it was guaranteed and that you weren't taking her by truck,' he shouts. Knowing he will not get paid properly until he has safely brought her to England, the smuggler says he has another plan. 'It's not a truck and it's totally guaranteed; different situation,' he boasts 'I'll call you back when it's confirmed.'

After a fitful few hours of sleep Emad wakes the next day in a serious depression. His appetite gone, he chain smokes, worrying about Nawal having to face another dangerous journey – and the mounting debts back in Britain. He does not believe the smuggler has a solution and Nawal is devastated seeing her son so upset. Though she knew he had issues with depression while they were apart, this is the first time she has witnessed it herself. 'Forget it,' she tells him, 'let's stop trying to get me to Britain. I want you to stop spending money; I don't want you to get into trouble. Just take me to Holland.'

Emad's lawyer had advised them that Holland would be a good place to go. It has a good health system and a better attitude to refugees than France and Italy. It would also be relatively affordable for Emad to visit her via ferry while he applied for her to be transferred to Britain. So he capitulates, with the caveat that if the smuggler gives the OK that morning they will try one last time. But when he calls the smuggler, all he says is a vague 'tomorrow, tomorrow.' They get back in the hire car and drive to Holland.

After such a grim four days they both feel relieved as they cross through Belgium and into Holland. At least they have a plan – and it helps that the sun is shining. Arriving in Osberg they have a sense of being on holiday again. There are flowers everywhere, the streets are clean and friendly people ride on old-fashioned bikes with baskets on the front; it was just how Nawal had dreamed Europe might be. Walking around Calais everyone had looked at Nawal and frowned at her hijab, but here everyone says 'good morning' and 'good evening' and smiles.

After a leisurely lunch they pull up outside a police station, ready to claim asylum. Emad walks around to Nawal's side of the car and opens the door to help her out. Then his phone rings. It is the smuggler. 'I've found something,' he says urgently, 'It can work and it should be ready in the next couple of days.' Emad has already made his mind up but he tells Nawal what the man has said and she begins to cry. 'Let's try,' she begs, 'You're going to leave me in Holland alone when I don't know Dutch and I know nobody and have no idea who to call for help?' Emad cannot argue with her. Over the last few days she has clung to him and he could tell – though until this moment she tried to hide it – that she was terrified of losing him again after her ordeal at sea.

'Don't worry, I won't leave you,' he says after a while, and they turn around the car, heading back towards the Belgian border. The next afternoon they are back in Calais. This time the smugglers are two British guys and they meet in daylight on a road alarmingly near the port. In their thirties and fat, with shaved heads and tattoos, these men look to Nawal like real criminals. Gesturing to two dilapidated estate cars, they usher Nawal and two Kuwaiti men without passports to the first one. Another three passengers prepare to get into the second. The cars have been specially modified so that the back seats lie flat but are hollowed out underneath. From a false bottom in the boot, Nawal is asked to climb inside and underneath the back seats. 'But I won't fit,' she says looking aghast at the tiny space that she and the other two men are supposed to squeeze into. The smugglers size her up, 'I thought you said she wasn't that big?' they ask Emad. Nawal is not enormous, but she is not petite either, and the men are clearly having second thoughts about the feat of human tessellation required to fit her and two others into the small cavity. But they press on, folding her in half and wedging her in, before pushing the other two men on top of her. One of the men has feet that smell worse than a ripe camembert. He has been living in a ramshackle tent in a migrant squatters' camp outside the town and has not washed in a very long time. For ten minutes in the stifling, airless space inside the car, the three of them wait. Police stop the car and give the boot a cursory search. Nawal can feel their hands pushing down on the false bottom of the boot, right next to her face. After what seems like hours – but is really only a handful of minutes – Nawal hears the rumble of the car on the ferry ramp. She has made it inside.

As people walk out of the car deck on the ferry, the men open the boot furtively and order their passengers to get out as fast as they can. Limbs stiff, they climb out and walk about the ferry's passenger decks in a daze. They need to find the foot-passenger exit but since none of them speak or read English and do not want to draw attention to themselves, they do not try to ask anyone for directions. When the ferry reaches Dover they begin to panic. How will they get out? After some deliberation they decide the safest route is to leave the way they came in. By the time they walk down the steep steps to the car deck, the lanes of cars are already beginning to move. All six of them – including the men from the second car – weave their way out, looking bedraggled in crumpled foreign clothes after their cramped journey. As they walk among the cars it is hard to imagine how they could stand out more from the other holiday makers.

When they reach the metal exit ramp they are spotted. A man in a high-vis jacket guiding the cars out holds up his hand in a halt signal and calls the police. The Kuwaiti men panic – with no asylum case, the arrival of police will mean Game Over for their escape strategy. Nawal is frightened too; without Emad there she worries they will try to send her back to France. The police arrive and the five men are bundled into the back of their van. When a policeman touches Nawal she cries out. He panics, thinking it is because she is Muslim and does not want to be touched by a man, but that isn't the problem: Nawal is just frightened at being caught. A policewoman is sent to deal with her and Nawal pleads with her, saying 'S riy , S riy ,' – the Arabic pronunciation of her home country. The officer understands and takes Nawal to sit with her and the other officer in the front seat of the van. They drive the two minutes to Dover Immigration Removal Centre, a holding place for migrants caught entering Britain without visas.

At the centre Nawal is asked so many questions, including many that would later make her laugh. 'Do you know anyone in Isis? Are you a member of Isis? Do you have any connection with the opposition? With the regime?' The questions seem to go on for hours and Nawal tells them she is desperate for a glass of water. It is another half an hour before it comes. When they ask why she is going to London, her answer is simple: 'Because of my son. I don't care where I live, but I want to be with him.'

One of the officers working there leaves a lasting impression. She notices Nawal's shoes are hurting her feet after trying to run on the car deck and she lies down on the floor in front of her to help take them off. At the end of the interview she kneels down again and puts them back on. Nawal would later say her behaviour was what made her certain that the people of Britain would be good. 'She was a beautiful woman. She did not speak Arabic but she knew my shoes were hurting and wanted to help.

When he had seen the car carrying Nawal safely enter the ferry, the smuggler organising the journey had called Emad. 'She's in,' he told him 'get on the next ferry'. Emad had made it onto the crossing and is now waiting in the car behind the immigration centre. He calls his solicitor to ask advice on what to do next. The solicitor is livid when he discovers what has happened 'My God, what are you doing!' he squawks down the phone, 'I said to go to Holland!' After calming down he asks Emad if she was fingerprinted anywhere. When he says no, the lawyer sounds relieved. 'They're unlikely to send her back to Calais because France won't accept her without a fingerprint record,' he advises.

The solicitor calls the centre for Emad and explains to them that Emad is Nawal's son and that he can pick her up. The officers tell him that the interviews will take several hours and that they cannot guarantee at the end of it she will be free to go. 'She may have to go back to France,' they say ominously.

At one in the morning Emad gets the call he has been waiting for. Nawal is free to go. Since he has been waiting so close by, he drives quickly round to the front and is inside the reception within seconds. When he sees Nawal hobbling towards him it is as if an enormous boulder has been kicked off his shoulders. She can go with him to London, having formally claimed asylum. In a few weeks there will be Home Office interviews and applications to worry about – but for now, nothing can impinge on his elation. Finally, they are together in Britain.

◆

Nawal has only been living in Emad's flat for a couple of days but it already looks unrecognisable. Everything is meticulously tidy and clean; his cupboard, which had previously been a mountain of clothes and paperwork, is now neatly arranged. 'She made me get up at 9.30 to tidy,' he groans like a teenager.

But the gripe is only in jest – having her there has given him new life. The worry has disappeared from his face and with freshly cut and dyed hair, he looks two decades younger.

Nawal stops regularly to pray, carefully washing her face, arms, hands and feet beforehand and putting on her best hijab. She is praying more than ever, feeling that God answered her prayers in the Mediterranean and again in Calais. She never used to be very religious; as a teenager she had worn short skirts and never prayed or fasted. When she was courting Emad's father she liked nothing more than riding on the back of his motorbike, clinging onto him. The mischievousness of that era has not gone from her face – or her personality – but to a stranger she could easily appear austere in her tightly tied hijab and dark, flowing clothes.

When Emad was fourteen he discovered God. He bought himself a prayer mat and wanted to be a good Muslim. He was embarrassed that his mum was not like the other parents; she smoked and did not cover her hair when he had friends over. She did not even avert her eyes from men. He asked her to pray like him and she did, encouraged by his example. Now she is a devout Muslim and upset to see Emad so uninterested in religion. 'I don't pray any more and she's not happy about it,' Emad says. Every time the call to prayer goes off on her mobile, she turns to him and says 'Shall we?' and he smiles and says 'maybe later'. She is lobbying hard but she can see the funny side. 'Now he's the smoker and I'm the sheikh!' she laughs.

Emad's flat had been full of Egyptian ornaments – gold plaster models of sphinxes and Pharaohs – but these have all been given away now. Also missing is the makeshift drinks shelf on his windowsill, previously home to assorted bottles of spirits for visiting friends. 'She tipped them down the sink because they're haram,' Emad sighs in mock indignation. In place of the ornaments is a simple china model of the Quran.

The first thing Nawal wanted when she reached London was a British phone contract. She is constantly glued to her smartphone, calling and texting everyone she knows to say 'I'm in London with my son!' Her phone bleeps and pings constantly with alerts from Viber, Skype and WhatsApp. 'My teenager mum,' Emad teases, as she stares down at its screen.

The only person she did not send her love to was Abu Kasim, the smuggler. Once safely in London she texted him angrily about the false promises he made – detailing the hell of the journey without food and water in a broken boat. He replied with a volley of swear words, saying he hoped she died. His last message was a threat: 'We took 200 people, we can take one back.'

Not everyone on Nawal's passage through the Mediterranean has been able to reach their chosen destination in Europe. Several of those who were rescued by the other two ships were forced to give their fingerprints in Italy. When they got to Sweden and tried to claim asylum, they were sent back to Italy straight away.

With the problem of being reunited with Emad now solved, Nawal turns her attention to finding him a wife. Walking along the streets it is Nawal and not Emad eyeing up the girls, nudging him in the ribs when she sees one she likes. On a trip to Primark within days of arriving, Emad was helping her find clothes, conscious that she would freeze in Britain in the thin black dress that was all she had with her. While Nawal was browsing the racks she noticed a beautiful woman speaking into her phone in Arabic. To Emad's mortification, she walked up to her and asked if she was single. The young woman was Moroccan and in Britain to study. 'I don't want a family life yet, sorry,' she said tactfully as Nawal tried to marry her off to her son.

At the doctors', the GP happily takes Nawal on, 'forgetting' to ask about her immigration papers. Emad is grateful. Until she gets refugee status she is not technically entitled to access non-emergency healthcare, but she has acute stomach pain and all her diabetes and heart medication has run out. The doctor is alarmed when he sees the cocktail of pills she has been taking, including an antibiotic she has been on permanently for more than a decade. In Syria she could call up the doctor, describe her symptoms and they would just tell her to go out and buy more drugs, typically without doing any tests. The GP puts her in for tests and, after discovering her dangerously high blood sugar levels, says that for now he will not give her medicine for anything except for her diabetes.

With Nawal's leg still permanently stuck in a straight line, Emad is more keen than ever to get them a car. His own disability, which often makes his joints too stiff to move, means he is eligible for a car under the government's Motability Scheme. Once his voucher arrives in the post he takes Nawal to choose a car. When the men at the garage hand over the keys to an almost new Volkswagen Golf, Nawal's eyes begin to water. She cannot believe the help they are being given: 'We're foreigners here and yet they treat us like we're British. They are giving you a car because you're disabled and they've given you a flat just because we're all human.'

♦

While Nawal is trying to play matchmaker among the aisles of Primark, Emad has already fallen in love. A few months before bringing his mother to Britain he had met Reem, a beautiful 23-year-old woman from Syria whose cousin is an old friend of their family. After some deliberation he decides to introduce her to his mother, realising that when he is living in a one-bedroom flat with his mum it will be easier if they meet. Nawal and Reem get on famously and for a few delicious weeks they all go sightseeing together, enjoying the last few days of the Indian summer as tourists in the city. Videos on Emad's phone show the three of them larking about on pedalos in Hyde Park, smiling outside Big Ben and play boxing in their flat. Reem looks even younger in the photos, her skin looking perfect beneath a white hijab. Emad has opened up his heart for the first time since his engagement was cursed by the Home Office. Yes, Reem is younger, but she is funny and smart and he has never felt his age anyway.

The three are inseparable and although Emad wants time on his own with Reem, having his mum there too makes Reem feel happier, since she worries it is improper for them to be alone together. After Nawal has been in Britain a month, Reem decides to tell her family back in Syria. They are furious when they hear the news. Rumours get back to them that Emad is not a good Muslim, that he hangs out with other women. They also learn that he is disabled and does not have a job. They want their daughter to marry a doctor, or at least someone her age.

Perhaps it is the new romance – or maybe the pressure of his mum asking every day – but Emad has started praying again and he has given up smoking. Now when the call to prayer sounds on Nawal's phone, they both stop what they are doing and begin to bend and kneel in prayer.

The tension in the tiny flat is building and Emad's depression is back. The debt he has built up, both from friends and

credit card companies, is frightening him and he worries constantly about his mother's pending asylum claim. He is still
looking for a job – the few applications he motivates himself
to make go ignored – and an agency that said it would help
him get a course to be a translator has still not found one. It
has now been more than a month since his mum arrived yet
he has been out of the house to see friends without her only
twice and the small room is starting to feel stifling. Nawal
can see how stressed he is and periodically disappears into the
toilet to cry alone.

Sometimes she wishes she had stayed in Turkey. People
were so friendly there. The young students she lived with gave
her a ring as a parting gift; they had become like daughters to
her. After Jordan, she was touched by how respectful people
were as she walked around. One day when she had wanted to
go and see the famous Blue Mosque in Istanbul, she asked
directions from a man on the tram who got off with her at the
right stop and did not leave until he found someone heading
there who could take her.

When Nawal goes for her formal Home Office interview
at Lunar House, the department's immigration headquarters
in Croydon, she hopes it will ease the tension. But she is so
nervous that she gets dates muddled and when she tells Emad
about it afterwards he becomes convinced that the Home
Office will see this as an inconsistency in her story and try to
send her back to Turkey. The translator was Iraqi and did his
best to put Nawal at ease. He said, 'Syrians are often afraid
in these interviews but you shouldn't be, it will be OK'. His
words did little to help her, the adrenaline of fear was coursing
through her, making her hands quiver and her heart thump.
Even simple 'yes' or 'no' questions she stumbled over. The

case officer said, 'If you lie to us and make a false statement we might send you back to your country'. The kind interpreter decided not to translate the threat but Nawal pressed him, asking what had been said. 'I don't want to tell you,' he said, 'it's better to ignore it'. But eventually he told her and the words would haunt her for weeks afterwards when she realised she had muddled the dates that her husband had been imprisoned.

His mother's ordeal in the interview – and his fears that after everything she may not be able to stay – eat away at Emad. 'The Home Office try to be tough but they are tough on the people here,' he says angrily. 'They're not tough – not even 1 per cent – on the smugglers.'

It is now more than two weeks since that interview and Nawal is being kept awake by nightmares. To add to her worries, her stomach has been painfully bloated and now doctors have found a lump they fear may be cancerous. Every evening she goes to sleep, only to be jolted awake in the middle of the night by terrifying dreams about Syria, Turkey and Jordan. In the latest one she sees herself in Damascus at a friend's house. When the laundry is hung out to dry she sees all of it is black and everyone is wearing black. In another, she is stuck in Amman with no money calling Emad for help and he doesn't reply.

The atmosphere in the flat is already tense, but the news that Reem's family have rejected Emad pushes him into an even blacker mood. Reem comes to talk to him about it and they try to resolve the situation. With nowhere private to go away from Nawal, in the end they just close the door to the narrow kitchen and sit on the floor. They talk all night trying to find a solution that does not end in them never seeing each other again. Emad hopes it will be possible to continue their friendship without her parents' approval but she does not want to disobey them. She gets up to leave, exhausted by the conversation and keen for a resolution. While she is in the bathroom putting on her hijab and readying herself for the journey home Emad grabs a bottle of his super-strength painkillers and gulps down around twenty in one go. When Reem walks back in to say goodbye she finds him there with the empty bottle.

Immediately calling an ambulance that arrives in minutes, Reem and Nawal get in with Emad and go to the hospital. All the way, Nawal is crying and shouting out with grief. Emad is the most precious thing in her life – if he is taken away, what has been the point of all the suffering of her journey to Britain?

'A lot of things came together,' Emad says later of what Nawal calls their Black Day. 'The problems all get bigger and bigger and swallow you.' In the hospital, the doctors keep him overnight, monitoring his heart and breathing. His blood pressure has rocketed but with treatment he recovers quickly.

Now Nawal stares at him as he sits on the sofa, his cheeks hollowed and black circles under his eyes. He is exhausted and wants space but she is too scared to give it to him.

◆

After the horror of their Black Day, Nawal helped Emad back to health. She gave him space, going out to the Egyptian kebab shop on the estate to chat with its owners so he could have time alone in the flat or see his own friends. She could sit for hours hearing their stories and watching people go in and out for their food.

Emad and Reem have stayed friends, though he hears less from her now. Her mother still does not approve of the relationship but Emad hopes one day she may come round. Using his old Syrian League contacts he is helping Reem's father try to negotiate her brother's release from a prison in Syria. A part of him wonders whether, if he achieves this, he might win the family round to the idea of him as a marriage prospect.

In a bid to curb the isolation and claustrophobia that led to Emad's overdose, he and Nawal also make more effort to go out and see friends. They see a lot of Anmar and Nemat, young parents who came from Syria a year before Nawal. The couple and their two beautiful little girls live not far from them in the top floor apartment of a white stucco mansion in an exclusive square in Earl's Court. It is the sort of council flat that would prompt squeals of horror from right-wing pundits but the family would have been grateful for any home.

Over dinner the two families share stories of their old lives – and their journeys to the new. Anmar had to try more than twenty times to get across the Channel. In the end he succeeded by clinging to the axles of an enormous truck as it trundled into the ferry at Calais. He had to get him and his family out of Syria in spring 2013. They were living in Qamishli in north-eastern Syria and Anmar was under constant threat of forcible conscription into the army or Kurdish militias. He got the family a three-month Emirati visa and a flight there with the money he got from selling the stock in his construction supplies shop. He wanted to keep them somewhere safe while he made the more risky illegal journey to Europe. He paid a Syrian smuggler with links at an airport in Greece to get a flight into Crete and then on to France. The Crete smuggling route had become notorious among Syrians and at least one of the people behind it has since been arrested.

The family of Anmar's wife Nemat is still in Deir ez-Zor, a city in the east of Syria that is under attack. As well as human casualties, she recently learnt of the loss of a landmark from her childhood, a beautiful suspension bridge over the Euphrates that was almost a century old. It was only for pedestrians and they used to go there for picnics, looking out at the glittering water below. Somehow its destruction came to illustrate to Nemat the way her home had been disfigured by war. After dinner she shows pictures of it on her phone, first looking magnificent, then mangled and splayed, its belly forced into the water by bombs.

Though the conversation is often sombre in topic, the mood is upbeat. Having spent several months in English lessons, Anmar is keen for a job and is starting to apply everywhere he can – Tesco, Costa, Starbucks – he is not picky. The whole family has refugee status now and he is hopeful they will stay in Britain for the rest of their lives. While the adults talk, their young daughters play hide-and-seek around the sofa, Nawal cooing at them as they pop out from behind it.

Nawal's spirits are lifted. She can see Emad is happier and she has now seen specialist consultants about the abnormal cells in her stomach. After further tests and scans, she now knows they are benign. They may need to be removed later, but for now at least, there is no cancer in her body.

On 12 November 2014, just 58 days after she first arrived in the country, Nawal hears a knock at the door. It is about eleven in the morning and Emad is out. She looks through the spy hole, sees a delivery man and opens the door. He gestures for her to sign for an envelope and she takes it inside. Although she cannot read English she recognises the name on the outside as hers and that it is an official letter. Emad is out with friends and not there to translate, so she opens it carefully and starts taking pictures of its contents on her phone. One by one she texts him photos of the pieces of paper inside, one of which has a photograph of her on it.

His reply is quick and thrilling. She is so nervous that she calls Emad more than fifteen times in half an hour to check he has got it right, but there is no mistaking it. The letter is from the Home Office and along with it is an ID card confirming she has the right to remain in the UK. When Emad comes home she sits looking at him in their tiny Chelsea flat and feels elated. At last, after more than three years of fleeing across Syria, Jordan, Turkey, the Mediterranean, Italy, France and the Channel, Nawal has a home again.

◆

CHAPTER 7

When Harry met Sai

The exact moment when Harry met Sai is a bit difficult to pin down. Sai likes to tell strangers they first locked eyes at a mutual friend's wedding in Thailand, her home country. Harry tells it differently. 'We met at the airport in Bangkok,' he says. 'She was there to meet me.' Their inconsistency is understandable: neither wants to be part of the Thai-bride-meets-foreigner cliché. But it is a bit unavoidable. Harry tries to explain: 'I had a friend who had a Thai girlfriend. I think she had said to Sai, 'Would you like to meet this guy?' and Sai said 'Why not?' It's a virtuous circle, there's a keenness to meet Western men and friends meet through friends.'

The couple are sitting in the living room of Harry's flat in a tree-peppered suburb on the outskirts of Edinburgh. Sai is 43, elegant and light-boned, with her hair cut in a dark bob, prominent cheekbones and slight wrinkles around beautiful almond-shaped eyes. Harry is 60, bald and squat, with a contagious smile and a more than passing resemblance to a billiard ball.

Sai left her accountancy job in Thailand in 2013 to move to the UK. She had already married Harry in 2012 after four-and-a-half years together. 'I'm a quiet person and I like to listen,' she says in halting English, 'but my husband, he talk, talk, talk.' Harry can certainly talk. An entertaining speaker, he has been heavily involved in politics, and campaigned hard for Scottish independence ahead of the referendum.

With the television paused in the middle of a recorded episode of Question Time, Harry tells the story of their court-ship. Sai listens quietly as he relays their meeting at Bangkok airport. 'Did you think I was gorgeous?' he teases, recalling the moment they first saw each other. Sai screws up her nose and shakes her head. A few moments later, she says: 'I never thought Harry was going to be short!'

Their first meeting in the arrivals hall was awkward. With typical geniality, Harry went over to give Sai a hug and a kiss on the cheek and she recoiled in shock. 'I was too shy, I didn't understand,' she remembers. 'It doesn't look good in Thailand if a strange man kisses you; it makes me look like a bad woman. In my country you just put your hands together, say 'Sabaidee' and bow your head.'

But they got over the initial hurdle and went travelling with the couple who had brought them together. Soon they got on well. They knew little about each other and had limited common language, but they managed to piece together their different life stories and interests. 'I wanted to meet someone from Scotland to learn English,' Sai said of her reasons for agreeing to the meeting. She didn't know much about Harry beforehand, 'just that he had a business'.

Sai grew up in a small village, where she worked hard in the family shop first thing in the morning and late in the even-ing. During the day she was a senior accountant for the local authority. Her rural upbringing is reflected in her nickname. Harry and other friends call her 'Rod', the Thai word for car and a reference to her birth on the back seat of one because it was too far for her mother to drive to the hospital.

When they first met in 2008, Harry was running a holiday company. Now he's largely retired, spending his time at home investing in stocks and shares.

They gently tease each other and are affectionate, with a rapport that belies the many cultural and language barriers. Harry is conscious of what people might think to look at them: 'It's one of those preconceptions. If you say to someone in the UK you've got a Thai girl they instantly think of a Bangkok bar girl, but she was a senior accountant. Younger than me, yes, but not ridiculously so.'

This is Harry's second marriage; his first ended in 1991 after four years. He went to Thailand seventeen years later in the hope of finding a new companion. He was amazed by the way Thai women took an interest in British men. 'It's the way it works in Thailand for some reason I don't really understand. Thai women seem to think that Western men are a great catch. I suppose we come from what must appear to be a much more sophisticated and cosmopolitan lifestyle. When Sai was a senior accountant in charge of ten other accountants she was earning £5,000 a year and could live perfectly well and support her family.

'Thai people are a physically beautiful race. Most people would say that among the peoples of the world they're considered to be very attractive. They also don't seem to have quite as much of an obsession with age. Whereas here it's a very stratified thing and if someone goes out with someone ten years older they're going "Imagine that!" You see a lot of things that are not greatly pleasant. You see guys in their 70s and 80s with girls in their teens and twenties. Common sense would say to me however they talk it up ... I'm not saying they're prostitutes but it's almost a cash transaction and I wouldn't expect a girl in her twenties to be interested in me. I met lovely young girls out there but to me they were children. I'd think, "She's pretty – but she's also a pretty young girl".'

After their week away together, Harry and Sai stayed in touch by email and Harry was impressed at her long missives in English. 'I thought, "Wow, she's good at this" and then I found out later she was translating it from Thai on her computer using auto-translate.' He wanted to be sure that they knew each other well – and that Sai had an idea of what life in Britain was really like – before they got married. For four years they took it in turns to spend time in Thailand and Edinburgh, staying at each place together for months at a time.

Sai first visited Britain in May 2009. It was just a short summer holiday and the weather was mercifully good, but she missed Thai food and family and friends. On the next visit, Harry wanted her to see winter so she knew what she would be letting herself in for. After a few weeks it began to snow and Sai was entranced. 'It was wonderful; I was so excited when I heard the 'pop, pop' of the flakes on the window and looked outside. It was nearly midnight and it was so beautiful, I just stood and watched.' Harry interjects with a guffaw: 'When the car wouldn't move it was less beautiful. We had to dig it out with a shovel.'

Both struggled with each other's living arrangements. Sai was shocked by Harry's flat, which is spacious by UK standards, but seemed minuscule compared to her family home. 'She calls it a box,' Harry says, 'but this box costs what a big house in Thailand costs.' Now that she lives in Britain, *Grand Designs* has become her favourite television show. 'I like dreaming about having a house like on the show. In my country, a house means upstairs and downstairs.'

Harry's longest stay in Thailand was for four months in 2010. For him, the problem was as much being out of the city as being in another country. 'She lives in a tiny wee village and I'm a city boy. Glasgow born and bred and living in Edinburgh. Everyone was lovely and gave me food and smiled but they didn't speak English. And her English was more limited then – and she was working. She'd work from 5am when the family store opened and then go to her office and work till 5pm or so and then back to the store till it shut at 8pm. I was lonely there all day while she was working. I had to say, "Look, we've got to spend time together."'

They married in Sai's village in 2012 and invited all her extended family and friends. In a large photo print of the day, the two look happy and proud. Sai is resplendent in a pink and gold silk dress and Harry, looking a bit like a novelty piper brought in for the day, is in knee-high woolly socks, a Royal Hunting Stewart kilt and a white open-neck shirt with a string fastening. 'They'd never seen a kilt in the village so there was a great deal of comment,' Harry laughs. He had picked up a bit of Thai – enough to order food and to wish people a nice day. On his wedding day he got a friend to translate his speech into Thai and write it out phonetically. He had already learnt how to say hot (*lon*) and cold (*mi lon*), though the former was more useful.

The day after the wedding, Harry fell very ill. 'It was partly the nervousness and running around Bangkok in the heat,' he recalls. They had to travel to the capital to make sure they filled out all the paperwork for the marriage. The British embassy gave them a document that needed to be translated into Thai and then signed and stamped at Thailand's own visa offices at the other side of the city. By the end of the day Harry was running a temperature of 103 degrees, with dehydration and gastroenteritis.

The process for getting Sai a spousal visa was more drawn out than they had expected. The law in Britain has changed so the British partner has to earn at least £18,000 a year or have considerable assets – or their new spouse cannot get permanent leave to remain in the UK. The application process cost £2,000 and Harry had to send bank records to prove he had enough cash and an income from investments after selling his business. 'We were together four-and-a-half years before we got married. She'd been here once on holiday and twice on a tourist visa for six months. She came on time and left on time and there was no question of her claiming anything. I would have thought that was sufficient evidence but their attitude to people coming in is terrible.'

Harry worries that the increased difficulty and cost of bringing over a foreign wife is a sign of the growing sway of right wing politics. 'We've not got any benefits, we don't think we're entitled to them. I've worked hard and had businesses for 30 years. I'm happy to support my wife. I don't like Ukip's attitude – it's sneery and nasty. Whenever you try and treat people as a homogeneous mass you're going to insult a huge proportion of that mass.'

Sai settled easily in Edinburgh and says she has never experienced any xenophobia or racism, something Harry thinks may be partly for cultural reasons. 'I think it comes down to attitudes. She would be identified as not British but she's quite attractive and her looks fit in,' he muses. 'Thai people are Buddhists so they've not got a hijab or any identifiable difference that singles them out – and she's very friendly.'

Sai has happily slipped into a routine with Harry, playing badminton together on Mondays, going to English lessons twice a week and working several hours as a cleaner. They like going away together too, visiting castles and exploring the islands around Scotland. Shopping is Sai's favourite pastime, though Harry is less keen. She often takes the bus to Princes Street in the centre of Edinburgh and likes to walk around the grand-fronted stores. It is Black Friday, the day of heavily discounted sales after America celebrates Thanksgiving – a consumer festival recently promoted in Britain. Sai is dying to go out to the shops with Harry. 'I've seen a pair of boots I like,' she says, looking at him hopefully.

She yearns to have more family around her. 'He likes socialising but I prefer to be home,' she says. 'We're different because he's social but I'm bored because we don't have children.' Harry interjects: 'Would having children make you less bored?'

'Yes,' she replies emphatically, 'I like children. I come from a big family and we have brothers and sisters and everyone is around the house and we chat.' Harry was an only child and both his parents have died. He has an aunt but does not see her often.

More than just assimilating into Britain, Sai has integrated into Scotland, embracing Harry's nationalism. She helped him give out thousands of leaflets for the Scottish National Party's 'Yes' campaign ahead of the referendum, and was excited to go and see its new leader, Nicola Sturgeon, give her first speech at the Hydro arena. 'I liked Nicola, she's strong and she looks like she has power,' Sai says. 'I saw Alex Salmond and clapped but why do they like him so much? I liked seeing Nicola, my country had a woman for a Prime Minister but she resigned because she was not strong enough for politics and people said her brother controlled her. There's a different idea of politics here. They don't fight like in my country, where sometimes people kill and burn things, they just talk.'

Sai wants to become a British citizen, but to do that will be a long process, taking years. Achieving citizenship was once little more than an administrative application that was either rejected or accepted. Now joining Britain requires a certificate in intermediate English, passing a test on British history and culture and making a pledge to the UK in a formal ceremony. Explaining her motivation for becoming British, she says: 'My husband was upset when Scotland didn't get independence. He thought it's not good and he doesn't want the government from England. He'd like to live in another country like France or Spain or Portugal, but I'd need a UK passport for that.'

Sai has enrolled in intermediate English classes and reads a book at home on citizenship test questions. She also wants to learn English in the hope that she can have a more mentally challenging job again. 'In my country I used my brain in my job. Cleaning is too heavy, it's hard. My muscles are very sore sometimes. For a long time, maybe two or three months, it felt difficult because in my country I was working every day. But here I was just staying home and doing English class with no job and I'm an active person.'

Sai has a Masters degree in Thai politics but grappling with Britain's complex political history for the 'Life in the UK Test' is a challenge. Harry sympathises. 'People from the Far East have no cultural reference points for here. If you say something dates from Roman times it means nothing to her, just as if she said this dates from the Sukhothai period I wouldn't know. I'm a keen quizzer: I've won thousands of pounds on television quizzes. But there's stuff on the Life in The UK Test I haven't got a clue about. Questions like, "What year did the civil war start?" Do you know? It's not even Scottish history, which is where she lives. 1642 by the way, that was the year. I had to Google it. It's one thing to say, "Do you buy a stamp in the butcher, baker or Post Office?" But some are impossibly hard. There are questions about English monarchy, the majority of which people don't know. I've taken mock tests and passed nearly all of them but I failed one. And that's being on the fringes of the Scottish national quiz team! She's had to memorise the answers by rote.'

Harry still hopes that if Sai gets citizenship they could start a new life elsewhere on the continent. 'I think it would be nice to go and live somewhere in Europe,' he says, hopefully. Sai isn't convinced. 'Then I'd have to learn another language again,' she says, eyeing her toes.

Sai's plans for the future depend on how long Harry lives. 'I think I'll stay here. The transport is good and if I get better at English maybe I can work as an accountant again. But if my husband dies I might go back to Thailand.' Her Scottish political awakening is still tempered by a longing for home. She says: 'If I can do something and vote I will always vote for Scotland and feel Scottish. But inside me I will feel Thai.'

♦

CHAPTER 8

Hassiba

The small classroom in Edinburgh's Southside Community Centre is hushed as lecturer Haidar Mahmoud explains the vagaries of the English language. The pupils sitting inside this converted church are all adults preparing for life in Britain and they are too focused to do anything but listen. This is where Sai attends classes along with around a dozen others, most of whom hope to become British citizens. Sitting across from Sai is Hassiba, a newly-wed who arrived from Algeria nine months ago. She is 25 and, despite her short stay in the country, already has some of the best English in the class.

Hassiba was not that enamoured with the idea of coming to Britain. She came to join her new husband but still yearns for home. In Algeria she left behind a burgeoning career as a geneticist, a luxurious life with her family in a pretty villa in reliably clement weather. In Edinburgh she works in a kebab shop and lives in a tiny flat beneath heavy slate skies. Learning English is her chance to win back at least part of that old life. She has a Masters degree in genetics and had been working in laboratories in Algeria; to have a hope of doing the same here, she will need a diploma in English.

She is slim and pretty, with large brown eyes that spark between a tightly wrapped headscarf. Speaking after class, she says: 'I know I'm different to some people who come. In

Algeria I had a nice, perfect life. A car, a big house, a job I loved. I was very happy. My husband came here to make his life better, but I only came because of him.' In another's hands, speeches like this about her old life could sound like arrogance, but she delivers it with such yearning and wide-eyed innocence that it is difficult not to empathise with her loss.

Hassiba knew her husband Rachid for two years before she married him. He had already been living in Britain since 1999 when he came to London from Algeria on secondment from one of the big oil companies as a petroleum engineer. The placement was meant to be for six months but at the time Algeria was in the midst of a civil war, with government forces clashing with Islamic extremists and terrorist attacks around the country. He is Algerian and proud of his country but he was desperate for the safety of Britain. When the six months were up and the company asked him to return home, he decided to run away. He found work as a chef in London and a few years later was offered another job cooking for an Italian family at their takeaway shop in Edinburgh.

After more than ten years living underground in Britain, Rachid sorted out his immigration status. Hassiba does not know exactly how it was solved, just that he hired a lawyer and that now he has a legal right of permanent residency in the UK. Given the length of time he was in Britain, it is likely this was solved because of an earned right of residence. Hassiba currently has a two-and-a-half year spousal visa with no recourse to public funds and she hopes for a permanent right of residence in the future. But the idea of British citizenship appals her. 'No, I would never like to be British,' she says, 'My country was colonised by the French and independence came at an expensive price. Until now the country is still under-developed. So being British is out of the question; with all that colonial history, I wouldn't want to do it.'

Hassiba first saw Rachid across the room at a child's birthday party in 2011. Her older sister is a teacher and she had been invited to a birthday party organised for the son of a colleague at the school where she taught. She was shy at the idea of going to the party alone and cajoled Hassiba into coming with her. The teacher hosting the party was Rachid's sister and Rachid was visiting from the UK for his nephew's first birthday.

Hassiba could see instantly that he was a good man. 'I felt something when I saw him,' she recalls with a girlish grin. 'I liked his smile. He played with the kids and joked a lot. And then he came to speak to me. Sometimes when people are immigrants living outside the country in France and places like that you can feel it in the way they act when they come back. But you couldn't with him; he acts like he still lives in a village. He's a lovely man with a white heart. If someone does something bad he forgets it straight away. If someone wants a job, he helps them.'

For three months Hassiba daydreamed about the beautiful smiley man she met at the party. Then one day Rachid contacted her sister and asked for Hassiba's number. She handed it over after checking with a very excited Hassiba. Soon they were chatting with increasing regularity, making plans to speak on Skype whenever possible, and Hassiba could hardly stop smiling. 'I liked him because he was modest and simple and intelligent. I liked everything about him.'

When he was in Algeria on visits they would meet together in secret. Under the country's Islamic tradition, men and women are not meant to meet alone before marriage but they wanted to get to know each other first. 'This generation has completely changed,' Hassiba says of their secret dates. 'But you still can't tell your mum and dad you're going to meet a man, it has to be secret.'

On their first tryst they went to a seafood restaurant on the coast. 'It's a bit like North Berwick', she says, grasping for a Scottish equivalent to their Mediterranean idyll. Soon they were meeting often at restaurants and coffee shops and going for long walks by the sea. Occasionally they were spotted by a neighbour but they could see they were being well behaved and did not report them to Hassiba's parents. 'We told each other about our lives and our families. I was in my third year at university and we talked about that. Then he went back to Scotland and I thought it was going to be just like that, no marriage.'

But once he was back in Edinburgh the relationship only intensified and they would talk for hours on the computer. 'He told me about the weather and his life here. He said: "It's hard to do Ramadan because when you go out for shopping you can see Scottish people sitting and eating and it makes it harder." In Algeria Ramadan is like Christmas here. When the sun sets it's important to have the whole family sitting around the table to share time together and eat together. He said to live here alone is hard, especially on an occasion like that. He didn't lie to me. He told me the reality that he hadn't got married because he didn't have his immigration papers. He told me he didn't want to get married to an Algerian woman and then not be able to bring her over.'

Rachid was also keen to avoid what some friends had done to avoid deportation. 'My husband knows a lot of people who got married just for papers. Arabic people marrying English and Scottish people. He has three friends like that. They came here illegally and then found a Scottish or English girl in a nightclub. The women say, "If we get married I'll sort your papers". Then they get married and they lose a lot of things. Like in one case he had to go to church with her. My husband did not want to get married to a European woman for papers because he can't live in this situation. If you have a child you wouldn't be able to give them a Muslim name. It's a horrible situation.'

When they finally had their wedding party in November 2013 Hassiba did not relax. Under Islamic custom you are not truly considered married until it is consummated and prayers have been said but she did not want to risk losing her virginity before the immigration paperwork came through. So the wedding party was more like an engagement; a holding celebration until they could confirm officially their life together in the UK. Once, a marriage would have been a fait accompli for a visa, but the rules have got tighter and tighter. She had heard of too many people getting married and sleeping with their husbands only to discover they would not be able to join them in Britain. To get the visa she had to prove their relationship, showing photos of the wedding, give evidence that Rachid had a secure job earning more than £18,000 a year and pass an English exam called A2. To take the exam costs £100 and it is not simple. Its cost and difficulty have marooned many spouses in their home countries. 'I met some women who failed the exam four times,' Hassiba explains. 'One was married in Algeria and was pregnant but lost the baby. She's stuck now.'

She used her virginity as an insurance policy. If they had not yet had sex the marriage would be nullified and she could have a future in Algeria with someone else. When it came to choosing where to live, Rachid had stood firm. Having let down his

Algerian employer and been out of engineering for more than fifteen years, he has no plans to return to his former career – even though the war is over in his home country. He has been working at the Edinburgh takeaway shop for so long that the family who own it have expanded the company to several branches. He is a trusted employee and is about to take over the management of the branch he works in. As a chef in Algeria he would earn a pittance and he loves his life in Britain.

After cramming for days before, Hassiba passed the English exam first time and got a British visa shortly afterwards. She arrived in London on 11 February and the next day she lost her virginity. She is so proud of her abstinence, and it formed such a crucial part of the marriage contract, that she came to Britain with a certificate of virginity. Signed by a gynaecologist, the certificate is kept in a file in her living room, next to the Quran and a hardback bound copy of her Masters thesis. It is a badge of honour that she was 'pure' when she married her husband.

Hassiba arrived in Britain in the dark and bitter cold of February. She has never felt more alone. 'Where my flat is you can go three hours and not see any people. It's so cold, really freezing. I imagined it would be cold, but not like this.' She was shocked by how hard everything was – even shopping was a struggle. She wanted to be a good Muslim but found it difficult to work out what foods were Halal and safe for her to eat, paranoid the ingredients would include traces of pork.

The tiny flats people lived in surprised her, particularly when she saw many had dogs in them. 'I couldn't believe people can live inside in small flats with pets. In my country if you have a garden you can have pets; otherwise not.' Her neighbours seemed cold and unwelcoming. 'In my country if you're cooking and you need something you knock on your neighbour's door and they give it to you. People are friendly. But here not so much. I have a new neighbour now; he's an alcoholic.' She had imagined she would see busy people everywhere, running to work. Instead, the estate was full of people listlessly hanging about. She was not sure what they did all day.

◆

Nine months later, Hassiba is sitting in the living room of the flat she shares with her husband. Her home is in a block in prime Old Town real estate, with nothing beyond but the green and grey of Arthur's Seat rising steeply into the mist. Yet somehow architects and town planners have contrived to make an unpleasant ghettoised cul-de-sac of clustered concrete buildings. Intimidating groups walk between them, their muscle-bound dogs a few paces in front, off the lead.

Hassiba has seen drug deals and fights on the estate and rarely ventures out alone. 'There are some people who take drugs in the area. They shoot up by the window, you can see them', she says. 'They go in groups. There are some in my block and some in the other block and they visit each other.' It is only mid-afternoon but she is already in her pyjamas – traditional flannel ones printed with pink roses. Inside without a headscarf on, her hair is thick and beautiful and her chocolate-coloured eyes look even more Disney. She cooks up a hot chocolate on the stove and gestures at the gathering gloom outside. 'This is my first November. In February it was OK; it was cold, but it wasn't like this. For me it's depressing when it gets dark this early, it's too much. If it's dark by 4pm I don't like to go out. Yesterday we went to Princes Street; I liked the Christmas lights and had my photo taken next to them. Then we had dinner in a Turkish restaurant.'

The Algerian television channel, Algerie TV, is on in the background. She finds it a relaxing reminder of home but makes herself watch British channels to improve her language. 'I like *This Morning* but my husband thinks it's boring. I think the BBC and the news are the best for learning the right English. Sometimes I put subtitles on to learn the words.'

She loves her husband and is happy in the marriage but she often has doubts about her relocation. 'People really suffer to go to another country and even when they arrive they suffer. It's hard. Sometimes I tell myself: "why all this?" I just have to prepare my suitcase and come back. My husband says everyone asks this question. But that we can't change it.'

When she was studying genetics in Oran at the University of Science and Technology Mohamed Boudiaf, her parents were very proud. They did everything to encourage her to keep at her books, with her mother doing all the cooking and cleaning and her father making sure she never had to do menial work. Hassiba got a part-time job analysing blood in a laboratory but never did anything unconnected to her studies. Her final project was an investigation into the genetics of obesity, which pinpointed a common gene present in 76 obese women. 'I haven't got this gene,' she laughs, looking down at her tiny frame. 'I eat a lot but I can't be obese'. She helped present it to scientists around the world, comparing findings with experts in the UK and China.

Her parents were excited at her success, having had their own educations stunted. 'My mum didn't complete her studies because she thought the world wouldn't be open to her. I wanted to help my mum around the house but she would say, "No, go and study. Cooking and cleaning won't help you. When you've done something with your life, then you can clean."' Her dad was working for a major petroleum company as a highly skilled welder and the family was well off but since neither he nor her mother had much education they wanted a better life for Hassiba. 'We say in our country that education is a long arm; it's a weapon for life,' she explains.

So it was with a bump that she found herself mopping the floor of a kebab house in Edinburgh. For the first few weeks she could not stop crying. Her husband was worried about her, not wanting her to sacrifice all her hard work. He helped arrange a meeting with a genetics Professor at Edinburgh University who encouraged her to get an extra English qualification so she could apply for a PhD.

In the meantime she needed to work a few days a week at the kebab shop with him, to improve her English and make sure they had enough money to stay afloat. Rachid had to clear all his debts before he applied for her visa – but he still owes money to the lawyer, and to Argos for a new kitchen for his wife. She is embarrassed by her new vocation. 'I've never thought about myself as a cleaner in a shop. In Algeria if I didn't find a job in a laboratory my parents would never allow me to work in a shop. In my country, someone who works in a shop or as a cleaner has no degree or anything. It's someone who has done badly in education. I just tell my family that I'm going out with my husband; it would be a big shock for them if they learnt I was a cleaner. I can't say, "Dad, I'm going to the shop just to learn English." He'd say, "I'll send you money and you can have a teacher at home." I don't want money from my parents now, I'm dependent on my husband. And I like earning some money. Yeah it's only £80 a week but it's good.'

She has been working since the end of March at the same takeaway shop as Rachid. They travel there together – in fact they travel almost everywhere together. 'I don't know the area and the people so my husband is scared a lot about me,' she says. 'I feel sometimes like a child. I need someone with me all the time. The first time I went to the hairdresser's he went with me to explain what I wanted. But now I can understand people. At first I knew it was English they were speaking but I couldn't understand the accent.'

When she started working two days a week at the shop it was largely just cleaning; she was not confident enough with the language to do more. She would work in the back while another girl worked out the front. She is paid just £40 to work from three in the afternoon until eleven at night. 'I think the other girls get more,' she says about the sub-minimum-wage pay. But she has accepted it as a toll on her inexperience. On a typical shift she will fill giant tubs with sauces, replenish the stacks of paper for wrapping battered food, fold cardboard pizza boxes and stock the fridge with juice. Once she has done all that, it is time to clean the dishes. She learnt the hard way that manning the phone was not a good idea. Someone called and asked for haggis and she had no idea what they were saying, so now she waits for someone else to answer and bags up the order. 'In my country we say "Fonta" not Fanta and when someone says "I want a Fanta and a haggis steak pie," I didn't know any of these words. I just knew chips.

'It was very, very hard for me at first because I didn't know anything. You can't ask the girl you're working with all the time what's being asked. You can only ask once because you feel shy. Sometimes I want to stop but my husband encourages me and says it's the best way because you can learn to speak to people.' She found all the food bizarre. 'All this food is strange and bad for me, it's horrible. Spring rolls, sausages and burgers are all frozen and when people ask for it they just fry it. It's unhealthy and it's very bad. In my country it's all fresh. They do mince pie, steak pie, sausages, fish suppers, pizza, pasta and doner kebab. When I saw fried pizza I was shocked. My counter was next to my husband and I said, "Rachid, they fry pizza?!" I was shocked and people ask for it a lot. Using so much batter also shocked me. Everything is battered or fried and a lot of customers are obese. They don't ask for one thing, they ask for a lot.'

Despite the hardship she is grateful to the boss. 'Whenever I see him I say thank you because despite not speaking English very well I have been able to work and learn a lot of things, like how people talk and eat and live.'

She also learnt about racism. 'Last Saturday I had a customer come back in who I had a feeling didn't like me to serve her. Some people see you with a scarf and don't like you. There's a girl working with me who's Scottish and she's lovely. She said, "No, no, it's fine". But every time I said to this customer "Hiya, can I help?" she didn't reply. She asked for a family meal, which is four suppers and a fried pizza, that's *this* big,' she says, extending her arms into an enormous circle to show its gluttonous size. 'I asked: "Do you want salt and sauce on the pizza?" And she just blinked at me and made a face. She had looked at me like I had germs on my hand. My colleague understood and took the box from my hand. Earlier, I had tried to join in a conversation about Christmas, saying, "Yes, there's a lot of shopping at Christmas," but she didn't speak to me. I left to do something in the back and came back to help when her food was ready. When she left the shop my colleague said "You were right, she is racist because while you were in the back she was speaking about Pakistani shops and she said

Paki and covered her mouth three times, saying "I don't like these people, Pakistanis, I don't like foreign people." I think the racism here is among lower class people who don't work. They see that these foreign people have a nice life.'

The prejudice she sees is not just at work, either. 'Once I was shopping and looking for hair colour and I took time because I have to read the packets and I wanted to make sure I get the right one. A security guard came and stood like this behind me,' she says, folding her arms and puffing her chest out, 'like I was going to steal something. In a lot of shops that happens. That's racism. We don't steal.'

Hassiba still daydreams about a better job. She is baffled by the lack of ambition for education among the Italian family who own the takeaway. 'None of them have completed high school but they're all telling me what to do. When you change your country you find you're in another place in society far from how you have been. Sometimes I'm washing up and I remember being in a white coat in a laboratory with my position, looking into a microscope and doing interesting things in life and now look what I'm doing. Now I understand why my parents said life is a thief.'

She is still hopeful that things will change. 'In time I think people will give me a job. I can't complain though because I don't speak English properly. I don't care about money because it comes and goes but I want experience and to learn how laboratories here work. Genetics grew up here in Britain and when you're in your own domain you feel much better because you haven't lost what you learnt.'

More than anything, though, Hassiba hopes to leave. 'If we save we can buy a house in Algeria. This isn't my country. Maybe in ten or fifteen years we can go back home, Inshallah.'

CHAPTER 9

◆

Aderonke

Aderonke Apata felt she had tried everything to persuade the Home Office she was gay. She sent letters from former partners – both in Britain and Nigeria – and piles of statements from friends supporting the idea that being sent back to Nigeria could lead to her death. But after her claim was rejected, she felt there was only one way of persuading a judge irrefutably that she was gay: sending a very personal home video.

It is June 2014 and Aderonke has been fighting to stay in Britain for almost a decade. Sitting with her girlfriend Happiness Agboro in a bar on Manchester's Canal Street, the heart of the city's gay scene, she recalls the decision to share the intimate footage. 'I was asked to bring supporting documents for my judicial review for the court to look at. What evidence do we have to compile apart from letters from people? I knew we had a home video of ourselves and I thought: why not just put it in? We've heard from people who have done such things and they got citizenship. When people just send letters from their partners and people who know them to be homosexuals, we are still not believed. I said: "I cannot afford to go back to my country where I will be tortured, so if I have to prove it with a sexual video then I have to do it."'

Her experience is echoed by many lesbian, gay and bisexual asylum seekers in Britain who have had to go to extreme lengths to persuade sceptical immigration officers of their sexuality. In spring 2014 Home Secretary Theresa May ordered a review of how border officials handled gay asylum claims after documents leaked to *The Observer* revealed inappropriate interrogation techniques were being used to make people 'prove' they were homosexual. In five hours of questioning one bisexual man was asked intimate questions about his arousal during anal sex; he was also subjected to a volley of inappropriate queries, including 'What is it about men's backsides that attracts you?' and 'What is it about the way men walk that turns you on?'

In this context, Aderonke felt she had no choice but to use all the evidence she had about her sex life. She still feels distraught at having shared such an intimate record of her relationship. 'I feel so bad that it's got to this stage,' she says. 'It's such a desperate and precarious situation to be in, very dangerous – because anything could happen to those pictures, those videos. People's details get lost, get destroyed, get misplaced – so some of these things could slip into society and get into someone's hands, and do you know what that could cost? If someone just uploaded a video one day on YouTube, it's horrendous.'

Aderonke started having relationships with women when she was sixteen but at first she had no idea what it was. 'We didn't know it was being gay; we didn't have a name for it,' she recalls. 'Our religion taught us that it was evil for women to be with women.' It took her a while to realise there was someone else like her at school. 'There was a girl in my class who everyone saw as weird. She was not conforming to the boxes of what people expected and they would bully and shout at her. One day she gave me a magazine and it had some funny pictures of women naked. I thought "Ooh, what is that?!" She had brought it into school and I wondered "Why did she give it to me?" Back at Aderonke's house they were alone in the bedroom she shared with her sister – and sometimes met in her backyard – but the fear of being caught was so intense that she ended it.

For years after that Aderonke assumed it had been a blip and one day she would have a boyfriend like other girls. Then, when she was studying Microbiology at the University of Lagos in the Eighties, she met her first proper girlfriend. Kemi was a chemistry student who Aderonke recalls as 'very smart, a brilliant woman' and they had a relationship in secret. After graduating they lived together for several years until they were reported to the police who, according to Aderonke, arrested and beat her, only releasing her from custody once she paid a bribe. After that they left Lagos and married men to cover up their sexuality, but their relationship continued in secret for twenty years. Aderonke's marriage was arranged in 1997 by a friend who knew about her sexuality. The plan was to get divorced but use the union to prove to society that she was capable of marriage. 'Divorce in my culture is still taboo but if I could show I was someone who attempted marriage it might end suspicions about me.'

In Nigeria most people did not talk about being gay but they knew Aderonke was different and would tease her. She recalls: 'They would say I was like a man; that there was just a little difference between me and a man, the fact that I don't have a thing in between my legs.'

When Aderonke first arrived in Britain from Nigeria in

2004 her asylum claim was on religious grounds. She came from a Christian family but had married a Muslim. Aderonke says she later learnt that her new husband's family had turned against her because they suspected she was gay. 'They were suspicious of me and my sexuality but they didn't have proof,' she explains. She says they took her to a sharia court in Ibadan where she was sentenced to death by stoning for fabricated charges of witchcraft and adultery.

In related vigilante incidents Aderonke says her brother and three-year-old son were killed. 'They came to the house with machetes and clubs. We fled the house and ran away.' Aderonke stayed in another town with Kemi, her former university girlfriend – now married – before she was introduced to someone who could get her a passport to leave the country.

It was May 2004 and after flying to Dubai, she decided to try to get to Canada, where she wanted to claim asylum. Her flight went via Heathrow but before she could get on the connecting flight she was caught with the fake passport she had bought in a hurry in Lagos. Over ten hours of interviews she explained what had happened, showing them her real Nigerian passport and telling them why she had needed to leave in a hurry.

They asked over and over: 'Why are you here, what are you doing here?' When Aderonke replied that she never intended to stay, that she was headed for Canada, they said: 'You can't go to Canada, we have to return you to Nigeria'. When Aderonke panicked and said she could not go back, she had to try to explain. She was still frightened about revealing her sexuality to strangers and just told the story of her marriage and the threat to her life. 'I'd had such a terrible experience with authority. I couldn't tell them about my sexuality,' she recalls.

As the interviewer took on more aggressive interrogation techniques Aderonke was terrified. 'She told me that I'd be put in
jail if I didn't tell her where I got my passport. I was scared. I
didn't know what to say. I didn't know if they had an arrangement with the Nigerian government. I was looking at the
guards, particularly the uniform – and she's talking about jail?
It was all too much.'

When the interview was finally over it was clear she
would not be put back on a plane. Instead she was taken to
Oakington immigration detention centre in Cambridgeshire.
After her terrible experiences with police in Nigeria, its
resemblance to a prison was disturbing. 'It's called immigration detention but to me it's prison: the high fences, the
guards, the keys. How is it different from a prison? After
what I'd been through the worst place I could find myself was
somewhere that felt like prison. I was in shock.' When she
first arrived she was completely lost and there seemed to be
little help on offer. 'I was just dumped there. Nobody talked
me through anything; if I needed to know where the toilet or
shower was I had to ask other people being held there. You
were given orders and there was no friendliness, no human
feelings – nothing. Nobody said "What's wrong?" or showed
me where to go for help.' She began to wonder if she had
made a mistake escaping at all 'It was a mix of bitterness and
a small ray of hope. There I might have been killed. Here I
don't think I'll be killed but I don't know what happens; I
might end up stuck in this jail.'

The days have blurred together in Aderonke's memory and
she finds it upsetting even trying to remember that time. She
believes she was there for around a week before someone came
to her room and said: 'You're being released'.

With no idea where she was going – and scant understanding of why she was being let out – she packed up her things and was driven to the nearest train station. She was handed a train ticket and told someone would meet her at the other end. The next thing she knew she was walking out on the platform at Stalybridge station, east of Manchester. Everything looked so strange to her as she waited to see who would pick her up. 'It was like being dropped in the desert somewhere or something, it was a very unfamiliar environment. I just stood there looking at the trains and thinking: "Where do I go? What if I can't find this person who is picking me up?"' She didn't have a phone number or an address for where she was meant to be going. Then a woman walked up to her and introduced herself. 'She must have worked out it was me quite easily,' Aderonke said later, 'I was looking like a lost child and I was probably the only black person in the station.'

The woman seemed kind and she drove Aderonke to her new home, handing her a towel and a small food parcel of basics, including rice and tomato paste. After she left, Aderonke sat alone wondering what would happen next. Her new room was a small box in a two bedroom flat. The bed was narrow and the space between it and the wall was narrower still; she could only stand sideways next to it. She felt completely lost but knew she needed to stay focused on clinging tight to this new country before it ejected her.

The block of flats housed asylum seekers from around the world and Aderonke got advice on finding a lawyer and began to fight her case. Her initial application for asylum and a further appeal were both refused. 'They didn't believe what I was saying; they didn't believe that a Muslim could marry a Christian and they said that even if it did happen I could go and relocate.' It was 2005 and all around her she could see what happened when someone exhausted their options in the battle to stay. At around four or five in the morning, when it was still dark, fifteen or more uniformed police and immigration officers would arrive at the block, bang on the door of the unlucky overstayer and drag them from the building. Aderonke could see out the window the way they manhandled people and bundled them into the back of an enormous van as if they were violent criminals. Aderonke had no desire to go through that, so when she got a letter saying she was to be deported, she slipped out of the flat one day and never came back.

For the next two years Aderonke kept away from that block, moving around Manchester without a home, trying to stay undetected. She slept anywhere she could: bus stops, churches, even sheds. 'People wouldn't know I was there. I would wait until it was late; there are some houses where you have fences and you can just sneak into the back of a shed and put your head back. I had to leave before daybreak and you always had one eye on the lookout. If I slept somewhere and I felt safer there I would go back. When I felt threatened I would move on. When I thought I might be suspected I didn't ever go back. I was never caught.'

'It was a terrible time. Painful and full of agony but I couldn't go back [to Nigeria]. Sometimes I might be lucky and someone would take me into their home because I'd started going to their church.' After all that time with no home and no job, Aderonke was willing to try anything. 'I met someone who said they could get my papers sorted for me. I thought it was genuine; he had been in the country for a long time and I assumed what they were saying was true. When he realised

I didn't have any money he said: "Just give me £50 as a transport fare." I said "thank you", and he gave me a passport. I saved the money by begging and it turned out to be fake but it allowed me to work.'

As her determination to build a life in Britain grew, Aderonke was helped by other friends. People she had only just met let her use their addresses to apply for work and soon she had landed a job in a care home for people with severe learning disabilities. Her only previous experience was looking after elderly relatives in Nigeria, but she was caring and warmed to the work. She thinks she might well have stayed on undetected but then she decided to report worries about some of the residents. 'It was a nice job but I was stupid. After about a year I saw people with unexplained bruises and I wanted to follow the procedure for reporting it. The executives didn't like that. They said if you report to the Care Quality Commission every time you see something, the care home will be marked in a negative way. That's when my problems started. I saw injustice, tried to do something and then got investigated. What made them investigate my status at that moment otherwise? Why didn't they do it at the beginning when I got the job?'

When they investigated further they realised Aderonke had no papers to be in Britain. She was arrested and sent to prison for three months. When she was released, she went underground a second time, finding new work and new false papers.

Around the same time she finally felt able to be open about her sexuality. On her first visit to a gay bar she was astounded by what she saw. 'My mouth was ajar in amazement. I just couldn't believe it; it was a very different experience in my life seeing women who could really show the world who they are. It was positive but it was painful that I couldn't do it because I didn't have the courage. I was going round watching people like watching a film, not believing it's happening.'

It was not until 2008 that she began coming out to a select few friends and making trips to Canal Street in Manchester. She had already made secret visits to Soho with a friend over the last two years and it was becoming harder not to talk about who she was. But at the same time this was going on, Aderonke says she was under pressure from the Nigerian church she was attending to get married and renounce her sexuality. 'The basic truth is that whatever country you come from, when you're here in the UK you end up in communities from your own country that are still the same as they are back home,' she explains. She asked the congregation to pray for her, to see if the 'evil spirit' could be lifted. 'But nothing left me,' she recalls, 'I had stronger feelings for women than I ever did.' Nevertheless, in 2011 she bowed to pressure and married a British Nigerian man. It solved the social pressure and it might also have solved her visa problems. But it only lasted a few months. 'There was no joy in it. How can you say you are married to a man when you've only slept with him once? And that once was like going to war in Afghanistan. So what's the basis of doing that? Why should I enslave myself to remain in the UK? I thought to myself, I won't be able to go on with this.'

They had a spousal visa application pending which would have concluded Aderonke's struggle to stay in Britain but she could not go through with it. 'I had to come out. At that point I felt I was deceiving myself and living a life that wasn't mine. So I told him who I was. I said: "This is who I am. I'm sorry;

I've been hiding this for a very long time."' Initially he did not believe Aderonke, thinking she was just joking. But when he realised she was serious they divorced soon after. Next she told her family, starting with a sister and an uncle living in Britain and then phoning other relatives in Nigeria. 'When I eventually spoke to them they didn't take it too badly. I think it was something they already had in their head that I was a different person, different to other females. "Oh yeah, I suspected," or "Oh yes, I knew," that was the sort of reaction I got.'

Back in Nigeria, discussions over new draconian laws for openly gay people were making Aderonke even more frightened of being sent back. She was right to be worried. By 2014, homosexuality could be punished in Nigeria by up to fourteen years in prison – or stoning to death if your case is tried in one of the Sharia courts in the north of the country. Until recently Britain did not necessarily accept asylum seekers on the basis of fear of persecution for their sexuality. But a test case in 2010 ensured that any LGBT person with a real fear of harm back home should be able to claim asylum in the UK.

In 2011 Aderonke was again arrested for working with false papers and sent to prison. The following year, while she was being held in Yarl's Wood detention centre pending deportation, she put in a fresh asylum claim. This time she was open that her biggest fear about returning to Nigeria was being persecuted for her sexuality. She says that a few months earlier she learnt that her ex-girlfriend Kemi had been brutally killed in an attack because of her sexuality. This latest asylum claim was also rejected, leaving Aderonke with what felt like no options at all.

In the meantime, things at Yarl's Wood had become tense. Aderonke remembers being bullied for her sexuality by other

Nigerians being held there; yet the Home Office still did not believe that she was gay. She was also becoming increasingly politically active and when she took part in a demonstration about the treatment of a woman being deported, she was moved from the detention centre to prison. 'I committed no crime, it was a peaceful demonstration, but I was taken to Her Majesty's prison. People weren't treated like human beings in Yarl's Wood. They were taken to the airport in handcuffs and beaten up.'

In 2012 Aderonke met Happiness. They were both staying in Yarl's Wood and Happiness noticed Aderonke straight away. At the time there was nothing more than friendship; Aderonke was already in a relationship with a woman from Jamaica whose asylum application had failed. When Happiness first asked her out, Aderonke turned her down, not wanting to be unfaithful. But shortly after Aderonke's girlfriend was deported she called from Jamaica to say the relationship was over. Happiness saw her chance. Like Aderonke, Happiness had fled Nigeria because of her sexuality. Her asylum application was more straightforward – the scar above her eye from a mob beating, along with threatening emails and images of her other injuries – meant her claim was hard to refute. After a short stay in Yarl's Wood, her asylum case was accepted just six days after applying.

Soon Aderonke was released too, and they began seeing each other. After only a few months they were engaged to be married. The relationship was a revelation to Aderonke. It was the first time she'd had a girlfriend where she had felt really comfortable with herself. 'It's the positive part of my life,' she says, sitting next to Happiness in her small room in a Salford bed and breakfast. 'Even after I came to the UK and had one or two sexual relationships I was not able to flaunt it, talk about it to people. It would always end and the feelings I had, or we had, for each other were behind closed doors. But now with Happiness I can walk around the streets, be who I am, be happy. Before I wouldn't go down the street holding hands, I wouldn't even be sitting this close to start with. I wouldn't think of wearing what I'm wearing today, what I'm comfortable in [a men's-style shirt and shorts]. It's quite positive and promising in a way, but I don't know how it's going to end. I don't know how long that joy will be. If I returned would I still be able to be myself? Would I be alive? If I returned would I be free in society? The law in my country now is fourteen years in jail and if I was in jail I'd stand the risk of torture or being killed by inmates.'

In January 2013 Aderonke was in detention, facing deportation, when an eleventh-hour legal intervention prevented it. Since then public support for her case has been overwhelming – more than 320,000 people signed petitions demanding she be allowed to stay in Britain. In spring 2014, after a long and noisy campaign, a judicial review was granted into her case.

◆

After Aderonke's case began to make headlines, the Home Office made a statement to the press saying: 'We do not remove anyone at risk because of their sexuality,' but sitting in Aderonke and Happiness's bedroom, the words seem hollow. It is now autumn 2014 and a backlog in the court means Aderonke has to wait until the following March before she has the chance to fight her case in the High Court.

Aderonke struggles to talk about the events of the last few years. The experiences have left her with severe post-traumatic stress that has twice had to be treated in hospital. 'My story is so complicated and it's a terrible thing. Sometimes when I think about what I've been through I ask myself how I managed to hold on. The time I've been in the UK I've been under immense pressure, terror and anger at just all the bad things in life that have happened to me. I want sanctuary, I just wanted to be protected, I want to be who I am.'

When Happiness and Aderonke began their relationship they lived in different cities because Happiness had a job as a chef in London. But after Aderonke was admitted to hospital a second time with post-traumatic stress, Happiness dropped everything to help. She hated the reputation that migrants were there to take benefits, so for months she lived off savings, staying with Aderonke and nursing her back to health. Eventually, when she was worried that she would end up spending all her savings, she went on Job Seeker's Allowance until Aderonke was better. Watching Aderonke laugh at a joke makes her overjoyed. 'When she's smiling like this it's lovely,' she says. 'When your mind is busy you're happy. But when she's lonely and thinking about her personal problems it's not so good.' Aderonke nods agreement. 'It's true; Happiness keeps me happy.'

Apart from the time she spends with Happiness, Aderonke has increasingly distanced herself from the Nigerian community in Britain. She used to go every Sunday to a Nigerian church but stopped after a young boy went up to her and asked: 'Are you a boy or a girl?' It is possible the question was innocent but it set off alarms for Aderonke. 'That really put me off – because the church is predominantly a Nigerian church so I said: "Okay, here we go again. I'm going to get another 'lesson' from here unless I move on."' So she moved to the Church of England, joining a local Salford church that welcomed her for who she was. 'It's been fantastic. They know about my sexuality, they know about us, and nobody is frowning upon anything. I couldn't believe it. Nobody in that parish is judgemental. People might have their reservations but they have never been shown to me.'

She has become so involved that she is now deputy warden, helping organise events and volunteering several days a week. Being able to go to a church where she can be open about her sexuality is a departure for Aderonke, who is increasingly becoming a champion of gay rights in Britain. Scarred by her own experiences, she sent a petition to the Home Secretary demanding that the deportation of gay asylum seekers be halted until a review had been conducted into their treatment by the Home Office. Her outspoken criticism has made her an informal spokeswoman for gay asylum seekers in the UK and she has given speeches at union meetings, gay rights symposiums and the North-West's Labour Party conference. In 2014 she made it onto *The Independent on Sunday*'s Rainbow list of the 101 most influential LGBT people in Britain and won a Positive Role Model prize at the National Diversity Awards. Dressed in a tuxedo and bow tie she walked up to the podium to accept the gong, saying: 'I dedicate this award to all the LGBT asylum seekers in the UK and those facing persecution all over the world due to their sexuality and whom they choose to love.'

When Aderonke went to Manchester Pride in summer 2014, she had to keep swapping T-shirts to march with all the different groups she now belongs to. All the while she wore a multicoloured umbrella hat on her head – and an enormous smile. 'It was beautiful. It's only the second time I've been to

Pride and it's freedom. Being able to walk around in a group of LGBT people and be myself with no judgement, nothing. It was heaven.'

At home, Happiness looks at her in admiration. 'The LGBT people and asylum seekers here see her as a voice to them. They see her as their spokesperson. There was one student that was doing some research. The lady they called said "I'm going to give you Aderonke's number because she's a role model to LGBT asylum seekers". If she was in Nigeria she'd be a chief. People really look up to her, they see her as a celebrity; a celebrity without papers.'

Being gay is still illegal in more than 70 countries in the world; and in five of these, homosexual sex carries the death penalty. Unlike Happiness, who sees homophobia in Africa as an insoluble problem, Aderonke is still hopeful that one day Nigeria and other countries will accept them. 'I believe that within another 40, 50 years there will be a different atmosphere in Nigeria; it will be more friendly. Just look at history. The same things that are happening now in Nigeria were happening around that length of time ago in Britain. People were disowned by their families, their societies. They were sent to Britain and even the government was against it. But then the law changed and people moved on. They realised that these types of people shouldn't be jailed. Just look at Alan Turing: he's been honoured now.'

Now 48, Aderonke's career has been disrupted or on hold for almost three decades and she wants to go back to education and retrain in something new. Until her immigration status is sorted she cannot enrol in a university – or work to pay the prohibitive fees. 'I'd like to go back to school. I was thinking prior to now that I'd do a PhD in public health as I already have a Masters but I might study law to do a specialism in immigration after all this. I've always wanted to be an expert and authority in whatever I do. I had my first degree in my country and a Masters in Britain. I've always wanted to be a professor. In every household in my home state there's a professor. Every house would have at least a PhD. I'd like to go to the University of Manchester; it's one of the best universities.'

The conversation is interrupted by a single ring on her mobile. The caller has hung up to save phone credit and wants Aderonke to ring them back. It is a childhood friend calling from Nigeria and experience tells her they will be asking for money. 'They don't understand it's not as rosy as they think. They didn't want to use air time but I don't have any credit to call them back, I'm not working. They don't understand. They just think you'll be picking up money as you walk along the street. I thought Britain would be a beautiful place, gold-plated like the places we saw on TV in Nigeria. In films the houses are always beautiful. I thought that's the way it would be, with streets glittering and dirt-free with no pot-holes. I couldn't believe it when I saw rats and cockroaches in England. If there are cockroaches here then as far as I'm concerned it's Africa.'

Britain may be grubbier than Aderonke thought: 'In Nigeria I didn't have bluebottles in my house,' she laughs, swatting one away. But more than ever, she cannot imagine living anywhere else. 'Manchester is more my home now. I've had ten years living in this city and I love the community: the church groups, the LGBT support groups, neighbours, friends. People are naturally receptive in Manchester. That's what you need really; they might not be able to solve all your problems but they still have time for you.'

Happiness gets up and makes a batch of pancakes on a small electric ring on top of the fridge at the foot of the bed. The two decide whether to watch *Ugly Betty* on Netflix (Happiness's choice) or BBC News 24 (Aderonke's). To many people in Britain these tiny lodgings would not seem much but they enable this couple to have a life together they could never have dreamed of in Nigeria. As Happiness tucks into a pancake, perched on the bed, she says: 'The thing is, you can be yourself here; you can be yourself at any time. Not being yourself at home? Now that is really challenging.'

CHAPTER 10

◆

Boston

If there is a single street that sums up how dramatically Britain has changed over the last decade, West Street in the Lincolnshire market town of Boston is it. Once home to boarded-up shoe shops and unloved hair salons, the road now has a bustling Lithuanian supermarket, a Polish restaurant, a Lithuanian cake shop, a Polish pub and several European-labelled stores. There's even an information centre offering translation, travel bookings and benefits advice to new arrivals from around Europe.

After Poland and seven other relatively poor Eastern European countries joined the European Union in 2004, the opportunity to work across the continent opened up – and towns like Boston changed forever.

An abundance of agricultural and factory work in Boston attracted migrants in droves. Now the small town has the highest proportion of Eastern European residents of any in Britain, with more than one in ten inhabitants coming from countries which joined the EU in 2004. In the decade from 2001, the number of Polish residents recorded in Boston jumped from 40 to 3,000, and the number of Eastern Europeans went from less than 1,500 to more than 8,000.

Daiva dropped the 'a' in her name to open Diva's Cakes on West Street in September 2013. Now 35, she lived in Boston for almost nine years before saving enough money to start her business. In her home city of Vilnius, Lithuania, she was a project manager for an advertising firm in charge of ten people. But when she first arrived in Boston with her husband Tomas, she took what work she could find, starting out on the production lines of a flower factory.

'The main reason we left Lithuania was because we wanted to earn quickly,' she says. 'Our idea was to go here for a couple of years and earn money and go back, but we're still here. I came from a small village originally and my parents were farmers so I don't mind hard work. We didn't come here to relax and have fun – we just worked and worked very, very hard. We often did sixteen hours a day.'

Now she and Tomas have a four-year-old daughter, Gabriella, who has just started school. 'When we go on holiday to Lithuania and it's time to go back to Boston we say "we're going home". This is our home now. We have a little pain in our hearts for our country. We still dream of going back there but we have a business here and our little one is going to school and will be a proper English girl. At the minute she speaks half-English, half-Lithuanian and we can't understand.'

Daiva taught herself to bake using YouTube videos after Gabriella was born. Now she makes impressively complex creations. The shop's Facebook page is almost all in Lithuanian and it's rare to see any non-Lithuanians dropping in for cake. Like the other businesses on West Street, it generates an unspoken – and perhaps unfair – feeling that the most welcome customers are those from the same country as the people running it. Daiva also has reasons to be less than enthusiastic about attracting English custom. An older man who wanted a sandwich came in one day after seeing a sign in the window advertising rolls and when Daiva explained it meant pastry rolls, like sausage rolls, he exploded: 'You need to go back to school and learn English.' Shopping at Boston market she has also heard xenophobic remarks. One man screamed at a lady shopping with her child: 'You immigrants go back to Lithuania, you're just here taking our money.' In her previous job Daiva says she encountered prejudice, with foreign workers expected to put in extra hours at the factory for no more pay and a perception that it was harder to get promoted if you weren't English.

Experiences like these have hardened her attitude to the indigenous population. 'Nothing will change,' she says. 'I'm still in my heart a Lithuanian person. English people would still see me as a Lithuanian person, they'd still see me as an immigrant. Even our daughter when she was born, we never thought about her as British. She's Lithuanian.' Later, she softens this view and acknowledges that over time her daughter 'will be like an English person,' but she bristles at the idea that she and her husband would ever be British citizens. Her experiences have made her guarded and she admits she finds it hard to trust people. 'In a foreign country you can't find good friends,' she says. 'I don't trust people. I trust myself and my family but I'm hard inside.'

Daiva believes that the benefits migrants bring to the town have been overlooked. 'The local people should be happy that the foreigners are here,' she says. 'There are not a lot of young people from here and foreign people are supporting the town.' There is some truth to what she says. The emergence of new businesses has enlivened the local economy, especially since many on West Street started in otherwise empty premises.

The numbers of people on Job Seeker's Allowance dropped by 200 in 2014, to 736, far below the national average and the peaks the town reached in the Eighties and Nineties. But some Bostonians refuse to see it that way. The West Street shops will never be for them and they resent the fact that so many popular High Street chains have left the town. A branch of Edinburgh Woollen Mill sits empty, while JD Sports and Millets departed long ago.

In a fiery edition of *Question Time* filmed in Lincoln in early 2013, Rachel Bull, a mother of two from Boston whose grandfather was a Polish pilot in the Second World War, made an impassioned speech against the impact of mass migration on the town. 'Boston is at breaking point,' she said, her voice cracking. 'All the locals can't cope any more. You go down to Boston High Street and it's just like you're in a foreign country. It's got to stop. The services are at breaking point.'

In a more nuanced interview later, she said: 'I don't blame the migrants. It's not their fault. They are only doing what the law allows them to do, which is come over here and work. I blame the government for not realising the impact it's having on ordinary people – or managing it.'

Andrew Brookes, former deputy editor of the *Boston Standard*, believes attitudes to migration are tied up with a sense that the town has been abandoned by local and central government. 'There have always been foreign workers but they used to be in smaller numbers; you had people from Ireland, London, Europe, but it was short-term. The problem is when no planning is done in advance and nothing is done in terms of infrastructure then there's going to be an issue. Although there is racism, a lot of the reason people are cheesed off is the feeling that services are stretched. If 10,000 people arrived from Bristol in a decade it'd be a problem.'

When Ukip did well at the council elections, it was, according to Andrew, partly because people felt that Lincoln and Lincolnshire County Council give Boston a raw deal. 'We feel we lose out to Lincoln, let alone London. Boston has been asking for decades for a bypass and they're not getting one but Lincoln is working on its fourth bypass. So some of it is frustration. Food manufacturers take lorries through the town all the time and when I was growing up in Nottingham we knew Boston as that place you get stuck in traffic on the way to Skeggy. So there's a separate feeling that Boston has been overlooked, regardless of immigration.'

When the town had an immigration inquiry in 2012, some people said the biggest social change they had seen was in the 70s and 80s when people came up from London and bought property, driving up prices. Rising rents is also an issue now, with many migrant workers unaware of the going rate and prepared to pay large amounts to live in cramped homes, sometimes with ten or more sharing.

Local services, such as schools and doctors' surgeries, were initially swamped and GP waiting times increased. But the increase in demand has a flip side. The maternity unit at the town's Pilgrim Hospital – where almost 40 per cent of births are to foreign-born mothers – would have long ago closed without migration. The new arrivals are also the impetus behind an enormous new GP surgery and extra funding in local schools. But economic and infrastructure arguments do little to assuage local concerns about the changes taking place.

The town's Central Park is five minute walk away from Diva's, where 56-year-old Bogoslav Grzyb is sitting on a bench with two friends, demolishing a carrier bag full of super-strength lager. It is lunchtime but the three are already drunk. 'My woman tells me to fuck off,' Bogoslav says when asked how he came to be homeless. Originally from Poland, he struggles to find regular work now and has been sleeping on the street for a week.

He's one of dozens of homeless migrant workers in the town who came for work but are struggling to survive. At Centrepoint, a homeless charity that provides showers and sustenance, the front room is packed with migrants enjoying a hot drink and cake. The centre helps between 50 and 60 homeless people at a time, 80 per cent of whom are migrants.

Viktor, 41, warms his hands on a cup of tea. He says he has been homeless on and off for about four years, after coming to Britain from Latvia nine years ago to work in flower factories. 'Now in England it's very difficult to find work. Many agencies only take people at busy times for one or two weeks and then that's it. I won't go back to Latvia. Here it's better because you can live if you can't find work.'

The high number of homeless and under-employed men drinking in the park stokes tensions in the town. One side-effect is a rise in human excrement found in public places, provoking the ire of residents. Gary Joynes, a neighbourhood beat sergeant for Boston police, says it's a constant source of complaint. Gesturing down a side street behind an unfortunately-named family butchers called The Boston Sausage, Sergeant Joynes says: 'The biggest issue that gets people most is people peeing and defecating in the street. This alley is notorious for it. I think it's a complication of homelessness and a lack of toilet facilities.'

But while Boston's longest-standing residents see public

defecation as a uniquely Eastern European problem, the evidence is slightly different. When the *Boston Standard* decided to publish CCTV images of people using the streets as toilets to shame them into better behaviour, they were inundated with complaints. Andrew Brookes recalls: 'We got abuse on social media saying, 'Why have you picked on English people not foreigners?' But the point was we didn't know, we just put up the CCTV. There's a double standard. As if when it's a foreign person weeing, they're weeing in our streets and when they're English it's an issue of insufficient public toilets. Or in a road traffic collision when someone dies and then it emerges they're Eastern European then it's less sad.'

The tensions sometimes translate into something more serious. The town has become notorious for its strained relations with migrants, which Sergeant Joynes jokes has replaced its previous claim to infamy: 'We were the fattest town in England but the Eastern European ladies don't tend to be a large build, so that's brought it right down.'

Dean Everitt is not laughing about the changes. He has organised several anti-immigration protests and isn't planning to stop. Dean, who works in plastic recycling, says: 'The town is a horrible place to live now. Ten years ago you'd know everyone and now the town is a stranger's town and you don't hear English. It's supposed to be called integration but there's no integration. We have Latvian shops, Polish and Lithuanian shops and it's all in their own language. They don't shop in our shops and we don't shop in theirs.'

Speaking about violence between English and Eastern European residents, he says: 'It's a tit for tat thing. We know about English lads beaten up by car-loads of foreigners and we know about foreigners beaten up by carloads of English lads.'

The amount of race-related crime registered in Lincolnshire leapt by 38 per cent last year, though police say this may be down to better reporting of incidents. Sergeant Joynes insists: 'You hear people moaning, saying it's raining and I can't park the car because of all the foreigners but it's very rare to get hate crime. I've worked here for seven years and there isn't an air of racial tension in this town. People moan but it's not a tinder box.'

Tinder box or not, the town is threatening to become a Ukip stronghold. Boston and Skegness, a Conservative seat taken by Mark Simmonds at the 2010 election, was so attractive to the party that at one stage Nigel Farage was rumoured to be considering it for 2015. In the end, 22-year-old local boy Robin Hunter-Clarke ran for the party. He won more than 14,000 votes but still fell more than 4,000 short of Matt Warman, the Conservative candidate. In a sign of Ukip's growing popularity, however, the party won the same number of seats as the Tories in the local election, with each getting thirteen representatives onto Boston Borough Council.

This is not the first time Bostonians have had an uneasy reaction to an influx of new residents. After Portugal joined what is now the EU in 1986, the numbers working on Lincolnshire farms grew steadily. By the mid-2000s an estimated 5,000 were living in Boston, roughly 10 per cent of the then-population. Like their Polish counterparts later, they were resented for the perception that they were driving up rents and taking jobs. Feelings were high enough that when, in the early 2000s, the *Boston Standard* decided to publish a Portuguese language pull-out to cater for the community, a swathe of English readers stopped buying the paper and the initiative had to be canned.

So when Portugal beat England on penalties in the European Cup in 2004, things turned ugly quickly. There had already been unrest in the town centre ten days earlier after a 2–1 defeat to France, with an angry mob throwing Molotov cocktails at police. But losing to Portugal was worse. Within minutes of the game ending the Portuguese-owned Volunteer pub was besieged, having most of its windows smashed as angry young fans hurled bricks. Riot police had to surround it to defuse the situation. The attack on the pub was not the first. Vasco de Mello, the pub's owner, who had lived in Boston since 2001, told reporters at the time: 'If I change the windows today, tomorrow they'll be broken again.'

Off the road between Boston and Skegness is Staples Vegetables, one of the biggest employers of migrant workers in the area. The 10,000-acre farm and packing site has up to 1,000 workers on its books at any time and most are migrants. In one field, a group of Eastern European labourers are hurriedly harvesting cabbages, chopping their stems and loading them onto a conveyor belt which takes them to a lorry where a group of women pack them into boxes covered in Union Jacks.

Vernon Read, the company's director, says a supply of labour from the east of the EU is essential to the business. 'Without immigrant workers we wouldn't be able to grow our crops in the UK. When we advertise locally we have hardly any applicants in the UK. Those English people who do come here don't stay long ... In the intake last year we had ten English people who started and within the first week seven out of the ten had dropped out. I think it's just because it's hard work.'

Mr Read believes immigrant workers are filling jobs English people will not take. 'They're not interested in benefits. They're hard-working, polite and very pleased to be employed rather than feeling they have a right to an income.' In contrast, he says, English job seekers rarely seem willing to take the work. 'We have a lot of problems with local people who can receive benefits. We have people who ring up and say "I'm ringing up because I've got to" and you get the impression they're at the job centre ... When you talk money they'll say I'm not working for £1 or £2 an hour. When you point out it's not £1 it's this much, their view is that it's a differential from what they can receive working compared to what they receive not working.'

Ben Semeniuk is one of Staples' longest-serving employees. Now 31, he has been working there ever since he left Poland for Britain in June 2004, a month after the borders opened. He had just finished school and took a job with them picking vegetables. He worked his way up to the pack room, to the print room and, most recently, to the office. He met his fiancée Agnieszka working at Staples and having sold property in Poland they are now looking to buy a house together near the farm. Now he believes that Lincolnshire is his home for the foreseeable future. Speaking with a slight Skegness accent, he says: 'I thought I would come for six months to earn some money but I never went back.'

Bostonian Adrian Dixon, who worked as a farm labourer for twenty years before turning to taxi driving, sees things differently. Out of every ten people who get into his taxi, nine want to talk about immigration, and he thinks places like Staples are behind the tensions in the town. 'People have a misconception that we're all voting BNP and we're all boot-wearing fascists. We're not. When I was a farm labourer the wages were £300 a week. They're worse now. Ukip will do well here and it's not from skinheads or hooligans or big boot wearers. It's normal people who want a fair crack of the whip. All you've got is greedy local farmers who wanted this in the first place. Staples is not the land of milk and honey they claim it is, I like to call it the death camp. It's slavery but it's not the farmers getting a bad reputation. There are some lazy people out there and we should stop their benefits if they don't want to work, but this is about farmers knowing they can pay less. It used to be if you were a farmhand round here you were made up. Yes, it was hard graft but you were paid fairly and it'd be you that had money to buy drinks in the pub and get a house.'

Adrian did some work driving farm labourers to and from fields in a minibus. The experience made him even more sceptical about working conditions. 'People aren't treated very well in farms and factories. The zero hours contracts are a scam. Sometimes people would be sent home in a shorter time than it took to drive there and back. They would just go along the production line and say "you go home". They treat them like animals. I've worked in a field picking cauliflowers next to boys from other countries who've been in medical school. Cabbages, brussels sprouts, I've done it all. I went into printing at a label factory called Paragon and when they made a load of redundancies, the land was always there for me, so I went back to work on the land.

'It's on the news all the time that if the immigrants left, the farms wouldn't be able to find staff. They would, they'd just have to pay fair wages.'

◆

It is parents' evening at Park Academy, a primary school in north Boston, and teaching assistant Klaudia Cichawa is in high demand. In her hand is a piece of paper with a list of eight time slots and Polish names. These are the parents who cannot speak enough English to discuss their children's progress and they perch nervously at blue dining tables on child-sized coloured stools dotted across the school hall waiting to be seen. The first couple who need translation arrive and go with Klaudia to their daughter's class teacher with their young girl sitting between them. The teacher smiles and the conversation flows warmly despite the language barrier.

With metal half-rim glasses, neatly brushed blonde hair and an impressively upright posture, 32-year-old Klaudia could be mistaken for severe. But it only takes a pupil getting a right answer, or for her toddler to start a fanciful soliloquy in the third person, and the stern veneer is replaced by a goofy smile.

She works in the most diverse school in what has become a very diverse town. There are eleven different languages spoken among the school's 329 pupils, including Burmese, Vietnamese and Hindi, as well as European tongues. Around 90 children have Polish as a first language and there is also a significant Latvian, Lithuanian and Russian-speaking population.

A sign in the entrance hall reads 'We all smile in the same language' and around the walls are colourful displays celebrating the school's diverse intake as well as what it means to be British. One home-made poster with the words 'Great Britain' in the middle has Union flags around it, each depicting its own British value written up by a pupil. Most are concepts, like 'individual liberty', 'the rule of law' and 'tolerance of different faiths, beliefs and cultures'. Another bubble asks: 'Do you think police are important?' Natalia, aged nine, writes in response: 'Yes, because they keep people safe.'

The headteacher, Claire Pinder, is young and enthusiastic,

exuding the positivity of someone parachuted in to improve a school's fate. She stands near the entrance, ready to speak to parents and encouraging them to write their thoughts of the school on a large piece of paper. The enormous sheet says, 'What would you like to see improved at Park?' in several different languages and parents have replied in felt tip using their own languages.

'A lot of people choose the school for the support for non-English-speaking families,' Mrs Pinder says. 'If we didn't have that support we wouldn't be able to do it. Without people like Klaudia we wouldn't be able to communicate. We have a buddy system so a new arrival is buddied with another Polish child and an English child. It's incredibly difficult. It's not just the language, it's the cultural change. They find that not only do they not speak the language but there's a new home, a new street and new friends. The biggest thing we want to do as quickly as we can is to get their understanding of English functional. We don't take them out of class but they might work one to one with translators. We use a phonic scheme which teaches them to read and write and older children use the same programme to learn English.'

She has been at the school a year, after working around the country as an educational consultant, but she says: 'You don't appreciate the challenges until you live them on a daily basis.' Casting about for an example, she lands on child protection: 'Culturally in Lithuania it's acceptable to chastise your children with a wooden spoon or a belt. Many leave children home alone as parents work different jobs. We have to respect their culture but they also have to respect the rules of our society. The best bit about the school is that all these cultural differences are celebrated. Kids don't see barriers they just see another kid. It widens their horizon in a way that other parts of Lincolnshire wouldn't give them.'

As Klaudia rests between appointments, a slightly flustered-looking teacher walks over. 'Can you help?' he asks, 'I don't think these parents are down on your list but we definitely need translation.' She leaps up and gets to work.

◆

Klaudia Cichawa's mother Alina was the first in her family to make the break to England. She had been trying to find work in Poland for about ten years, living in a village just outside the city of Radom in the south. For a woman of her generation in Poland, especially one with three children, she was relatively well-qualified, with A-levels and the equivalent of a BTech in horticulture. But at 49 she was competing with younger people for scarce jobs. At job interviews people would say 'you're too old' and she was getting disheartened.

A good friend from her village had moved to Boston to work on Lincolnshire farms and suggested she join her. Alina had worked in the fields as a child and she was worried about money and having a paltry pension after a decade out of work. When her friend said, 'You can come for three months and if you don't like it you can come back', she thought, 'Why not?' Klaudia and her husband Karol tried to teach her a little English before she left but by the time she arrived in Boston she could still only just about introduce herself and say hello.

It was May 2006, just two years after Poland joined the EU. In those first few months it was hard to leave her home and her family behind for the first time. At Christmas and Easter, the times when she was used to being surrounded by her three noisy, loving daughters, she felt totally alone. Her husband had come to work in England too, but they had long lived separate lives, so when he found work in Leicester he chose to stay there alone.

She was so low on money that she couldn't afford a day off and a journey back to Poland was out of the question. She would chat to her daughters online as often as she could but it was an exhausting time. With little grasp of English, she worked in the fields initially, before getting a job in a factory.

Since the work was through an agency there was no contract, so she took all the hours she could. Thanks to EU membership, the more she worked, the more she would contribute towards her state pension back home and hopefully create a more comfortable retirement in Poland. By the following year she would work a twelve-hour shift in a flower factory during the day, come home, have some food and then work a full night shift cleaning the machines in a food factory and exposing herself to a cocktail of chemicals. At her peak she was clocking in around 70 hours a week but she could only sustain it for a few months. Exhaustion kicked in and when the food factory gave her a proper contract for her night shifts she took it, savouring the chance of having just one full-time job.

It was not long before she had persuaded Karol and Klaudia to join her. 'Why not?' she said to them. 'You both speak English well, you could come for a year or two and make some more money.'

Klaudia and Karol had lived abroad before. In the summer of 2005 they got a student visa to America and went to work in Virginia Beach for four months and save money for their wedding. It was their first work abroad and they liked the adventure. 'I saw all these black people with a comb in their hair and with trousers with the belt round their knees so you can see two pairs of pants. I felt like I was in a movie because there weren't many black people in Poland,' Klaudia recalls. They did not have a car so she walked three miles every day to and from her day shifts at McDonald's and her evening shifts at Dairy Queen ice cream. They came back with enough money to throw a wedding for 200 people a fortnight later.

After Poland joined the EU, England was the obvious choice for a longer stint working abroad. Many of the other strong economies, such as Germany and Austria, delayed opening their borders to Polish workers, and England's decision to let Polish workers in made them seem tolerant and open. Klaudia was also good at English. At school they had not just learnt the language, but the history and culture too. This was not the language of America or Hollywood – she can still remember the pictures of Big Ben and the Houses of Parliament from her text book. 'I saw that and thought, wow, that's a country I'd like to visit.'

When Klaudia landed at Luton airport one October evening in 2006 she barely noticed her surroundings. It was her first time in Britain but she was focused on just one thing: seeing her husband Karol. They had only married a year before and had been living apart for three months. She was nearing the end of her teacher training in Poland while Karol had gone ahead to Boston to start saving for their future. Klaudia was unable to join him for good until the following summer, when she had completed her studies.

This first trip was just a visit during a half-term break from her university, and the night she arrived they hardly got any sleep. They were so excited to see each other that they stayed up until morning catching up and doing, as Klaudia later recalled with a smile, 'other things'.

The next morning when Klaudia went out in Boston she could find almost nothing to like about England. She had been told of the miserable weather, but had not been prepared for such unrelenting wind and grey. All the buildings were a lurid red colour and even the parks irritated her. How could they be called parks when there were only a handful of trees? In Poland parks had been like forests. Places of retreat full of trees, plants and space. In Boston, a park was a handful of trees, some mangy grass and a few drunks on benches.

The other thing that puzzled her was the way strangers would say 'Hello, how are you?' and then walk away before she had a chance to answer. In her village, asking how someone was took time; people would stop in the street and unburden their problems. At first she took offence at the empty question but she would later appreciate it as a friendly gesture.

She had always been good at English but she found she could hardly understand what people were saying; they spoke in an accent that sounded nothing like the language she had seen on television or been taught in lessons.

Karol's first impressions of Boston were better. It helped that it was August when he arrived and the sun was shining. Alina, his mother-in-law, took him around, showing him the shop, the pharmacy and the place everyone new in Boston goes: The Stump. This is the unusually high tower of St Botolph's, a medieval church that is arguably the town's only major attraction, unless you count an old windmill on its outskirts.

Karol's own mum had not been happy about him leaving. His sister was seven years older and had long since left home, so Karol was her baby. On the few occasions he has been able to come home since, she always demands to see more of him. The encouragement he needed came from Klaudia's 83-year-old grandmother, who told him to 'go out in the world and find your place'.

And the place he found was right at the bottom. Karol has a Masters in specialised electrical engineering and is qualified to mend MRI scanners and other complex hospital equipment. But he knew the available work was unlikely to use his skills so when he was offered shifts in a dog food factory he accepted them. He had worked in dull and repetitive jobs before, but he had never been anywhere that smelt so bad, so he was pleased when the next temporary job offered by the agency was as a cleaner. He was taken in a van to Skegness to clean up the chalets in Butlins. It was peak season and he was one of several agency staff brought in to make up the gaps. The hours were unreliable, the pay was minimum wage and he spent most of his day scrubbing toilets. He knew if he really wanted to improve his circumstances he'd need to get contract work.

Alina had helped him find a place to stay – a bed in a room he shared with two other guys, one from Portugal and the other from Poland. The men were kind, showing him what to do and where to go and reminding him to pronounce Lincolnshire like 'sheer' not 'shire'.

He finally found settled work in a ready meals factory in Holbeach, a small town seventeen miles south of Boston. There were a mixture of English and foreign workers – though more of the English workers were in supervisor or senior roles. People were welcoming and he quickly made friends with the other workers and earned the trust and respect of his managers. One English manager, who eventually went on to marry a Polish lady who moved to the town, recognised Karol's hard work and intelligence and promoted him to supervisor. Later still, Karol became a manager too.

Outside work he was not always as well received. Karol is bald with smiling eyes and a broad, kindly face of the sort that most people would stop to ask directions from, not pick fights with. But one night he was out in the pub with Polish friends and a group of English lads tried to beat them up. 'We knew something was going on,' he later recalled. 'These guys kept looking at us and then talking to each other. So we decided to leave the pub, but as soon as we got up they followed us.' After a lot of pushing and shouting the police arrived and told their assailants to leave them alone. 'We were very calm, we just wanted to go home', Karol explains, looking sad at the memory of the uninvited trouble.

Karol is not blind to the problems caused by his fellow newcomers, however. If anything, he feels their misbehaviour more acutely than their xenophobic critics. Over a cup of tea at home, he says: 'Sometimes when I see Polish or other different nationals in the street not behaving as well as they should, I feel embarrassed personally because I know how you behave and what you do, you're representing your country. I know that people who see a Polish person drunk on the street will say all Polish people are drunkards and that they don't work and are stealing stuff. If you want English people to say good things about Polish people you need ten good people or 100 good people. But when they want to say a bad word, one is enough.'

Karol has some empathy with those who are aggressive towards newcomers like him. 'I understand there's a lot of change. A lot of different languages around the town and a lot of different shops. It must be a strange situation. But we don't do anything wrong coming here, that's the thing. We didn't swing through the clouds to come here. My people don't understand it. We're here because someone allowed us to come here. Even if we apply for benefits we do it because we can – it is the law. If the law changes, fine. People need to understand that most of us come here to find a future and a better alternative or to feed their families. I know people who are really poor and they came here because it was their last chance. I know people who came here in their 50s when it wasn't an easy decision to come and leave their homes and their families to earn money. It means they were in need and desperate. The human aspect is very important. There's a lack of understanding from the British community for us. The British need to understand we're not here to drink and get your money, because we work for it. We don't get anything for free, just as British people don't. If you open a newspaper like *The Sun* you will only hear about someone committing fraud for thousands of pounds. Nobody gives the figures for how few Polish people are on benefits. But this is what Ukip thrives on.'

Some of the most overt xenophobia in Boston is expressed by teenagers. Klaudia's cousin Anita arrived in Boston at the same time as her. Anita initially left her two sons with her mother in Poland but two years later when they were eight and ten she brought them over. They are teenagers now and the eldest has been beaten up several times. 'For teenagers it's more dangerous or unsafe. I know a few stories where teenagers outside of school have been picking on and beating up and bullying Polish children and one was my nephew. He didn't want to go to school and because of the language barrier sometimes he didn't even know when people were picking on him,' Klaudia recalls. 'When someone doesn't quite understand they sometimes answer "yes, yes" and nod their heads. They were picking on him because he did that and said "yes, yes" because they were the only words he knew. He didn't want to go to school and he would cry and hold the door and his mum would have to push him out. It's hardest for teenagers arriving because little children get used to it much more quickly. It's also a hard time for them as human beings and then finding yourself in a different country where you know only a few words like colours and animals, basically that's what they learn at the beginning. It was about two years later the boys came. The younger one adapted much quicker.

'Teenagers are influenced by parents. Parents wouldn't dare to shout at me in the street because I'm Polish but their teenagers can. If you think something, your children will think the same unless they're grown-ups; so if teenagers hear at home that foreigners are blamed for everything then they will do the same.'

Greta, a Lithuanian teenager who arrived in Boston when she was nine, says there was a noticeable increase in racist bullying when she got to secondary school. Now seventeen, Greta says she still hangs out only with Lithuanians, often visiting Diva's cake shop on West Street as her mum is an old friend of Daiva's. 'In primary school there was no racism but in secondary school there was, and in town too. I think Boston is the most racist town in England. When I go in town and talk in Lithuanian people say "go back to your country" but I ignore them. There are some nice English people who like foreigners but I don't really have English friends; they are more likely to stay in their English groups. All my friends are Lithuanian. I go to college now and in my class of 30 maybe ten are Lithuanian.'

In class the teachers tried to mix foreign-born students with English ones to help with their English language development and encourage a sense of community. But outside of lessons people largely stuck to their own national groups. Greta is at college now studying public service and would like to be a police officer in a bigger town, hopefully somewhere nearer London. She still has a strong Lithuanian accent but says she feels Britain is her home.

'I mostly go to places where people aren't English, like the Lithuanian shop and restaurant. I don't know why. I don't eat English food. I don't know what English people do. I did have some English friends at school but not so much now. All my friends that have boyfriends or girlfriends, they are Lithuanian. My boyfriend is Lithuanian and all my boyfriends were. In college [English people] are nice and friendly and I get on with everyone.' But later in the conversation she contradicts this, saying: 'I just don't really like English people, they're so nasty. It's mostly children that are nasty. Adults keep it to themselves rather than say it out loud. There's nothing to do here in Boston so [teenagers] go and smoke weed and say whatever they think.'

◆

Klaudia had worked hard at her Polish teaching degree from Maria Curie University but when she first moved to Boston she could see no prospect of using her skills. She thought, 'If I can just make a bit of extra money then I can go back to Poland and get on with life'. Her first job was at a chocolate factory in Skegness. She was packing seasonal Cadbury chocolates, which meant wrapping up lots of eggs and Valentine's hearts.

Her next job was at FreshCook, where Karol already worked, preparing ready meals for Marks & Spencer. The idea of a meal in a box was alien to her and Karol, who always cooked their food, even after long days at the factory. The work was tedious but she was grateful for the money.

After she had been there two years, the company announced they would be making redundancies. Klaudia recalls they were trying to make people move onto new contracts. 'They hoped that plenty of people would leave because they wanted more people to work nights. Once they fired you, they re-employed you on a new contract. Less money, less holiday. There was a union and we were in it, but they said to the union either we do it like this or there will be no factory.'

The shake-up was what she needed. Seeing time pass by, she had been worrying that her teaching skills were mothballing, so she started volunteering at a nearby primary school. She would work twelve-hour shifts at night, sleep for a handful of hours and then go straight to Park Academy. She quickly became an indispensable classroom assistant, helping out three days a week as a translator for newly arrived children and a helper to those who were struggling in class.

After three months she was offered ten hours' paid work helping at the school. It was such a victory. She hated the factory by then and was desperate to start using her brain.

Soon afterwards she saw an advert for teaching assistants at Skegness Junior School, a short drive away. She was one of a handful from the 100 or so people who applied that were offered an interview. Part of the assessment process was preparing and delivering a twenty-minute lesson. The thought thrilled and terrified her. As a qualified teacher in Poland, she had plenty of experience in planning and delivering lessons, but she was nervous at the thought of doing it in English.

She decided to teach the children the legend of the Wawel dragon in Krakow. As the story goes, the dragon ate all the sheep in the neighbourhood and terrorised the townsfolk. Knights and other brave men had been thwarted in their attempts to slay it, but in the end it was one young boy who managed the impossible. He stuffed a lamb with sulphur until the dragon got so thirsty that he drank the entire Vistula – Poland's biggest river – and exploded.

In the middle of the lesson she was asking the children to think of words that she could write on the board to describe how the dragon might make people feel. They said all the usual words like 'scared' and 'frightened' and then one boy put his hand up and said 'petrified'. She froze. She hadn't heard the word before and she glanced nervously at the adjudicator. With no idea how to spell it, she took a guess and decided to be honest. She told the class: 'I'm not sure how to spell that one but I'll write it up on the board and then check it in the dictionary.' Her hands were shaking when she opened the dictionary, but she had guessed right. The headmaster said it was the best lesson he'd seen and that he was pleased she had used a dictionary. The next day she was offered the job and soon she was driving to Skegness every morning to work with a special needs boy and then back to Boston in the afternoon to continue her work as a teaching assistant.

Klaudia's obvious talents at her job did not always bring her good fortune. 'It's against the law to say something racist at work,' Klaudia would later recall, 'but sometimes you feel it'. It was an Ofsted inspection a few years ago that revealed the scale of a fellow teaching assistant's resentment towards her. She was British and now works elsewhere. Like Klaudia, she was qualified only to assist lessons, but with staff in short supply, both women were given the opportunity to teach some themselves. They would divide up the work so that sometimes

Klaudia was the teacher and this lady her assistant – and sometimes the other way around. Klaudia had been given a group of low-ability children, most of whom were new arrivals struggling with English, and the other assistant was responsible for another class. The previous headteacher at the time observed both of them at work and recommended that when Ofsted came, Klaudia should be the teacher for all their lessons. Sure enough, when the inspectors arrived, it was Klaudia standing at the front of the class. In the feedback afterwards she was worried that her accent or word choice might have caused problems, but the inspector looked thrilled. All her comments were positive and she judged the lesson to be brilliant, particularly praising the way that Klaudia's own experience of having to learn English made her so good at explaining it.

After that the other teaching assistant was livid. She had once been a friend but after school that day Klaudia remembers her shouting 'Maybe I'd like to go to Poland to teach Polish now' and that it was unfair Klaudia had positive feedback when she could not even pronounce words properly. According to Klaudia she then began to mimic the way she pronounced work as 'wark' and made no attempt to hide her resentment. Klaudia explains: 'She was jealous. She didn't see it as a good thing that I did well. She sees it that I'm foreign and I'm teaching English even to English children and it's not fair.'

There have been other moments too. When a middle-aged Polish man was stabbed to death after making a drunken pass at an eighteen-year-old English girl on her way home one Saturday night, much of the town's reaction was in sympathy with the British killer. The killer, Stephen Sleaford, claimed his actions were all to defend the young woman but this was not accepted by a jury and he has since been convicted of murder.

Klaudia recalls: 'We are blamed for everything. Mostly it's absolutely fine but when I hear someone picking on Polish people I get emotional and cross. I heard people say this Polish guy tried to rape the girl and that's why the English guy stabbed him, but his daughter told me that story was wrong. When I was talking about this stabbed man in the staff room, people felt they could say something else nasty about Polish people. Nobody seemed to talk about the bad English man who stabbed him, just about the man who was stabbed. Then they started to blame Polish people for double parking, which was nothing to do with it. Now when we drive around, me and my husband say "Look, it's double parking" and the cars are English. You can read the names on the vans and they're English.'

◆

At the same time as her career was taking off in the British school system, Klaudia spotted another opportunity to teach. It was 2009 and migration from Poland to Britain had been in full swing for five years. All around the town she could see Polish children starting to grow up without their mother tongue and she wanted to help them hold on to that heritage. At mass one day in St Mary's, the town's Catholic church, she asked the priest to read out a notice that she was offering Polish tuition. She thought maybe one or two parents might be interested but after the service she had a list of 44 people all keen to learn and within a few weeks the number of prospective pupils had risen to almost 100.

Such a large number would not fit in the church hall, let alone her living room, so she decided to hire out some class-rooms at Park Academy and turn the idea into a Saturday school. She found other former or practising teachers prepared to volunteer their time and then she set about sorting out the practical arrangements. This turned about to be more of a palaver than she could have predicted. At the bank she discovered that without an Ofsted number she could not call it a school, so she had to hastily rename it the Polish Saturday Club and then there were all the criminal records checks and public liability insurance. Within four months it was open and it now has around 100 six- to sixteen-year-olds studying not just Polish but also extra English, geography, history, religious studies and maths lessons too.

'Some parents think if their kids are in England they need to speak only English so they don't see the point of the Saturday school. I don't agree with that,' Klaudia says. 'Some of them think "we don't want to put too much on them". But it's fun, not just strict teaching and learning, although they do have homework. At home you don't speak in beautiful full sentences so it's not enough otherwise. There are benefits too. I would say 95 per cent of those who come to our classes are high achievers in school. Learning other languages helps you with everything. They are thinking quicker.'

Klaudia is a founder member of a committee for minority weekend schools in Lincolnshire and used to be its chair. The group meets every few months to support the work of fourteen supplementary schools in the county, teaching Chinese, Arabic, Hindi, Bangladeshi, Lithuanian and Latvian as well as Polish. Although she is passionate about maintaining some Polish identity in the next generation, Klaudia is not blind to the importance of integration. In her own life she makes an effort to forge friendships with British neighbours and colleagues and she is aware that a club just for Polish children could be quite insular. So when a charity promoting community cohesion asked Klaudia if they could work with her Saturday school she leapt at the chance. She was excited the day the agency came to the school, thinking it could be the start of something positive for the town. But rather than arrange for other pupils of different backgrounds to come along, they just got her pupils to write some poems about Boston and sing a few songs. Klaudia was confused – she had expected them to arrange something which brought all children together and would encourage Polish people to mix with others in the town. Instead everything seemed to be separate. 'I later heard that agency got paid £70,000 for that project and they just delivered a few sessions. They came to our school, they didn't support us financially and then they were able to tick the box and say they had worked with Polish children. I think they were targeting the wrong people anyway. The children are already integrating at school with their friends in the week. They should be targeting the people who aren't really welcoming us. Until all people learn that it's to our benefit to come together it's not easy.'

◆

It is 8.45 on a cold Saturday morning in November. As most of Boston's kids loll about in their pyjamas watching television, almost 100 Polish children are queuing outside Park Academy.

Ranging from six to sixteen, the younger ones are soon clattering around the hall playing tag – or in the case of the handful of teenagers, leaning against the wall trying to look nonchalant. At the door a register is taken and the kids, each with a rucksack and a lunchbox, look prepared as for any school day, aside from the lack of uniform. It is the last Saturday before Advent and a £1 coin is collected from each child for an afternoon party to celebrate the start of the Christmas period.

The chattering mass hurtles around and around until they are brought to attention by the teachers and lined up according to age group. Klaudia has been there since eight in the morning despite sinusitis, no sleep and a tough week at work covering for a difficult class whose usual teacher is off with stress. A young Polish priest, dressed in black and carrying an acoustic guitar, stays in the hall to teach a class of eight-year-olds who are preparing for their first communion. The remaining children file out to classrooms with their volunteer teachers.

Klaudia's first class is with nine- and ten-year-olds. There are nineteen of them and as she takes the register each child answers 'jestem', Polish for present. The best-behaved girls in class gather in the seats next to her. The class is quiet and well behaved, listening attentively. Their textbooks look dry and full of laborious exercises, but Klaudia manages to enthuse them. At a table further away are the boys who are less keen to be there. One of these boys explains in hushed tones that they are learning about adjectives and nouns and their homework was to learn which was which. His accent is perfect Bostonian English, with no hint of his Polish roots. Another boy, older than the rest of the class and with more of a cockney accent, looks bored and crabby. 'Polish is well hard,' he says, adding, in case it weren't clear, 'English is way easier'.

He is in a class with younger children because he has not been brought up speaking the language as much. 'If I had to choose between staying in Poland or England I'd choose England. I was born here,' he says. He starts to lean back on his chair and swing his legs. 'I just don't like it, it don't feel right,' he scowls. He's clearly struggling to understand the questions, waiting for the others to fill out their workbooks before copying their answers. He says he didn't want to come but the rest of the class seem happy to be there.

With pictures of zoo animals, the class have to add in the right descriptive words. Eager to please Klaudia, they wriggle in their seats when she asks a question, their hands stretched in the air. The majority of these kids don't look or sound any different to other British children; they are already assimilated but this is their parents' attempt to hold onto their heritage.

Klaudia's next class is the group of eight-year-olds who were having their religious lesson with the priest. One girl, who has already been through her first communion, is there early. She has china doll looks, with tightly curled light brown hair and porcelain skin, and looks as composed as a grandmother. She was born in Lithuania but her family are Polish and they moved here. She is nine but already speaks Lithuanian, Russian, Polish and English fluently, and talks eloquently for her age. 'I came here when I was six,' she says. 'My cousin taught me English. When I came I only knew hello and 'bye. Nobody was playing with me because nobody understood my language.'

She takes a seat silently and soon the other children file in. One young boy has a pencil case full of Angry Bird cards and a small plastic car which ends up confiscated within minutes of the lesson starting. Dressed in a perfectly ironed button-down shirt, his English accent is prim Home Counties though his parents are Polish.

The class is on syllables and they try to clap out the number of syllables in words as Klaudia dictates them. When the kids say the vowel sounds in English she has to correct them and teach the Polish way. With each word, more than a dozen hands go up, straining to be asked.

After a brief morning break, Klaudia's next lesson is a rehearsal for the nativity play. The characters of Mariya and Józef are played by two of the school's young teenagers and Józef looks distinctly less interested in the part than his stand-in wife. While Mariya delivers perfectly remembered lines about her imminent birth of a Messiah, Józef has his hands deep in his hoodie pockets and seems preoccupied with showing off his best Jay-Z impression before knocking on the door of the inn. The nativity play follows the Bible story closely and includes traditional Polish carols, something Klaudia is keen to keep going at a time when British schools are increasingly rejecting the Christmas story in favour of a vague Winterval celebration.

Next Klaudia takes the school's four oldest students who are preparing for a GCSE in Polish as a second language. It is one of the things that makes the school popular with the pupils' parents and regular teachers, as it all but guarantees them at least one A or A* in their exams. Each of the students has written a formal letter to Santa Claus in Polish saying what they want for Christmas ahead of the 6th of December, when he is traditionally said to visit in Poland. They read out their letters and the English words in their wish list – *Assassin's Creed*, Busted and McFly – are typical of any British teenagers.

She shows them the history book called *Dywizjon* [*Squadron*] *303* that they will be reading in their next class. Written in Polish, it has an RAF bomber on its cover and tells the history of one of three squadrons of Polish pilots fighting in the British air force in the Second World War. Klaudia explains: 'Not many people know about this bit of history. They hated Germany so much that these pilots risked their lives all the time. They destroyed so many German planes. These guys are fourteen and fifteen and they sometimes say their teachers don't have enough knowledge and don't teach about the Polish role in the war at school. It's really important for them to know about this.'

At noon the children have half an hour to eat and play and the teachers gladly retreat to the staff room. Klaudia has spent her week taking a class of 30 low-ability children and looks in desperate need of a sofa. 'A class of 30 with only seven girls,' she says, her eyes full of horror. 'The teacher got stressed and went off. So now I'm teaching her class. It was a really hard week. Next week she won't be back either.' The previous night she and Karol had gone on a long-awaited date to the cinema despite her week from hell. 'I felt really unwell but I knew it was the only night for this month and next month that we'd get to go out because my mum could babysit. Afterwards we went to Tesco to do the big weekly shop. That was the date!'

◆

It had never been Klaudia and Karol's plan to stay in England. Their roots in Boston were largely financial – it was the place that could help them raise the money they needed to have a better life in their real home. But one night in Poland changed all that.

Klaudia was 27 weeks pregnant with her first child when she and Karol got on a plane home for her cousin's wedding. She had been nervous about flying so far into the pregnancy but a doctor checked her over and gave her a permission slip, saying she would be fine until her 38th week. A week after arriving they were celebrating her sister Patrycja's name day at the family's home in her village. In Poland your name day, a designated day of celebration for the saint you were named after, is like a birthday. People bring flowers and chocolates and often party long into the night. It was late afternoon and Klaudia had a tummy ache. Patrycja, who had two boys already, told her not to worry. 'Sometimes it's like that,' she said, 'it will be fine.' But the pain did not go away, and feeling exhausted, Klaudia went up to bed. As she lay in bed the pain would rip through her and then disappear. She kept thinking to herself, 'OK, that was bad, but I'm OK, if it happens again I'll call an ambulance'. By 2am it was excruciating and she couldn't stand it any more. Karol called an ambulance and when she reached the hospital the doctor informed her she was in labour. The news was shocking – she had not even brought a toothbrush or a pair of pyjamas with her – but it made sense. By the time they were in the ward the contractions were every eleven minutes and there was no denying what it was.

The doctors at the hospital were helping reluctantly. They were on strike that day and had vowed not to touch any patients, but with a mother in labour they had little choice. Klaudia had always had a weak heart. She was born with a hole in it, which had to be operated on when she was ten, and as a teenager she would suffer palpitations which made her weak and dizzy.

Though they tried to stop the labour they were too late, and being forced to give birth at such an early stage in the pregnancy set her heart racing in panic. Soon it was going at 200 beats a minute and she was getting weaker by the second. She has since heard that a caesarean would usually be offered with such a complicated birth but it was not. She is unsure now whether that was because it was a small, local hospital with inexperienced staff, or because those staff were on strike. Either way, the longer the labour continued, the more it looked like mother and baby were unlikely to survive the night.

As the pain continued, the hospital staff seemed unbothered. Perhaps, she wonders now, they were trying to get her used to the idea that she was likely to lose the child. Certainly someone – she cannot remember if it was a nurse or a doctor – told her the baby would not make it. Hours in, when she gasped for a glass of water, a sullen nurse replied 'What, now?'

'We didn't know what was happening, we didn't know why I was in labour,' she recalls, anguished at the memory of being kept in the dark. 'The doctors did not want to touch patients all day because of the strike but they did. I think they had no choice. If they had not we both would have died. They asked Karol to leave the room and then I had no family around me and just doctors and nurses telling me to push.'

Soon there were ten people gathered round and a cardiologist and another doctor were arguing across her bed, oblivious to the distraught woman between them even as they quarrelled about her. Klaudia's heart had been thrashing at 200 beats a minute for more than two hours, and the cardiologist wanted her to stop pushing so he could use electroshock pads in an attempt to force a stop and slow it down. The shock did not really work but after 22 hours of labour and near cardiac arrest, Klaudia gave birth to Helena.

There is a ten-point scale for newborns, with ten being the healthiest. Helena scored a one – her heart was beating and that was the only positive thing to say. She was so tiny that she weighed just two pounds and she could not breathe unaided. The hospital's meagre facilities would not be enough to keep her alive and the consensus was that she was too small to survive. But Klaudia and Karol did not want to give up hope.

After two days Helena was still alive and she was transferred to a specialist antenatal unit in Warsaw, leaving Klaudia behind in hospital to worry. Soon afterwards, while Helena was still fighting to stay alive, Klaudia had an emergency operation to correct her own heart's irregular rhythm. Ten days later she was finally able to join her baby. It was a relief to be in a hospital where they were treated like human beings. In the weeks afterwards Karol took his paternity leave and all the holiday he could, but eventually he had to return to England so that he did not lose his job.

Klaudia stayed on in Warsaw. At night she stayed in her youngest sister's flat, sharing a single bed with her, and in the day she was in hospital watching over Helena as she went through two head surgeries, having a shunt inserted to drain fluid from her brain. At the same time she was learning how to be the mother of a baby whose legs were as thin as her own fingers and who she was too scared to touch for fear of hurting her. It was three months until Helena had developed enough to breast feed and was finally strong enough for Klaudia to take out of hospital.

By this time Klaudia and Karol knew Helena had cerebral palsy and would be unlikely to develop like other children. Suddenly a future life in Poland looked less certain. They looked around and noticed every staircase and step. The buses, the trams, the underground, they all had steps. Pavements ended abruptly where they reached the road and now that they thought about it they could hardly remember seeing disabled people in Poland – not because there weren't any but because they were forced to stay inside at home. A disabled person in a block of flats with no lift would simply live inside with occasional visits to their balcony. Klaudia believes the prohibitive cost of wheelchairs – and their impracticality even in cities – conspires with poor wages to make sure that a disability can be tantamount to a life sentence indoors. Having the child inside constantly means a parent must always be there too, and would probably have meant only one of them could work, leaving them with minimal income.

'You don't notice if you don't need it, but little things become big things when you need them,' Karol explained later. 'Here we have good access to most places we want to go with her and can spend more time together because of that. We're not locked in the house. We've been given this opportunity to have a normal life, even with our daughter. Simple things are easier in Britain. When you go outside, everywhere, the pavement and walkways are all for wheelchairs. In Poland it's not. New buildings maybe, but normally nowhere is accessible at all. Our life would look completely different.'

So when Klaudia picked up her seven-month-old baby, who still weighed only four pounds, and got on the plane to London, it was with a sense for the first time that she was coming home. Karol was so relieved to see them after months of worry and still has a latent fear that something else will go wrong. Even seven years later he still calls Klaudia at eight every evening, when he gets a break at work, to check that nothing has happened to Helena and that everything is OK.

In those first few years they worked opposite shifts so that someone could always be at home looking after the baby. But charities and the NHS meant things were easier to cope with. An occupational therapist came and played with the baby several times a week just to see what she was able to do. Equipment like potties and shoes are provided whenever Helena grows out of them, and she is taken by taxi to a special school. Klaudia was sure that none of this would have been possible in Radom, and the knowledge made her feel that a future in Poland was no longer what they were working towards.

◆

When Klaudia first moved to Boston she did not go to church often. She would make a special effort at Easter and Christmas but not with the enthusiasm she had back home. She found it easier to pray in Polish but she could usually follow the service and say the prayers aloud in Polish while people beside her spoke them in English. She wasn't familiar with the hymns but there were some songs in Latin, like the 'Ave Maria', which she knew from her childhood. St Mary's, Boston's only Catholic church, was used to a congregation of a handful of people, sometimes fewer than twenty, most of whom were retired. But many of the new arrivals accepted the language difficulties and swelled the congregation every Sunday. Klaudia recalls: 'The priest said he was so happy – he had never seen so many people in the church.'

Soon the number of Polish churchgoers was too large for the small building to cope with, and in 2008, with increasing demand for a Polish-language service, a Polish priest was brought in to take extra masses. Now Father Piotr takes three masses in Boston in Polish on a Sunday as well as extra services in Skegness and Spalding.

At quarter past eleven on the last Sunday before Advent, the overflow car park at St Mary's church is already double parked and the shop car park up the road is rapidly filling up. Inside the modern red-brick church are hundreds of people – more than there are pews. Young families arrive with their children, yanking off hats at the door and nudging them towards the holy water at the entrance so they can dip their fingers in and make the sign of the cross.

At 11.25 Klaudia arrives with her youngest daughter Hanna. They are still early for the service but the pews have long since all been taken. There are enough seats for about 200 people but far more are crammed onto them, with a small child on every other lap and families packed together in tight units. Behind the main block of pews are another five rows of people who have to stand throughout the service, which is where Klaudia takes a place with Hanna. Behind them, in a glass entrance porch with only a distant view of the altar, are another two rows of people sitting on chairs. A final group of parents with young babies hover in the doorway with prams.

It is hard to comprehend how full the church is. For a country where the norm is a congregation of pensioners that struggle to fill even a third of the pews, this is a religious rave by comparison. Every step of a steep staircase has at least one small occupant. Some of the younger children gather by a small bookshelf at the back, pulling children's books off the shelves and sitting between the feet of standing adults to read. An older boy reads *Topsy and Tim* quietly in English to Hanna, who manages to stay silent throughout the hour-long service.

There could never be enough service sheets or hymn books, so instead the service is projected onto the back wall to the right of the altar. Everyone seems to know the hymns by heart, singing along loudly and tunefully. The youngish priest walks around the front of the church with a microphone making jokes and engaging with the congregation, many of whom seem to be listening intently. His sermon – paraphrased by Klaudia later – is about being kind to children, being ready for Christ and minimising sins during Advent. Everyone is asked to pick one sin which they will not commit in the run-up to Christmas.

The air is thick with incense and hand bells are rung at each stage of the sacrament. The collection plate takes a while to go round and the contributions are almost all coins – most of the pockets here are not deep. What little extra is made from work in a factory is typically sent back to Poland to help families.

When it comes to going up for communion, Klaudia stays put. 'I couldn't go,' she says later, 'I've done too many sins and I haven't been to confession.' She laughs exasperatedly: 'Everything is a sin. I said swear words this morning so that's it. But I only go about twice a year to confession.'

The 11.30 service is followed by another at 1pm which is expected to be even busier and Klaudia expects a final service at 7.30pm will also be full. The church is now so popular that on busier days, such as Christmas and Easter, crowds gather outside to take part in the service in the cold open air. Those standing outside can sometimes go into the hundreds. People carry napkins so that when they need to kneel they don't get their knees grubby on the damp concrete of the car park. This is familiar to Klaudia who as a teenager used to stand outside for services in Poland, though largely because it was a rare opportunity to hang out with boys.

St Mary's now seems to be two churches in one place: a very popular Polish church alongside a scarcely attended English one. The church would seem a logical place to pro-mote union between Bostonians and newcomers but Klaudia is not aware of any attempt to integrate the two communities. She says religion has a special significance for Polish people and that 'British families it seems aren't bothered'. History has amplified loyalty to Catholicism in Poland. After it was banned under communism and priests played such a key role in securing freedoms, the church is seen as something to be cherished rather than a boring historical part of the establishment. But while some of its congregants are believers, Klaudia knows many simply go out of habit, or to show off their latest outfits.

◆

After the trauma of Helena's birth, it was five years before Klaudia and Karol felt ready for another child. Even then, Klaudia was so worried something would be wrong that for the last three months of the pregnancy she kept a packed overnight bag nearby. Hanna Cichawa was born in Pilgrim Hospital in October 2012 after a twelve-hour labour with no complications. The nurses and doctors were attentive, Klaudia's heart was fine and when it was time to go home she could take the baby with her. Helena is now seven and uses a wheelchair a lot of the time. She cannot speak but she can communicate and move around the house unaided. She is often happy and her two-year-old sister gets excited when she hears the door open in the afternoon and knows Helena is home from school.

The final step in making life in England permanent was buying a home. A year after Hanna was born they found a bungalow in Swineshead, a small village south-west of Boston which was close enough to Spalding for Karol's commute to the factory. Every room is accessible for Helena and outside there is even a special swing that her wheelchair can be clipped onto, donated by Scope, a charity the family now raise money for. Their pretty garden ends where the fields begin, with rows of cabbages ready to be picked by migrant labourers when they are ripe.

Their first thought on moving in was to have a barbecue and invite the neighbours over. The party went well. Their neighbours are British and older, in their 50s or 60s, and Karol and Klaudia were nervous about what they would make of having foreigners next door but they were very welcoming, having regular chats over the garden fence. At first they thought they were the only Polish family in Swineshead but they have since heard that there is another at the other side of the village.

Karol is still working in a food factory as a night shift trainer in Spalding, though he is unsure what he will do long-term. He says he has sacrificed his career for Klaudia's because she had a chance to do what she was actually qualified for, but he talks of this with pride rather than resentment. He takes quiet pleasure in being one of the few husbands among their friends who cooks the dinner and does most of the childcare. He used to work all night but now his shift finishes at 2am so he can get a few hours' sleep before getting up with the kids.

After the inspectors rated her lessons so highly, Klaudia went back to school at Boston College in the evenings. She got GCSEs in maths, English and science – the requisite exams to get onto a short course to qualify as a teacher in the UK. She knows she will be a teacher in Britain soon but she has postponed the training until Hanna is older. In the meantime she has a job as Park Academy's cover supervisor, which means she can step in and do the job of a teacher free from the burden of lesson planning and marking.

It is the school holidays and Karol and Klaudia are enjoying a rare day at home all together. They look relaxed and content, each pleased to have the other's company. A week ago they celebrated their tenth wedding anniversary and the 40 friends they invited gave a glimpse into how deep their

roots in the area have become. There was Margaret, a British
teacher in her 60s at Park Academy, and Anna, a Portuguese
teaching assistant, now two of Klaudia's closest friends and
confidantes; then there was Kinga and Mateusz and Ania and
Tomek, Polish couples who have stayed alongside them as they
shared the challenges of settling in a new place. British and
Polish friends of Karol's from the food factory came too and
there was even family – Klaudia's mum, cousin and nephews,
all of whom share this exile in Lincolnshire together. Except
for Klaudia and Karol it has stopped feeling like an exile.

On a flat-screen television *Fireman Sam* dubbed into Polish
is playing via satellite while Karol and Klaudia drink Earl
Grey tea. Karol is in a reflective mood and speaks eloquently
about their new identity: 'I feel British as well as Polish. When
we're in Poland and we're coming back here we say "we're
going home",' he explains. 'I'm not trying to be more British
than British people are but I'm trying to understand British
people and British culture as much as I can because I know if
you live here or somewhere else you have to be a part of it. You
cannot be a separate island on a British sea because if you're a
part of the community you have to truly be a part of it. I still
have my own traditions, Polish traditions within my family
like at Christmas time, but I also try to make my children to
know British tradition and culture as much as Polish because
I know it will be better for them to know in the future.'

Sitting on a sofa in jeans and a football shirt, Karol looks
every bit the British dad at home, were it not for the fact that
the strip is a team from Poznan. 'I'll still be a Polish person
inside of me,' he says, 'but if you don't integrate with the
community you live in, you'll never be a 100 per cent happy
person because you'll be afraid to speak to your neighbour,

you'll be afraid of the guy in the shop or the guy on the corner. It wouldn't be good for me. I'm quite a social person and
I couldn't lock myself in the house and watch telly and drink
beer all day because it's not for me.'

Klaudia is proud to be Polish and of her roots and says
she would not want to be a British citizen but she is unde-
niably a Bostonian. Her accent is noticeable as much for its
Lincolnshire vowels as its Polish lilt these days. She has started
picking herself up when her Monday turns to Moonday and
stamp to stump. In the evenings she still reads in Polish to
relax and is on the fourth book of *Game of Thrones* – or, more
accurately, *Gra O Tron*.

She has now been asked twice to stand for the local council
by councillor and Labour General Election candidate, Paul
Kenny, who recognised her involvement in the community and
determination to integrate. But as far-right feeling in the town
continues to percolate, she is unenthusiastic about being seen
as a spokesperson for the community. She worries about the
anti-immigration protests and antagonising people in the town
unintentionally. In the last few years they have had plenty of
Ukip leaflets through their door and she is aware of the direc-
tion of feeling in the town.

A day or two earlier David Cameron made a speech saying
the government would be clamping down on EU migrants and
preventing them from taking benefits. The changes are minor
but the rhetoric upsets Klaudia. 'After Mr Cameron's speech
there won't be plenty of people coming,' she says. 'People are
worried about finding work and not benefits. The guys who
hired Polish people who went on *Question Time* said that if you
ask an Englishman to get up at 4am and work all day in the
field they won't come, but if you ask Polish or Lithuanian they

will be there working really hard. Employers of minorities can see the difference.'

Klaudia's mother Alina, now 57, plans to retire to Poland once she runs out of strength to work. The toil in England has already meant another nine years of bumping up her state pension and she has some savings to make life there more comfortable. But Klaudia and Karol are more settled than ever.

When England played Poland in a World Cup qualifying match in 2013, Karol was interviewed by BBC Radio One about who he was going to support. Ever the peacemaker, he promised to watch the game in a Polish shirt with an English scarf around his neck. Karol recalls: 'They said it was a diplomatic answer but it's how I feel really. I'll always be Polish but living here has already changed me and will change me more. I'm more open to people. I think it's because here every day I meet a lot of different people and I would not have this opportunity in Poland. I meet people from different countries and different cultures and I learn a lot about them, about their life and lifestyle and that has definitely made me more tolerant. It doesn't matter where I'm from – especially here where you meet people from so many different countries – you see that we're the same.'

Klaudia nods in agreement: 'We all want to work, we all want to have some fun and we all want to be happy. We just look different or speak different languages. I think now we can't be more tolerant. We're a minority living in another country, we've got a disabled daughter and with all our experiences that we've been through we are open-minded, tolerant people. You can't be more so I think.'

At home the family usually talk in Polish but read to Hanna in both languages and are relaxed about their daughters' dual identity. 'Hanna will be more British than us because of the education and the people she'll meet,' Karol says. As if to confirm his thoughts, Hanna ignores the dubbed television for a while and becomes absorbed by an English book about Peppa Pig in the snow.

When Hanna and Klaudia go to eat their dinner in the kitchen, Karol stays in the sitting room dancing with Helena. As he holds her upright and swings her around the room, her laughter and squeals of happiness carry around their home.

Epilogue

Klaudia and Karol want to be part of Britain. They are proud of their Polish heritage, yes, but they are also keen to contribute to their new home. Their feelings towards this country are echoed by many others in the book who want to be included in the UK. Yet for several, this desire for integration remains unmet.

Researching this book meant spending time with people at dramatic moments in their lives: crossing borders together; observing the first days of a strange new marriage; watching as judges decided futures here. But the bulk of the time was spent in people's homes letting them talk. In several cases this was the first time a British person – other than the immigration authorities – had shown an interest in getting to know them. Whatever political decisions are made about how many people we allow into the UK in the future, the way we interact with those already here demands greater thought.

It is only by engaging with each other that we will achieve a more integrated, happy society. If new arrivals are to settle properly as fellow citizens and not aliens, we need to share their experiences. The worst case scenario for integration is lived out in towns like Boston. It has the highest proportion of Eastern European migrants in the country and feels like several towns in one. Rapid change, a lack of foresight and an increasingly hostile indigenous public, creates an atmosphere of division which puts up unseen walls between Eastern European areas and British, souring the community and prompting mistrust on both sides.

Digital breakthroughs have made us all less social. For new migrants it is even easier to stay with one foot in the country they have just come from. Almost everyone I met had television beamed in from their own country – or at least in their own language – and stayed in touch with relatives via video chats. The internet provides useful forums for scattered diaspora, with groups like the Bulgarian one Hristina found on Facebook bringing welcome support at times of isolation. But all of this only makes it easier to live a separate life from other British people.

So how can we patch up these divisions? If there were easy, natural ways for new arrivals and long-standing residents of Britain to do more together, many would leap at the chance. Existing institutions like schools, churches, workplaces and sports clubs can all do more to encourage this, according to the Social Integration Commission – which recently found segregation costs the British economy £6bn a year. The study showed people in the UK increasingly seek the company only of those most like themselves, with profound consequences. The resulting drop in social mobility and increased isolation between groups means that problems are emerging in areas from employment to health, costing the UK the equivalent of 0.5 per cent of GDP. Matthew Taylor, chair of the Commission, cautioned that without action on integration – between classes and ages, as well as nationalities and races – Britain's society would be characterised by 'ugly' divisions. 'Britain's becoming more diverse and if we don't think about this and we're not willing to act on it, the danger is that we'll become more separate,' he said.

There are straightforward moments when we can come together – the challenge is whether we harness them. There was something uplifting about seeing the previously neglected Catholic church in Boston reborn with a Polish congregation. But how much more so if the British and Polish congregations were mixed and singing each other's hymns? Difference can be celebrated without preventing us from doing more together.

Targeted integration projects can work: just look at the Maryhill Integration Centre in Glasgow, which provided much-needed warmth and community to Hristina when she first arrived from Bulgaria. But badly executed ones can exacerbate the problem. In Boston, Klaudia was saddened when her students were asked to participate in an integration project and never actually interacted with British kids as part of it.

We can also improve life in Britain by learning from other cultures. Hassiba and Sai, among others, were shocked at how little neighbourliness and interaction there was with those living around them. More of this could help bring down divisions.

As the bus journey from Bucharest to London showed – when just four of its passengers were going to London and only one for the first time – the scale of migration rarely lives up to the hype. In all 37,000 Romanians and Bulgarians arrived in the year to September 2014, a tenth of what was predicted. There is a tendency to imagine the situation is much worse than it is. The British public believes that a quarter of its population is made up of immigrants, when in reality they represent just 13 per cent. The same Ipsos MORI poll revealed people in Britain are convinced that one in five of the population is Muslim, when actually it is one in twenty. Contrary to widely held pessimism, the number calling themselves

Christian is still at 59 per cent, despite beliefs that just over a third would consider themselves as such.

There is nothing new about migration. William Wordsworth observed with pleasure in *The Prelude* the variety of immigrants that made up London when he visited in 1791. 'Among the crowd all specimens of man,/ Through all the colours which the sun bestows,' he wrote, before listing nationalities from every continent. This is not to say there is no cause to worry about how society integrates. But it is a plea for calm.

I have tried to give a snapshot of the lives of immigrants in the UK but it is not scientific. There are four chapters in this book where asylum has been part of people's reason for being here. I included them because I wanted to tell their stories but they are not a representative number. In 2014 asylum seekers made up 4 per cent of all migration to Britain. I don't want to give credence to the myth that those seeking sanctuary make up a large portion of immigration and we need to curb their numbers. They don't, and we don't. To imply so risks undermining the vital help we offer to those in desperate need of safety.

Some stories have been almost impossible to verify, particularly for those claiming asylum. In these circumstances further enquiries in the country of origin can risk putting an interviewee in greater danger if they are later deported. You can check a country's recent history to assess plausibility but you still have to rely heavily on personal accounts. Where possible I have cross-checked using other sources, looking through countless signed testimonies, Home Office correspondence and court documents. I have seen the letter from the Home Office after Emad's passport was lost; read the evidence of witnesses to Harley's astounding NHS work and scoured contemporary reporting of the Farooq family attack in Pakistan news sites. But sometimes there is nothing to prove categorically that an event has happened. On those occasions I encountered a similar dilemma to the one the Home Office faces when considering the veracity of asylum claims.

The Home Office has previously been criticised by the Chief Inspector of Borders and Immigration for its 'culture of disbelief'. Some of these cases certainly suggest more humanity and common sense could be deployed. Without it you get Aderonke in a loving relationship with a woman still feeling she needs to send a sex-tape to prove her sexuality; or Emad paying smugglers because Britain would not believe – or take steps to check – that the woman who wept and praised God while she held him at Milan station was his mother.

To an extent, Home Office scepticism reflects a public desire for a system that is seen to be tough. But the experiences of the people I encountered in this book show that once someone has made a home in Britain, what they need from other citizens is empathy and welcome. If we fail to offer this there will be many more divided towns like Boston.

Acknowledgements

I am indebted to the people whose candour, trust and generosity enabled me to write the ten stories in this book: Mihai, Roxy, Ummad, Shaiza, Zain, Harley, Chris, Clive, Hristina, Georgi, Emad, Nawal, Harry, Sai, Hassiba, Rachid, Aderonke, Happiness, Klaudia, Karol, Daiva, Greta. Also to Emily, Tony, Samira, Anna and all those who gave their time – but whose stories didn't get told.

Without the imagination and support of my agent Chris Wellbelove at Greene & Heaton this book would never have happened. Thanks to my excellent and wise editor, Duncan Heath, and to Kate Hewson for taking a punt on an unpublished author. Also at Icon, thanks to Andrew Furlow, Steve White, Leena Normington and Sara Bryant. For the cover, I am grateful to designer Dan Mogford and photographer Abbie Trayler-Smith.

Many local experts, volunteers and charity workers were generous with their time as I learnt about the issues affecting migrants in their area. Thanks to Gary Joynes and Andrew Brookes, for nuanced analysis of Boston and invaluable background on the town; to Haidar Mahmoud and everyone at Edinburgh College and the Southside Community Centre for letting a stranger interview their students; to Sunny Singh and Robina Qureshi at Glasgow's Positive Action in Housing and Margaret Sweeney and Phil Jones at the men's night shelter; to Jim Brady at Glasgow Clyde College and Tony Openshaw at Asylum Support Housing Advice in Manchester for useful background.

For accommodation and encouragement in Edinburgh, Manchester, Glasgow and Newcastle, thanks to Stu Cadge and Calum Guthrie; Anna Stopes and Harry, Nina and Greta Cormack; Mel McDevitt; Emma Cockburn and all at the Sidney Grove house.

For legal advice, I am grateful to Colin Yeo at Garden Court Chambers. Also to Nick Armstrong at Matrix Chambers for years of excellent tips on immigration law – and with apologies for handing him what turned out to be a stinker of a case. For overturning what could have been a disastrous gagging order, I am obliged to Louise Hayman and Charles Green.

At *The Independent*, thanks to news editor Matt Moore for encouragement, friendship and a very timely book loan; to Amol Rajan, Lisa Markwell and Dan Gledhill for their support – and to Sean O'Grady for agreeing some very generous time off. To all the Indy's reporters who make coming to work a pleasure, particularly Cahal Milmo who has been an unofficial mentor and pulls off the rare coup of being a brilliant reporter and a thoroughly nice man.

I am indebted to photographer Jason Alden for years of reporting companionship – and for that long-awaited fry-up after 52 hours on a bus. I am grateful to former colleagues Sarah Morrison and Nina Lakhani for their infectious idealism and John Mullin, for the Glasgow pep talk and being the sort of editor that makes you a better journalist. For their specialist knowledge, thanks to Lizzy Davies for working out where Nawal might arrive in Italy and to Issam Ahmed for advice on Pakistan.

I am grateful to my brother Chris, who was working

abroad while I was researching this but still patiently listened to me bleat about it on Skype. His absence gave me an idea what it must be like for the families migrants leave behind. To my granny, Dr Jill Duncan, for teaching the importance of being open-minded about people – something she has not lost as she enters a tenth decade. To my parents, Sally and David, for making everything possible. I owe a particular debt to my mother for checking chapters and showing by example how to write a book – as well as giving hundreds of hours of company in the British Library.

I am forever thankful to my husband Oly, for love and proof-reading. There can't be many people prepared to share their first year of marriage with a laptop and a group of strangers from around the world. There must be fewer still who would do it with such kindness and encouragement.

References

PROLOGUE

'An inspection of the UK Border Agency's handling of asylum legacy and migration cases', John Vine, Independent Chief Inspector of Borders and Immigration, March–July 2012

'Thousands of Romanians and Bulgarians "Plan to flood to UK in 2014" as employment restrictions relax', Nick Craven and George Arbuthnott, *The Mail on Sunday*, 27 January 2013

'385,000 from Romania and Bulgaria "poised to flood in"', Martyn Brown, *Daily Express*, 5 December 2013

'Emergency plans to cope with floods of migrants', *Daily Telegraph*, 11 December 2013

'Migrants are ready to flood to into UK', Jonathan Petre and Simon Walters, *The Mail on Sunday*, 29 December 2013

1. THE BUS

'A 52-hour bus ride – and the dream of a new life', Emily Dugan, *The Independent*, 6 January 2014

'Benefits Britain here we come!', Giles Sheldrick, *Daily Express*, 1 January 2014

2. UMMAD

'Pakistan: Prosecute Ahmadi Massacre Suspects', Human Rights Watch (hrw.org), 27 May 2012

'Over 100 Ahmadi graves desecrated in Lahore', Rabia Mehmood, *Dawn*, December 3 2010

'Pakistan: Massacre of Minority Ahmadis', Human Rights Watch (hrw.org), 1 June 2010

'Pakistan's Ahmadiyya: An "absence of justice"', Asad Hashim, AlJazeera.com, 7 August 2014

'Targeted attack leaves one Ahmadi dead; three hurt', Faraz Khan, *The Express Tribune*, 20 October 2012

'Student shot in the forehead in Pakistan has bullet removed through his NOSE', Anna Hodgekiss, Mail Online, 6 November 2012

'Wounded man (Ahmadi) dies', *Dawn* (Lahore), 29 November 2012

'Pakistan's Ahmadis faced with death or exile', Beena Sarwar, Inter Press Service, 20 October 2014

'Abdus Salam: Nobel-winning Pakistani physicist who predicted the "God particle" is shunned in his own country because of his religious beliefs', Mail Online, 9 July 2012

'A towering minaret, huge prayer halls ... but is it a mosque?', John Ezard and Sally James Gregory, *The Guardian*, 3 October 2003

3. HARLEY

'Fury at Border Agency over case of NHS therapist', Emily Dugan, *The Independent*, 13 November 2013

'We let Bulgarians work here but not Aussies. Why?' Allison Pearson, *Daily Telegraph*, 14 November 2013

'Child therapist is ordered to leave UK after 9 years', Lucy Bannerman, *The Times*, 15 November 2013

'Lauded therapist still in limbo as battle to stay in Britain drags on', Emily Dugan, *The Independent*, 20 August 2014

'I feel like I've been let out of prison. It was like I was under house arrest', Emily Dugan, *The Independent*, 3 February 2015

4. CLIVE

Glasgow Girls, book by David Greig; musical by Cora Bissett, Citizens Theatre, Glasgow, 31 October 2012

Glasgow Girls, directed by Brian Welsh, BBC Three, 14 July 2014

'UNHCR 2013 Global Trends Report', United Nations High Commissioner for Refugees, 20 June 2014

'Mapping Statelessness in the United Kingdom', Asylum Aid/United Nations High Commissioner for Refugees, November 2011

5. HRISTINA

'Rema is named the UK's Refugee Woman of Year', Catriona Stewart, *The Evening Times*, 12 March 2013

6. EMAD AND NAWAL

'Syrian embassy accused of threatening protesters in UK', Matthew
Taylor, *The Guardian*, 23 June 2011
'Syria accused of torturing relatives of overseas victims', Sam Jones,
The Guardian, 4 October 2011
'Government to allow 500 Syrian refugees into Britain' Andrew Grice
and Jamie Merrill, *The Independent*, 29 January 2014
'UK resettles just 50 refugees from Syria', refugeecouncil.org.uk,
27 August 2014
'Countries vow to resettle more than 100 Syrian refugees: UN', AFP,
10 December 2014
'Migration Statistics Quarterly Report', Office For National Statistics,
February 2015
'Libya's boat people, and Italy's tragic folly', Nicholas Farrell, *The
Spectator*, 6 September 2014
'Departing Milan, destination unknown', Emily Dugan, *The Independent*,
8 September 2014
'Migrant Arrivals by Sea in Italy Top 170,000 in 2014', International
Organisation for Migration, 16 January 2015
'UK border police 'to consider entry' for Syrian refugees waiting in
Calais', Henry Samuel, Telegraph.co.uk, 4 October 2013
'An immigration crisis on Britain's doorstep', Cahal Milmo, *The
Independent*, 15 February 2014
'Hundreds of migrants try to storm ferries at Calais in a desperate
dash for Britain', Miranda Prynne, *The Daily Telegraph*,
5 September 2014

9. ADERONKE

'If you don't believe I'm gay, I'll send you a video that proves it', Emily
Dugan, *The Independent*, 9 June 2014
'Theresa May orders review of gay asylum handling', Press Association,
29 March 2014
'Gay asylum seekers face "humiliation"', Diane Taylor and Mark
Townsend, *The Observer*, 8 February 2014
'Nigeria's president signs law imposing up to 14 years' jail for gay
relationships', Associated Press, 13 January 2014
'The Situation for LGBT people around the world', Stonewall.org.uk,
updated 2014

'Aderonke Apata wins National Diversity Award', Stefano Fumagalli,
     Red Pepper Blog, 7 October 2014
'The Rainbow List', *The Independent on Sunday*, 9 November 2014

10. BOSTON

'They came, they worked, they stayed in Lincolnshire', Emily Dugan,
     The Independent, 23 March 2014
'The mother who dared to tell the truth about immigration on the BBC',
     Barbara David, *Daily Mail*, 27 January 2013
'Boston jobseeker figure falls and is far below 1980s and 1990s peak',
     Boston Standard, 30 January 2015
'Chance to fight for a Boston bypass', *Boston Standard*, 21 June 2012
'Census reveals rural town of Boston has most eastern European
     migrants, Helen Pidd, *The Guardian*, 11 December 2012
'Boston is fattest place in England', *Boston Standard*, 10 October 2006
'Portuguese in Boston, Lincolnshire', *The Guardian*, 23 January 2006
'Dywizjion 303', Arkady Fiedler, M.I. Kolin, London, 1942

EPILOGUE

'385,000 from Romania and Bulgaria "poised to flood in"', Martyn
     Brown, *Daily Express*, 5 December 2013
'Migration Statistics Quarterly Report', Office For National Statistics,
     February 2015
'Perceptions are not reality: Things the world gets wrong', Ipsos MORI,
     29 October 2014
'An inspection of the UK Border Agency's handling of asylum legacy
     and migration cases', John Vine, Independent Chief Inspector of
     Borders and Immigration, March–July 2012
'Faith and free schools "breed social and racial segregation"'
     (interview with Matthew Taylor), Emily Dugan, *The Independent*,
     1 January 2015
'Social integration: A wake-up call', Social Integration Commission UK,
     20 October 2014